Dollar Origami Treasures

Over 50 Exciting Projects

Second Edition

Books by John Montroll
www.johnmontroll.com

General Origami

DC Super Heroes Origami
Origami Worldwide
Teach Yourself Origami: Second Revised Edition
Christmas Origami
Storytime Origami
Origami Inside-Out: Third Edition

Animal Origami

Dogs in Origami
Perfect Pets Origami
Dragons and Other Fantastic Creatures in Origami
Bugs in Origami
Horses in Origami
Origami Birds
Origami Gone Wild
Dinosaur Origami
Origami Dinosaurs for Beginners
Prehistoric Origami: Dinosaurs and other Creatures: Third Edition
Mythological Creatures and the Chinese Zodiac Origami
Origami Under the Sea
Sea Creatures in Origami
Origami Sea Life: Third Edition
Bringing Origami to Life
Bugs and Birds in Origami
Origami Sculptures: Fourth Edition
African Animals in Origami: Third Edition
North American Animals in Origami: Third Edition

Geometric Origami

Origami Stars
Galaxy of Origami Stars: Second Edition
Origami and Math: Simple to Complex
Origami & Geometry
3D Origami Platonic Solids & More: Second Edition
3D Origami Diamonds
3D Origami Antidiamonds
3D Origami Pyramids
A Plethora of Polyhedra in Origami: Second Revised Edition
Classic Polyhedra Origami
A Constellation of Origami Polyhedra
Origami Polyhedra Design

Dollar Bill Origami

Dollar Bill Animals in Origami: Second Revised Edition
Dollar Bill Origami
Easy Dollar Bill Origami

Simple Origami

Fun and Simple Origami: 101 Easy-to-Fold Projects: Second Edition
Super Simple Origami
Easy Dollar Bill Origami
Easy Origami Animals
Origami Twelve Days of Christmas: And Santa, Too!

Dollar Origami Treasures

Over 50 Exciting Projects

Second Edition

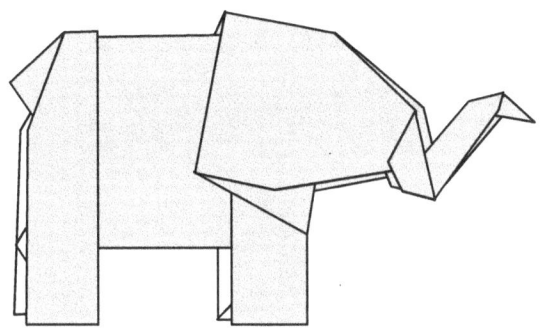

John Montroll

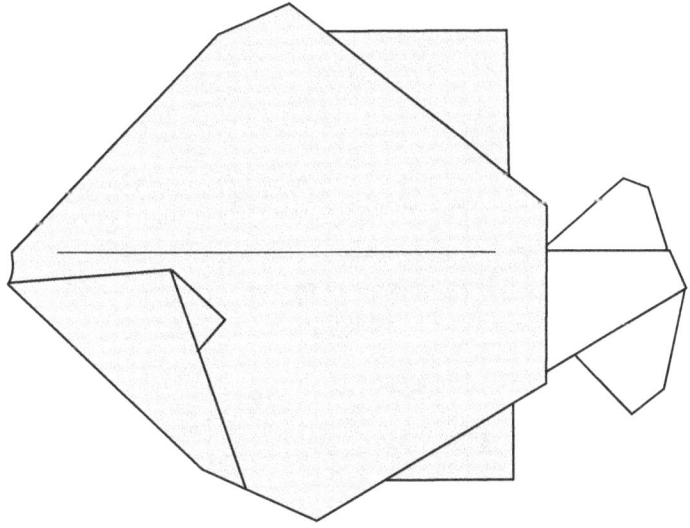

Antroll Publishing Company

To Steve, Sally, Bobby, Billy, and Charlie

Dollar Origami Treasures
Second Edition

Copyright © 2018 by John Montroll. All rights reserved.
No part of this publication may be copied or reproduced by any means without the express written permission of the author.

ISBN-10: 1-877656-41-0
ISBN-13: 978-1-877656-41-5

Antroll Publishing Company

Introduction

Folding dollar bills has become very popular. The bills are made of quality paper, well suited for origami. There is no end to the varied models that can be folded. Here is a collection of over 50 models in categories of objects, boats, hats, bugs, birds, sea creatures, mammals, and dinosaurs. Most are my original designs, a few are traditional favorites, and some are modified from traditional models. This work features more models in my growing list of dollar origami books.

The models range from simple to complex, but not too complex. The difficulty levels are shown in the contents. Clear step-by-step instructions show how to fold a simple sailboat and a challenging crab. Along the way you can fold a kimono, ocean liner, parakeet, moth, piggy bank, and tyrannosaurus.

It is up to you which side of the dollar bill should show in finished models. Although the diagrams use white and shading to represent the dollar bill's two sides, you may choose which side of the bill you wish to show; the diagrams will show each finished model with mostly the shaded side.

It is not necessary to fold from dollar bills. Any paper can easily be cut to form the proportions of a bill. There are methods, shown on page 12, which show easy ways to approximate the proportions given a square or rectangle. The illustrations conform to the internationally accepted Randlett-Yoshizawa conventions. Origami supplies can be found in arts and craft shops, or visit OrigamiUSA at www.origami-usa.org.

I thank Russell Cashdollar for the cover design and Neil Sood for the photographs. I also thank Steve Rollin, Jan Polish, and Brian Webb for their continued support. And I thank the many folders who proofread the diagrams.

John Montroll

www.johnmontroll.com

Contents

Symbols 9
Basic Folds 10
Dollar Bills from a Square 12

★ Simple
★★ Intermediate
★★★ Complex

Objects *page 13*

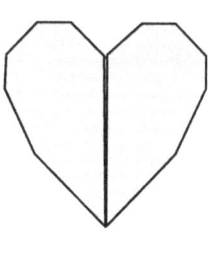
Heart
★
page 13

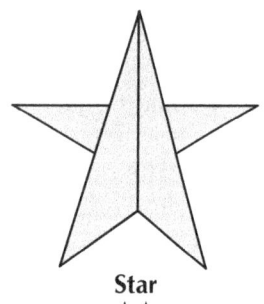
Star
★★
page 14

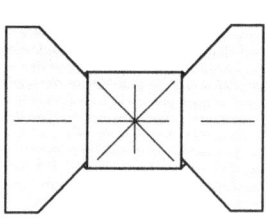
Bowtie
★
page 15

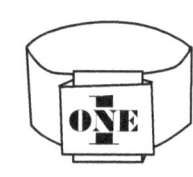
Ring
★
page 16

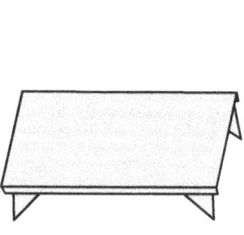
Table
★
page 17

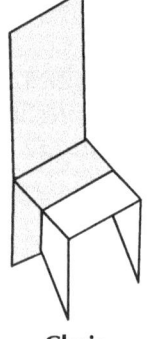
Chair
★★
page 18

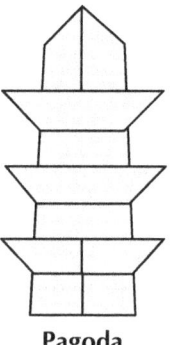
Pagoda
★★
page 20

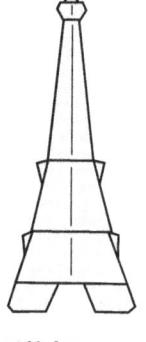
Eiffel Tower
★★
page 22

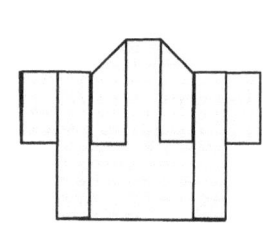
Kimono
★★
page 25

Boats & Hats *page 26*

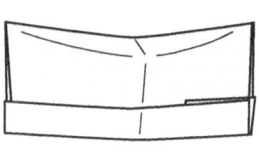
Navy Cap
★
page 26

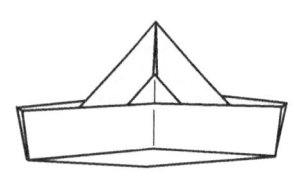
Pirate Hat
★
page 27

Samurai Hat
★★
page 28

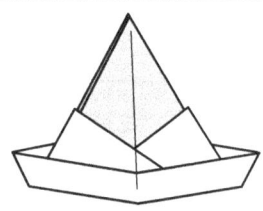
Party Hat
★
page 30

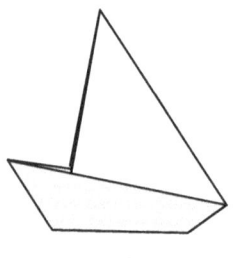
Yacht
★
page 31

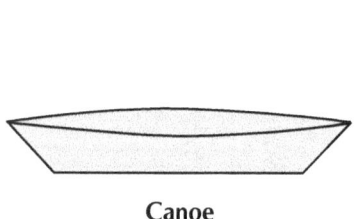
Canoe
★
page 31

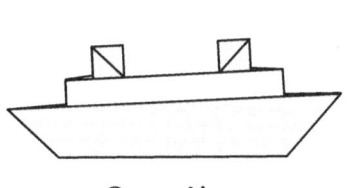
Ocean Liner
★★
page 32

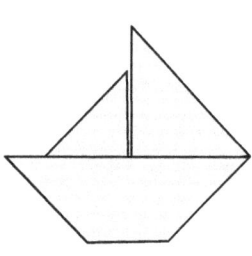
Sailboat
★
page 34

6 *Dollar Origami Treasures*

Bugs & Birds *page 35*

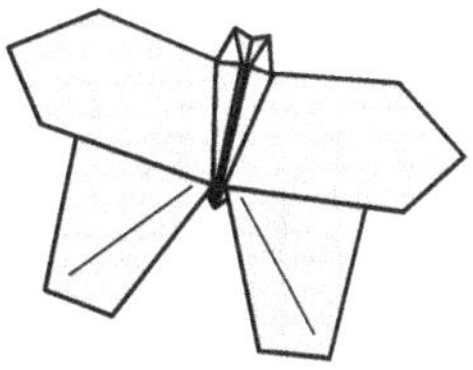

Butterfly ★★ *page 35*	 **Flying Crane** ★★ *page 37*	 **Standing Crane** ★★ *page 38*	 **Parakeet** ★★ *page 41*	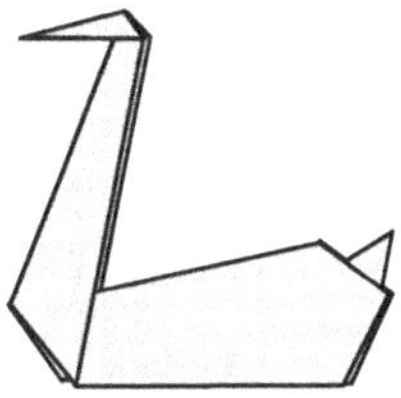 **Swan** ★★ *page 42*
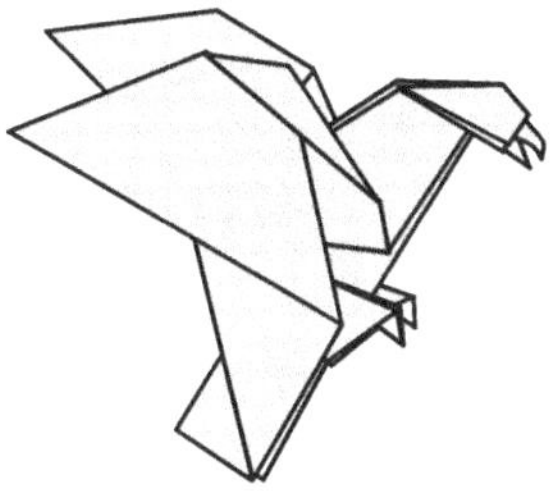 **Eagle** ★★ *page 44*	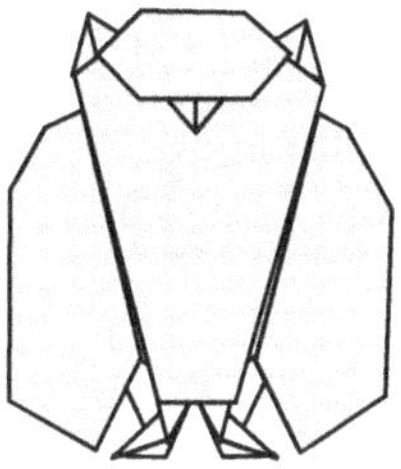 **Owl** ★★ *page 46*	 **Hummingbird** ★★ *page 48*	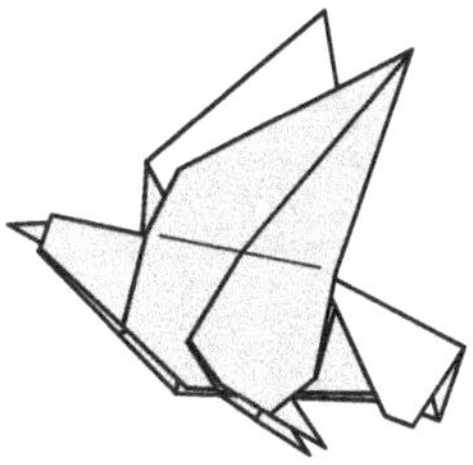 **Pigeon** ★★ *page 50*	
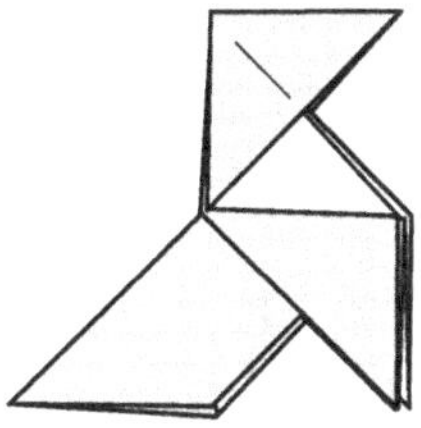 **Pajarita** ★★ *page 53*	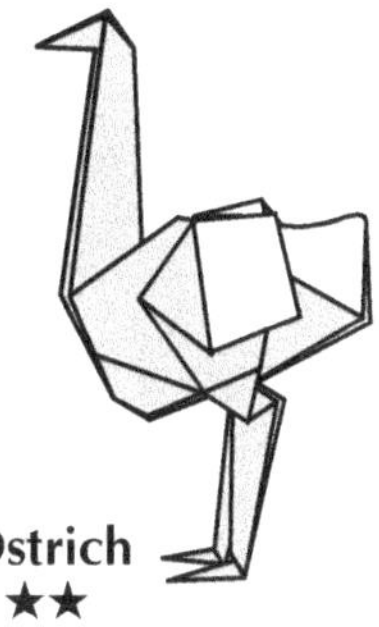 **Ostrich** ★★ *page 56*	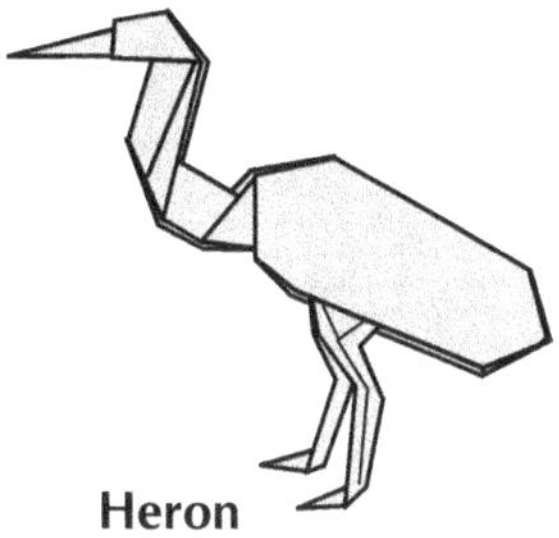 **Heron** ★★ *page 59*	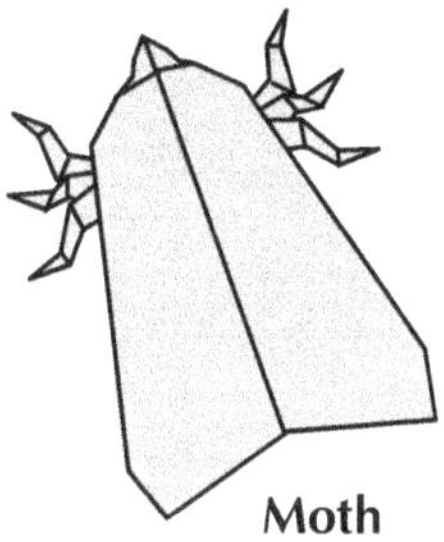 **Moth** ★★★ *page 62*	

Sea Creatures *page 65*

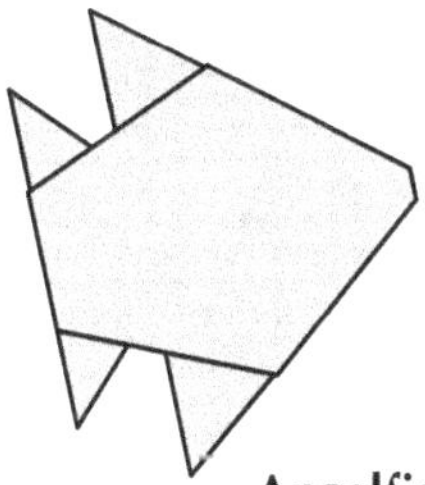

Angelfish ★ *page 65*	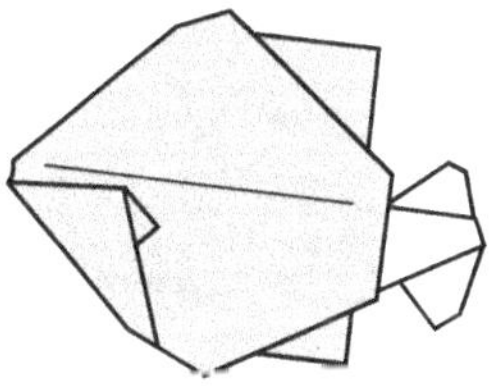 **Tropical Fish** ★★ *page 66*	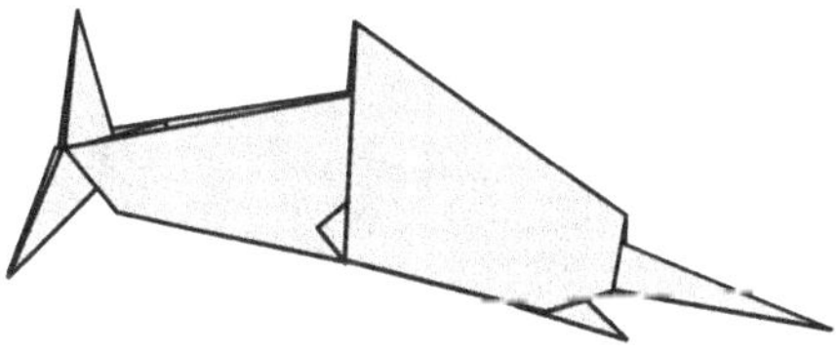 **Swordfish** ★★ *page 68*	
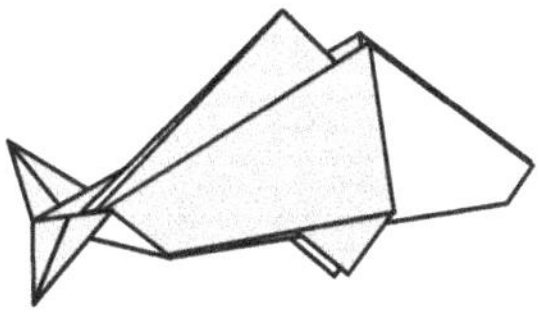 **Carp** ★ *page 71*	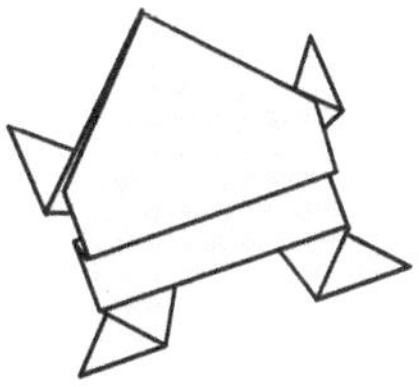 **Frog** ★★ *page 72*	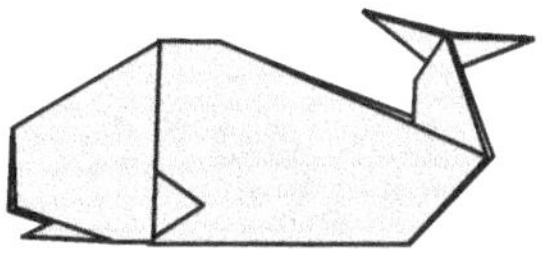 **Whale** ★★ *page 74*	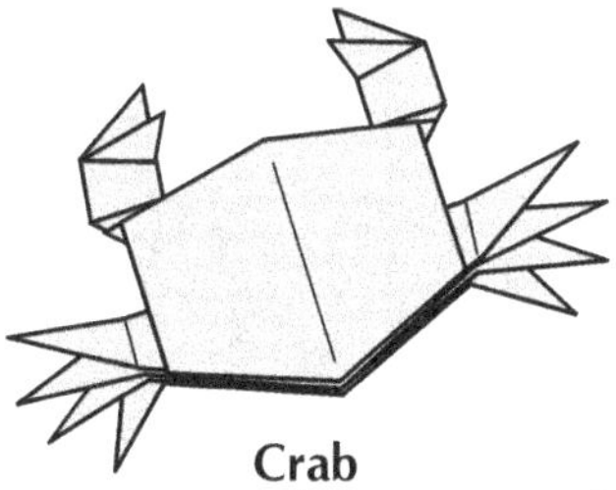 **Crab** ★★★ *page 77*

More →

Mammals *page 80*

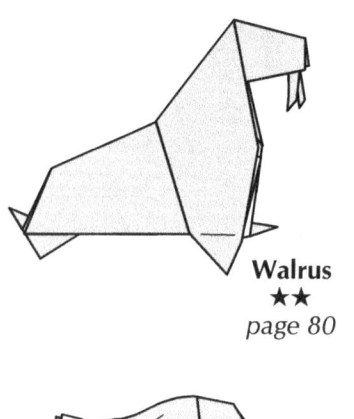
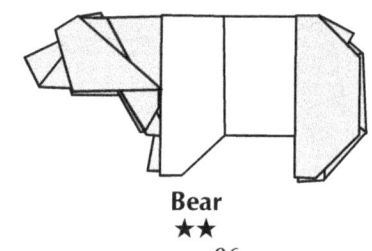

Walrus
★★
page 80

Sheep
★★★
page 83

Bear
★★
page 86

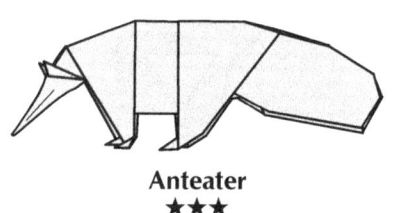

Mouse
★★★
page 88

Raccoon
★★★
page 91

Anteater
★★★
page 94

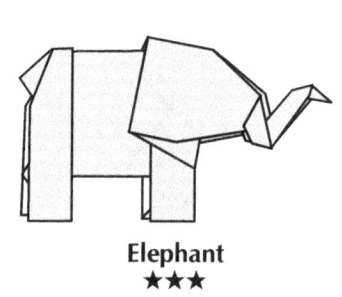

Dromedary
★★★
page 97

Piggy Bank
★★★
page 100

Elephant
★★★
page 104

Dinosaurs *page 107*

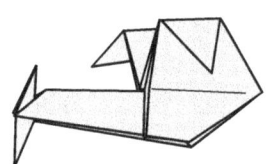
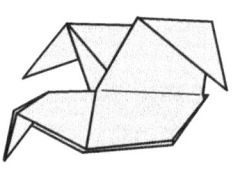
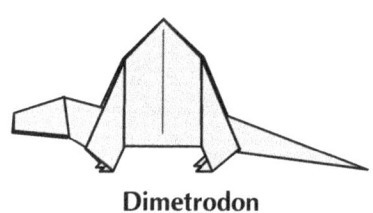

Quetzalcoatlus
★★
page 107

Pteranodon
★★
page 108

Pterodactylus
★★
page 109

Dimetrodon
★★
page 110

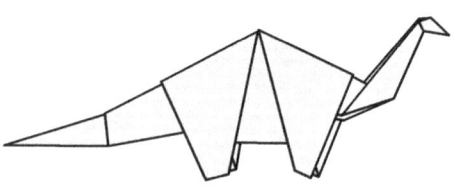
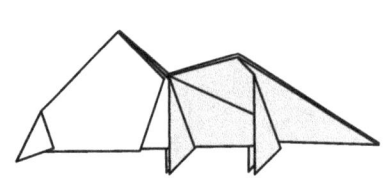

Apatosaurus
★★★
page 112

Protoceratops
★★★
page 115

Tyrannosaurus
★★★
page 117

8 *Dollar Origami Treasures*

Symbols

Lines

— — — — — — — — —   Valley fold, fold in front.

—··—··—··—··—··—   Mountain fold, fold behind.

————————————   Crease line.

···   X-ray or guide line.

Arrows

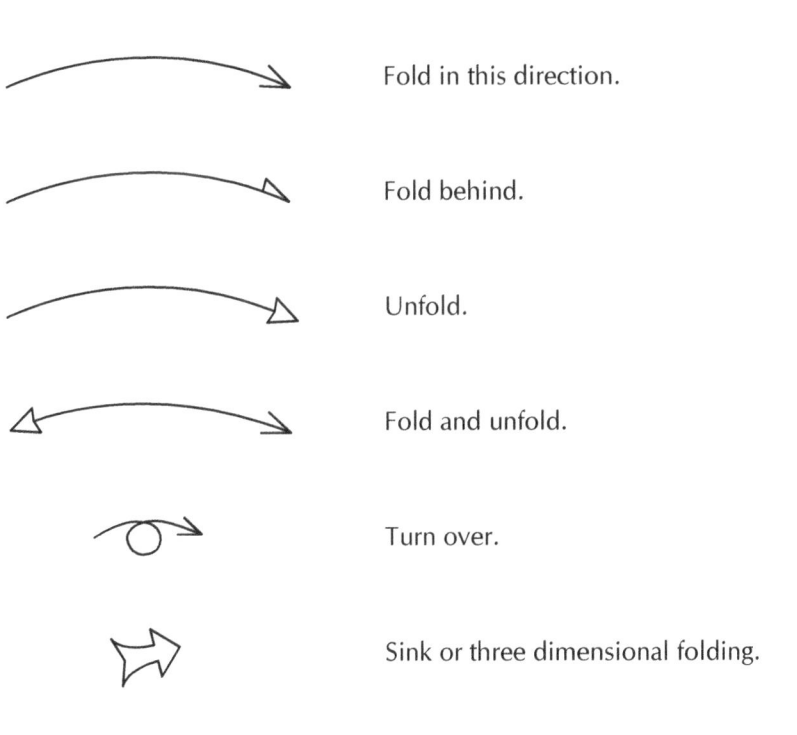

Fold in this direction.

Fold behind.

Unfold.

Fold and unfold.

Turn over.

Sink or three dimensional folding.

Place your finger between these layers.

Basic Folds

Pleat Fold.

Fold back and forth. Each pleat is composed of one valley and mountain fold. Here are two examples.

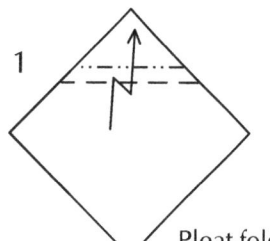
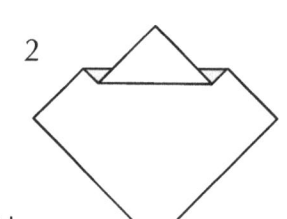
Pleat-fold.

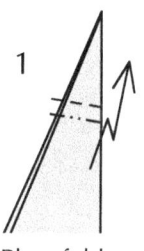

Pleat-fold.

Squash Fold.

In a squash fold, some paper is opened and then made flat. The shaded arrow shows where to place your finger.

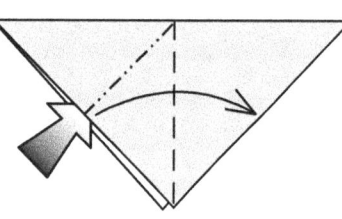
Squash-fold.

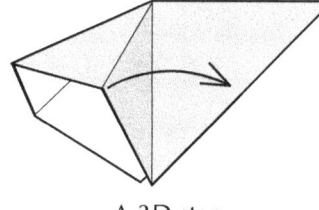
A 3D step.

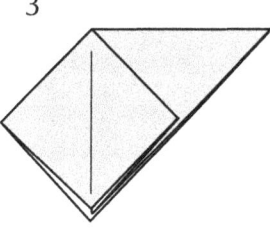

Petal Fold.

In a petal fold, one point is folded up while two opposite sides meet each other.

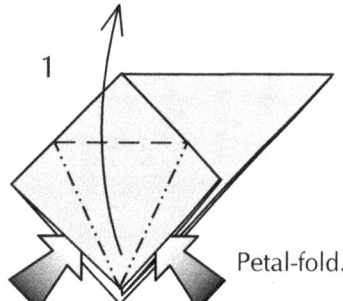
Petal-fold.

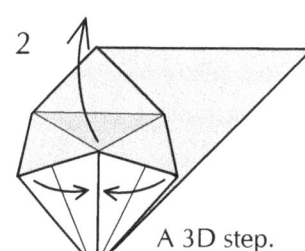
A 3D step.

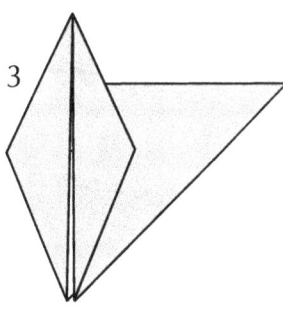

Rabbit Ear.

To fold a rabbit ear, one corner is folded in half and laid down to a side.

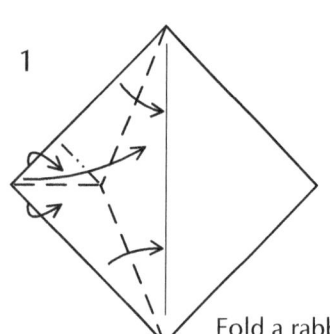
Fold a rabbit ear.

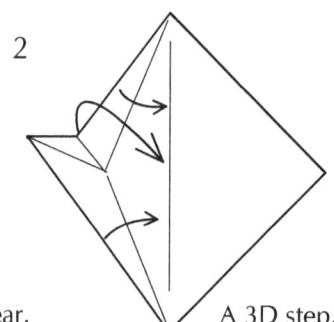
A 3D step.

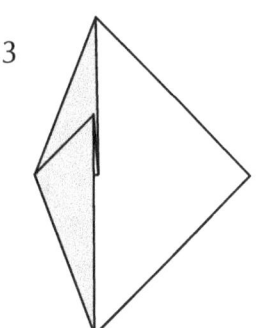

Inside Reverse Fold.

In an inside reverse fold, some paper is folded between layers. Here are two examples.

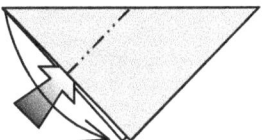
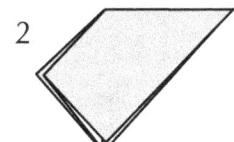
Reverse-fold.

 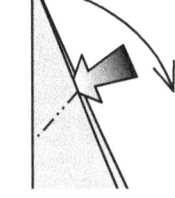 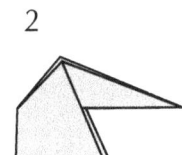
Reverse-fold.

Outside Reverse Fold.

Much of the paper must be unfolded to make an outside reverse fold.

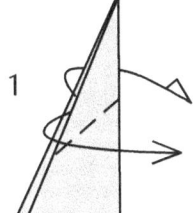 
Outside-reverse-fold.

Crimp Fold.

A crimp fold is a combination of two reverse folds. Open the model slightly to form the crimp evenly on each side. Here are two examples.

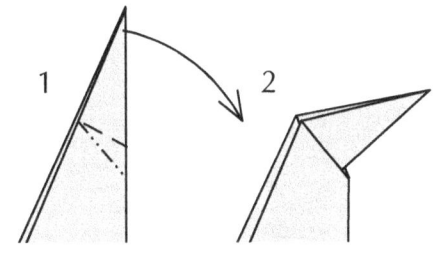
Crimp-fold.

 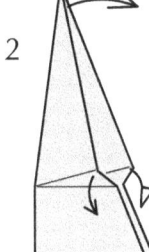 
Crimp-fold.   A 3D step.

Sink Fold.

In a sink fold, some of the paper without edges is folded inside. To do this fold, much of the model must be unfolded.

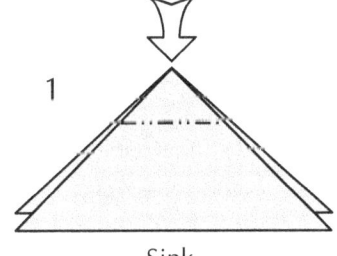 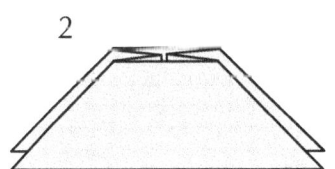
Sink.

Spread Squash Fold.

A cross between a squash fold and sink fold, some paper in the center is spread apart and then made flat.

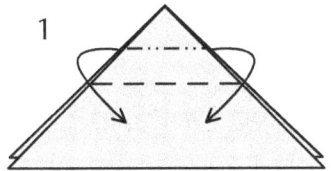 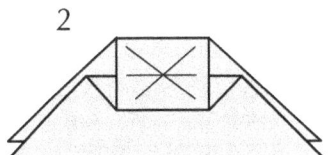
Spread-squash-fold.

Basic Folds

Dollar Bills from a Square

The dollar bill has dimensions of approximately 2.59 inches by 6.094 inches. This ratio is 1 by 2.35. There are several ways to approximate this proportion from a square or rectangle. One is to use dimensions 3 by 7 (1 by 2.333). Another method is to create a rectangle with the diagonal at a 22.5° angle as shown here; the ratio for this method is approximately 1 by 2.414.

An 8.5 by 11 inch rectangular sheet of paper can be cut into thirds to create the proportions of a dollar bill. This method is shown here, and the resulting ratio is 1 by 2.318.

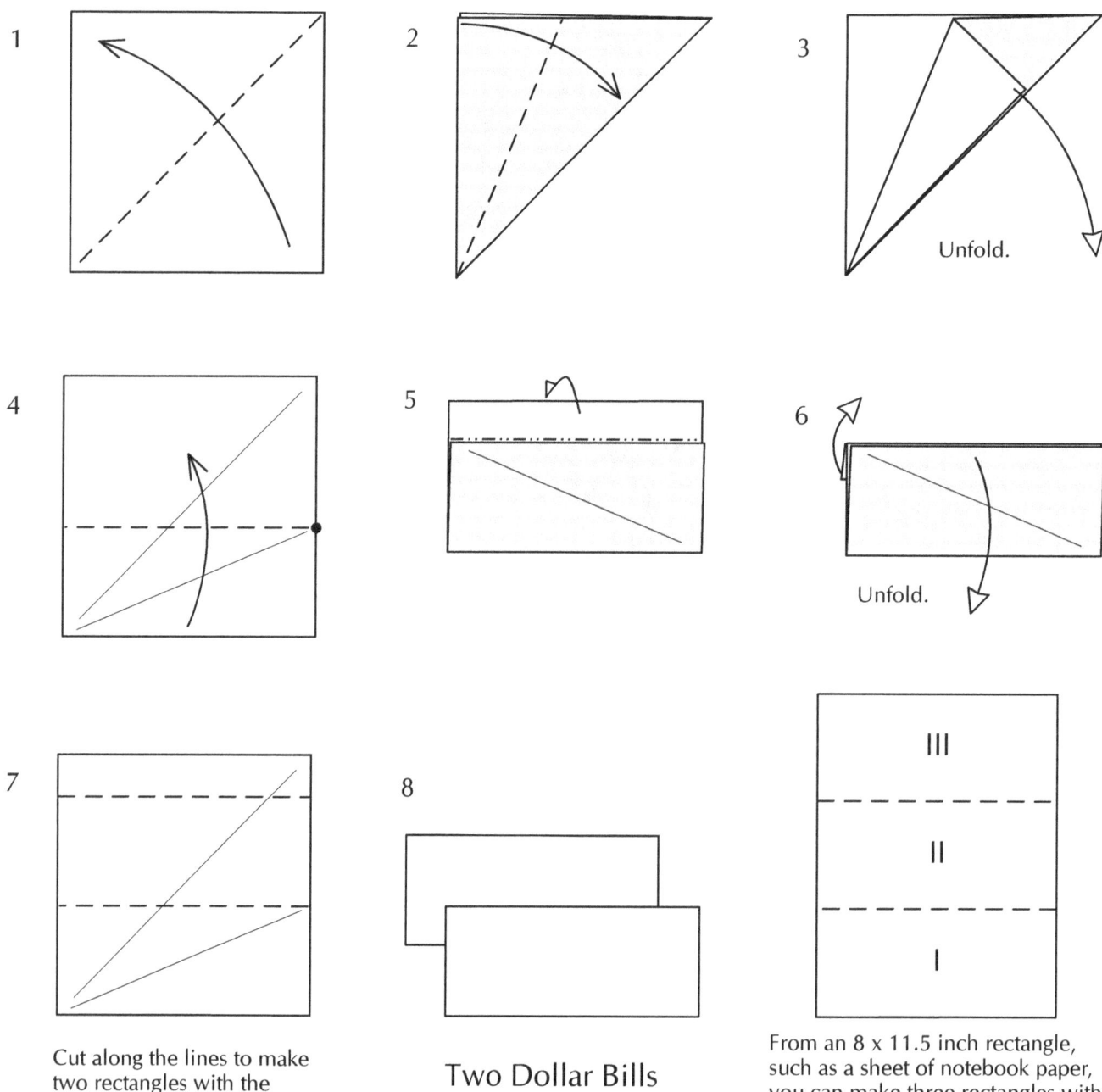

7. Cut along the lines to make two rectangles with the proportions of a dollar bill.

8. Two Dollar Bills

From an 8 x 11.5 inch rectangle, such as a sheet of notebook paper, you can make three rectangles with the proportions of a dollar bill by dividing the paper in thirds.

12 *Dollar Origami Treasures*

Objects

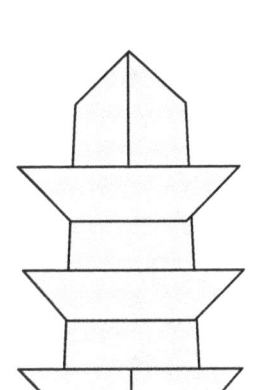

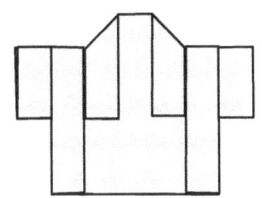

Here is a collection of nine objects. The ring and bowtie are traditional favorites. The traditional kimono is from a square so I designed a variation from the dollar. The rest, including the pagoda, star, and chair are my designs.

Heart

1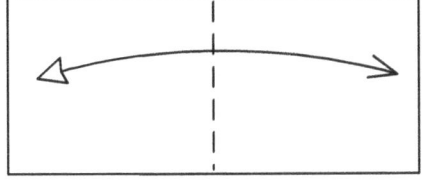

Fold and unfold.

2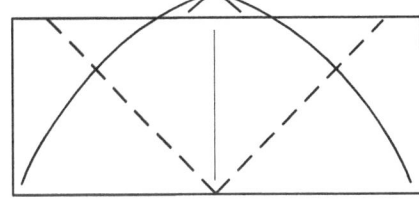

3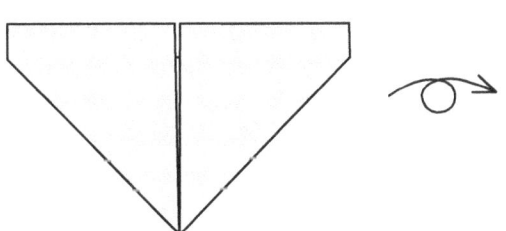

4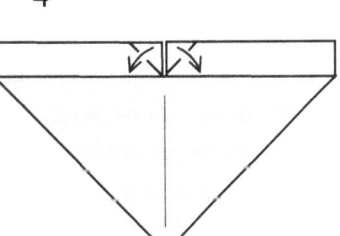

5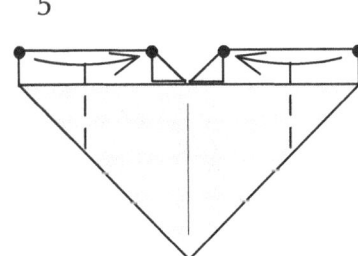

6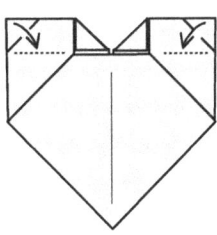

7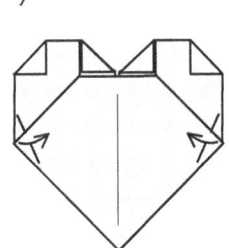

8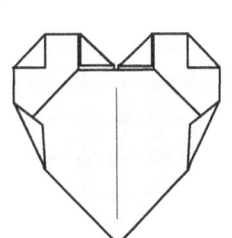

9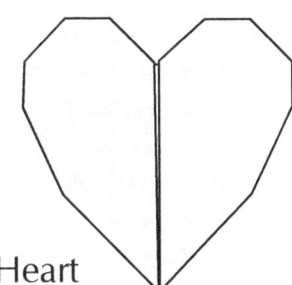

Heart

Heart 13

Star

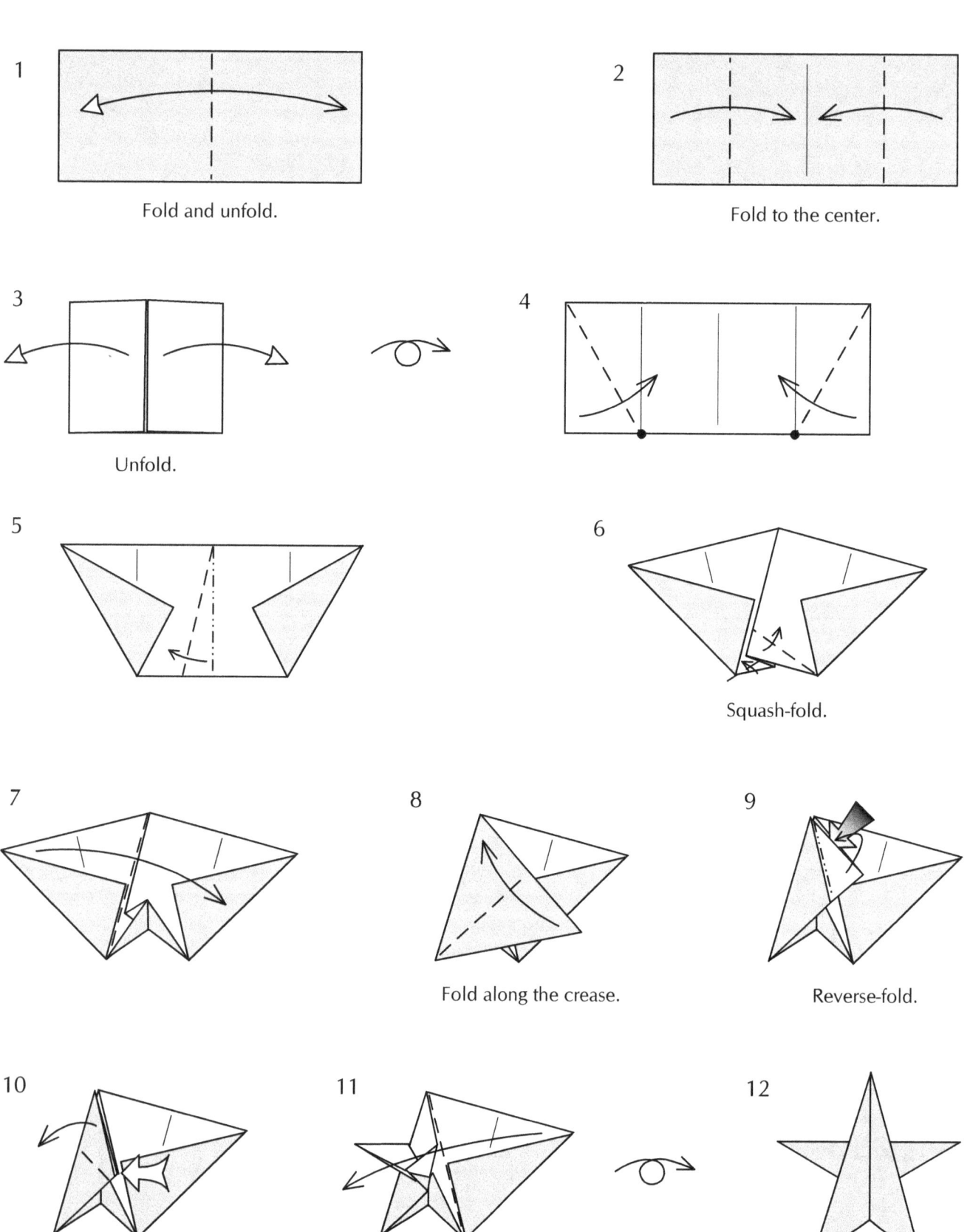

Bowtie

Traditional

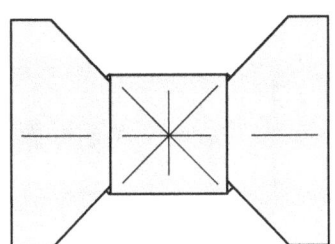

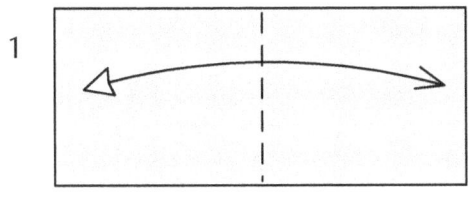
Fold and unfold.

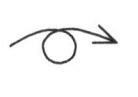

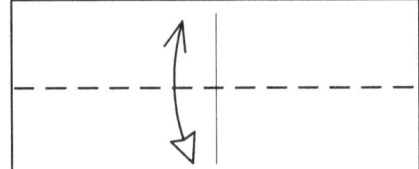
Fold and unfold.

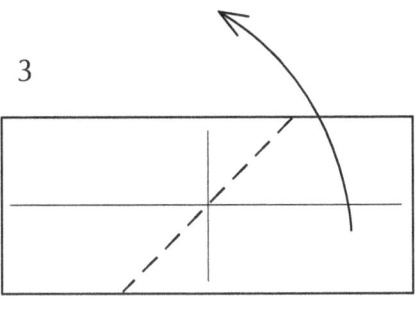

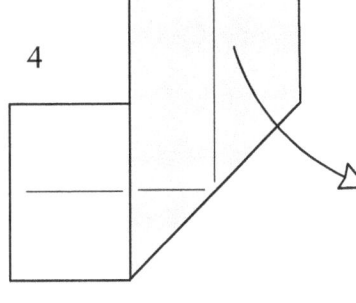
Unfold.

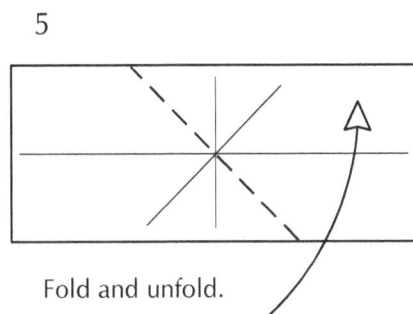
Fold and unfold.

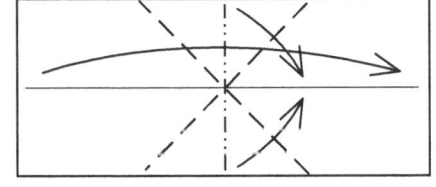
Fold along the creases.

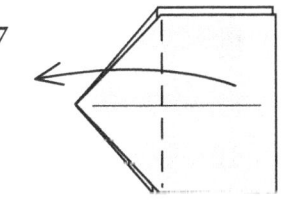
Repeat behind.

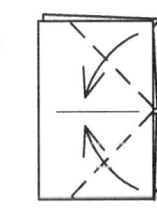
Repeat behind.

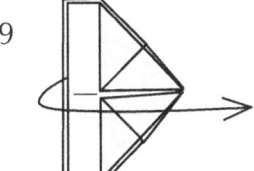
Bring the top layer to the right and open the model.

This step is 3D. Push the center in, so it flattens into a square.

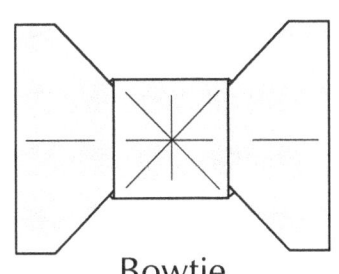
Bowtie

Ring

Traditional

1

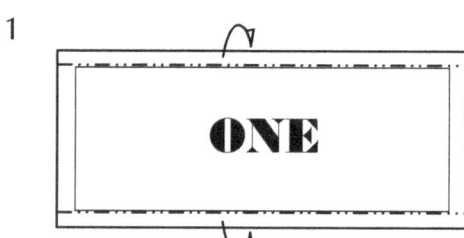

Begin with the side showing ONE in the center. Fold behind along the borders.

2

3

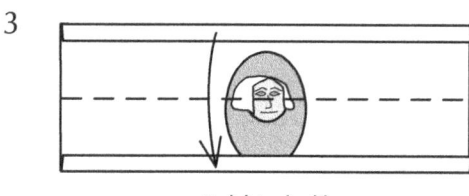

Fold in half.

4

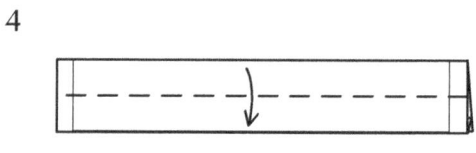

Fold in half.

5

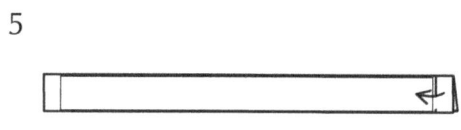

Fold by the margin.

6

Fold to show the ONE on the right.

7

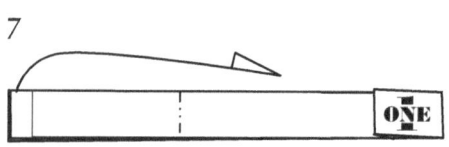

The length that is folded behind affects the size of the ring. The more that is folded behind, the smaller the ring.

8

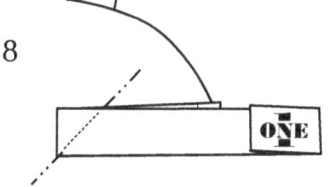

9

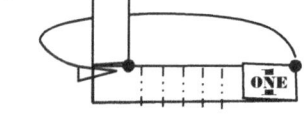

Wrap the band around from behind so the dots meet.

10

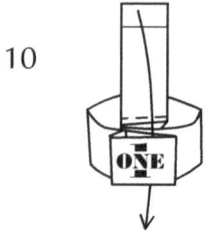

Fold between the layers.

11

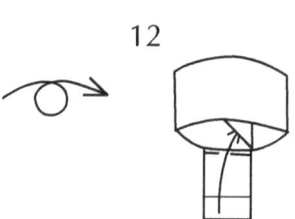

12

Tuck inside.

13

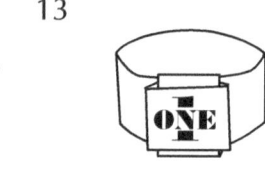

Ring

16 *Dollar Origami Treasures*

Table

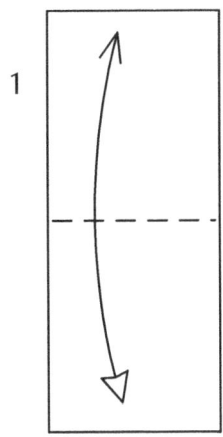

1 Fold and unfold.

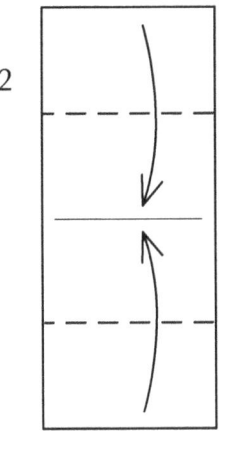

2 Fold to the center.

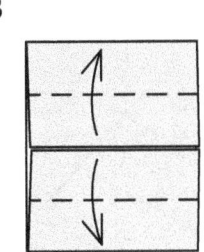

3

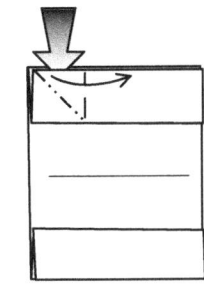

4 Squash-fold.

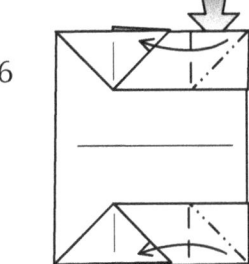

5 Squash-fold.

6 Make squash folds.

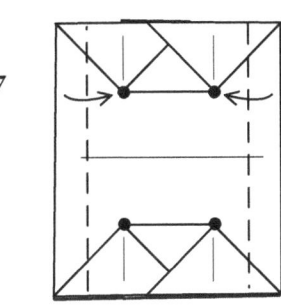

7 Fold the edges to the dots.

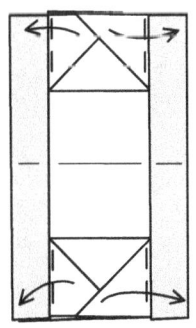

8 Spread the legs so the table can stand.

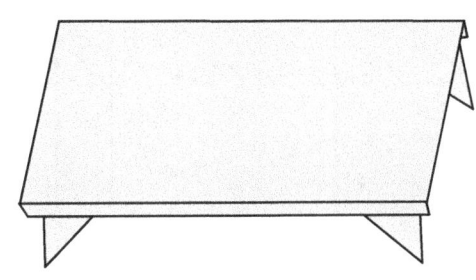

9

Table

Chair

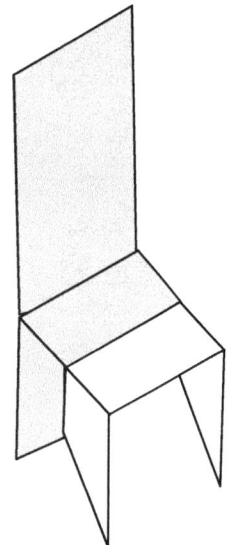

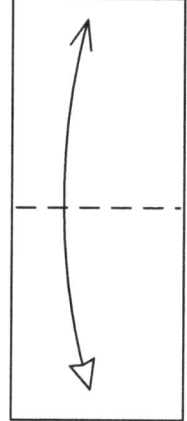

1

Fold and unfold.

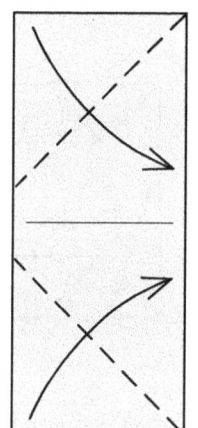

2

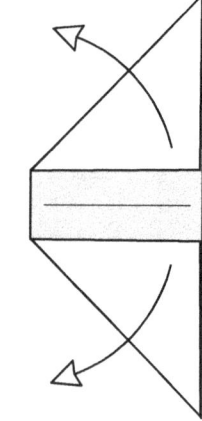

3

Unfold.

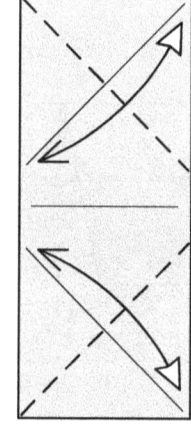

4

Fold and unfold.

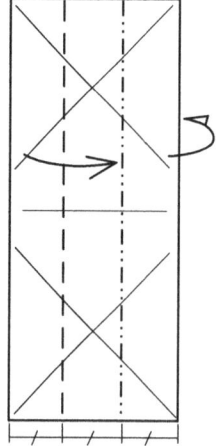

5

Fold in thirds.

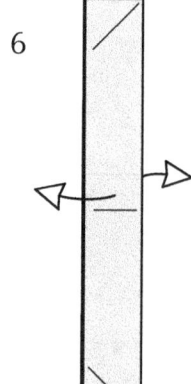

6

Unfold.

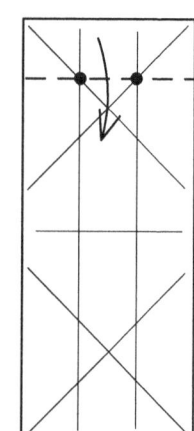

7

18   *Dollar Origami Treasures*

8

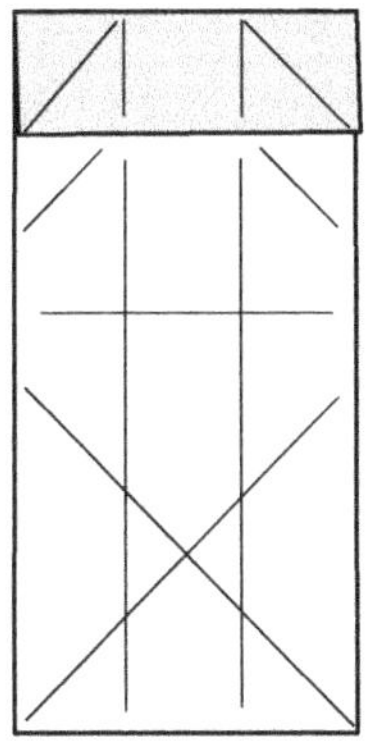

9

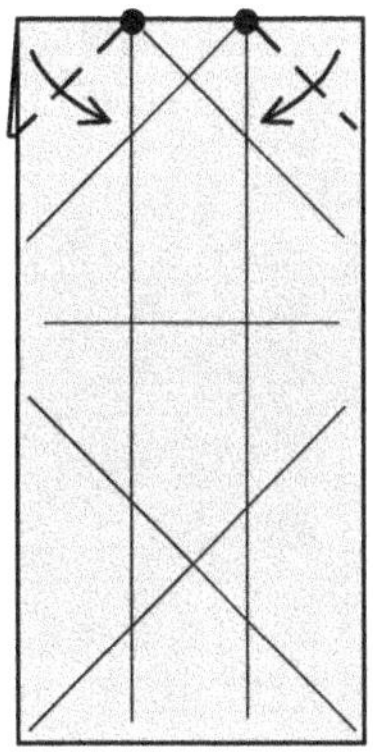

10

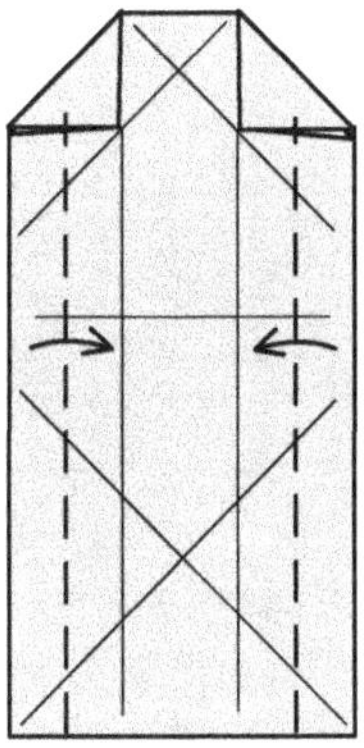

11

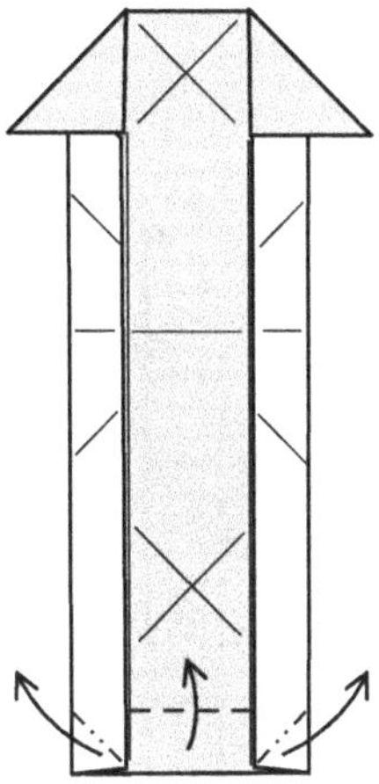

Petal-fold.

12

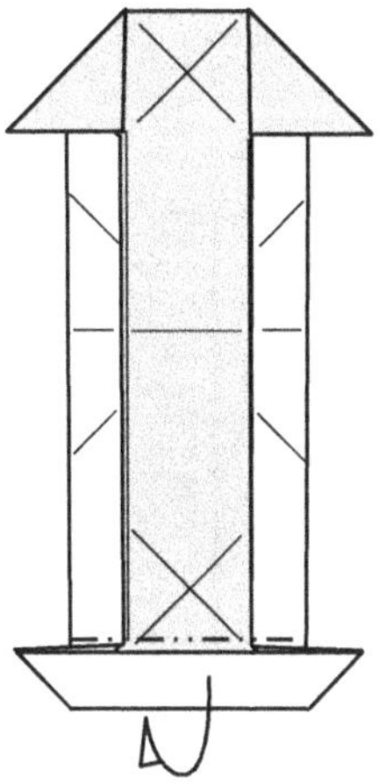

13

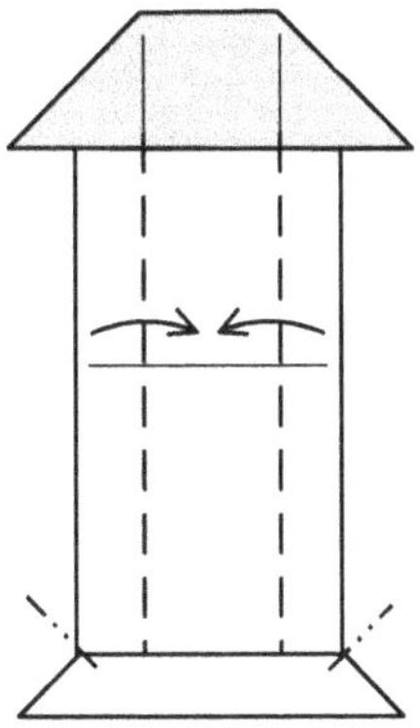

Fold to the center.

14

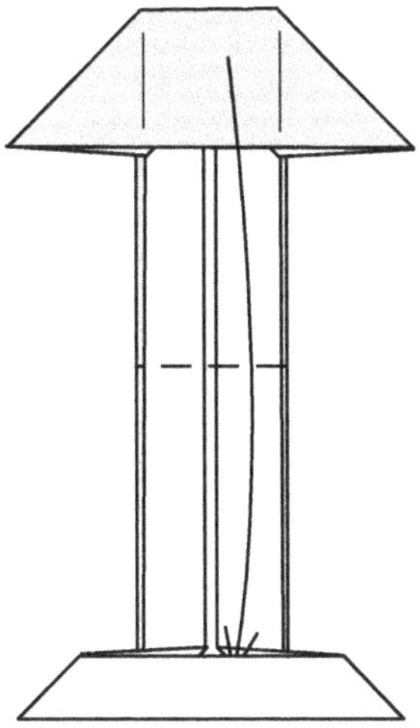

Fold along the crease
and tuck inside.

15

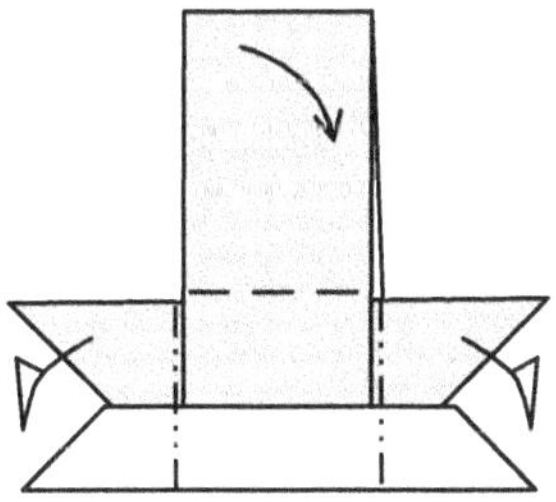

Shape the chair.

16

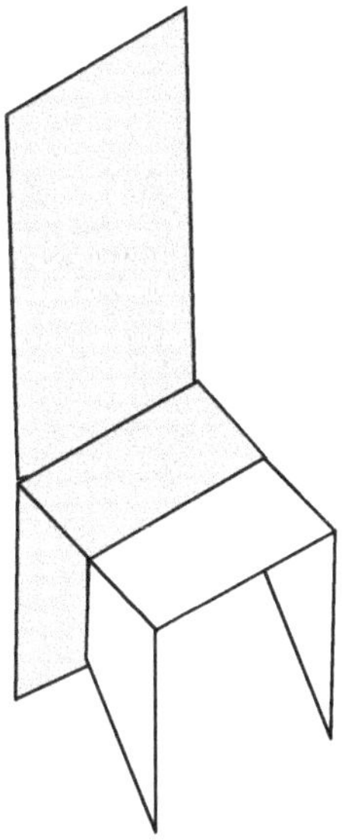

Chair

Pagoda

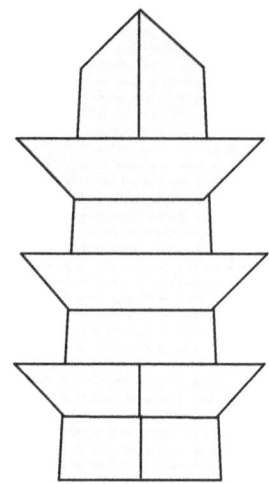

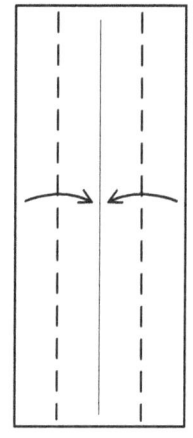

1   2   3   4

Fold and unfold.   Unfold.

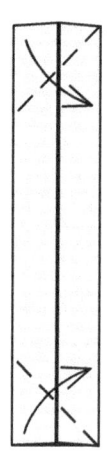
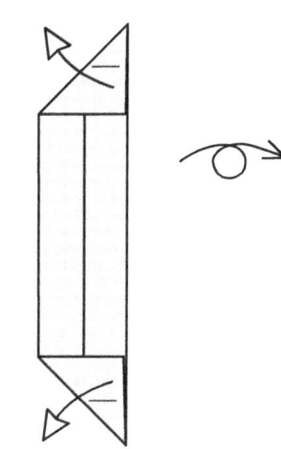

5   6   7   8

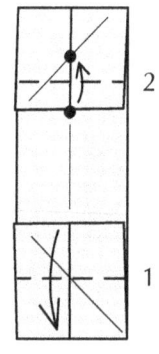
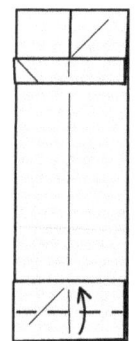
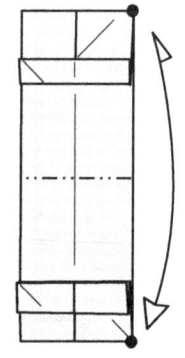

1. Fold at the dot.
2. Fold slightly above the dot.

1. Fold down.
2. Fold to the dot.

Fold in half and unfold.

20   *Dollar Origami Treasures*

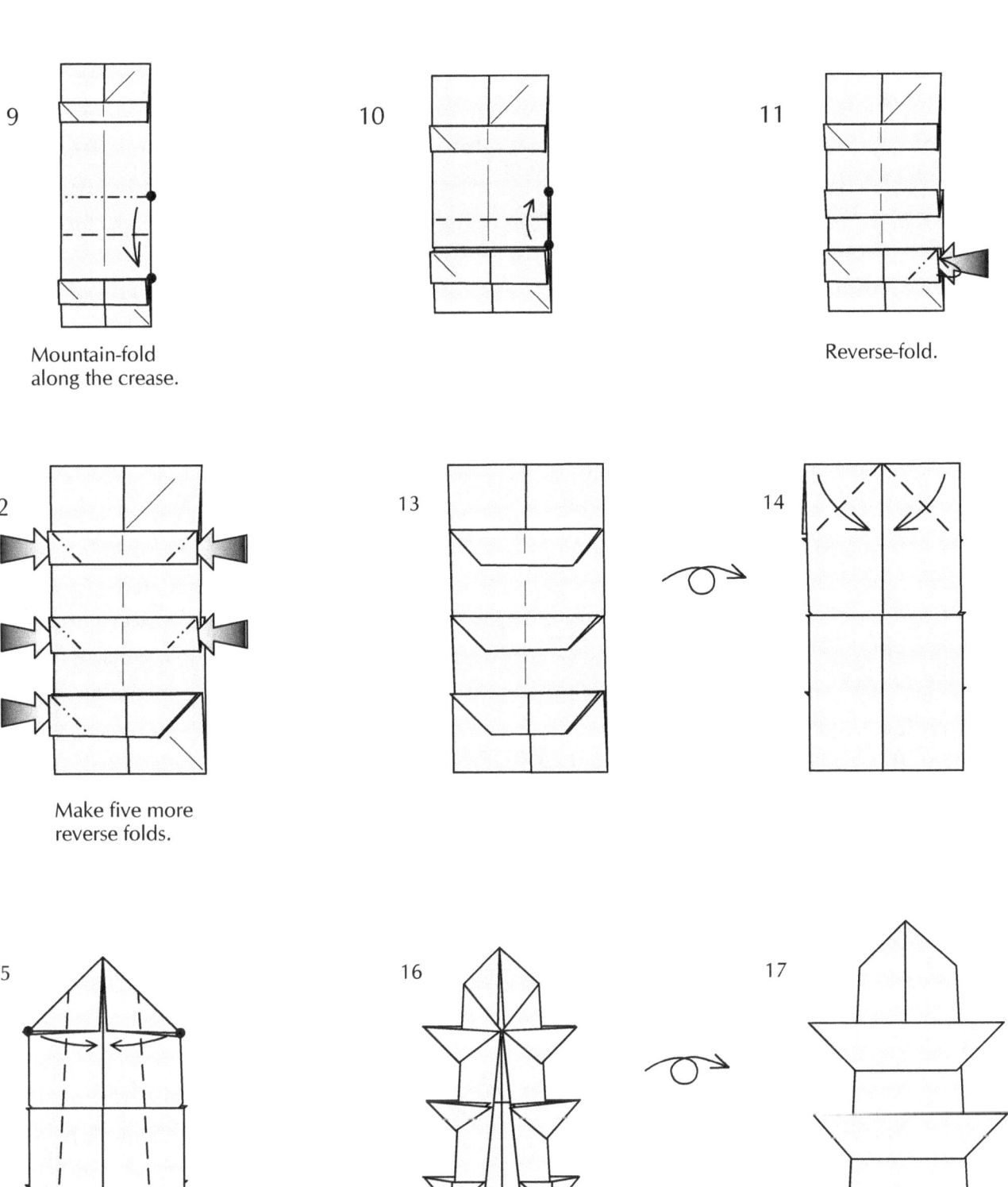

Pagoda

Eiffel Tower

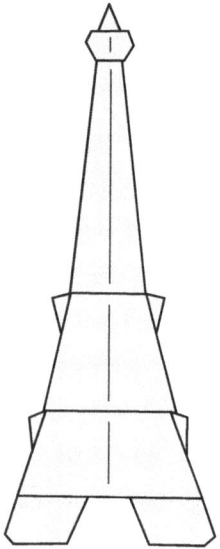

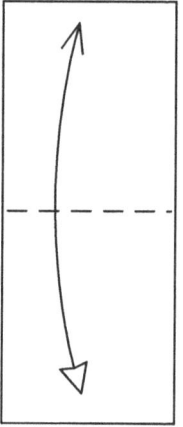

1

Fold and unfold.

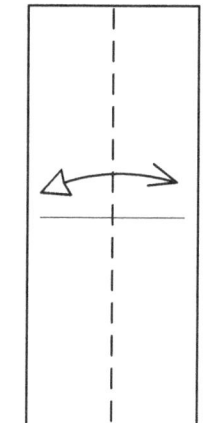

2

Fold and unfold.

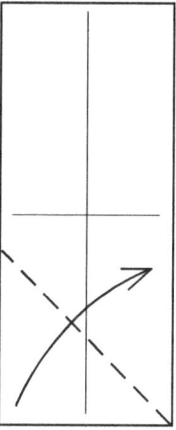

3

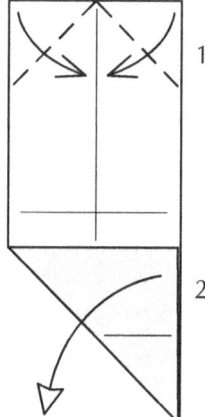

4

1. Fold to the center.
2. Unfold.

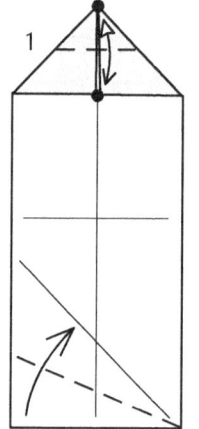

5

1. Fold and unfold.
2. Fold to the crease.

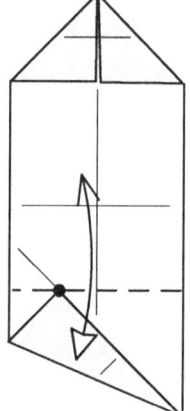

6

Fold and unfold.

22   *Dollar Origami Treasures*

7

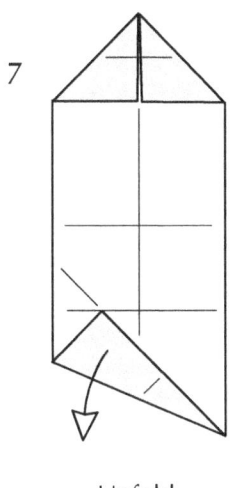

Unfold.

8

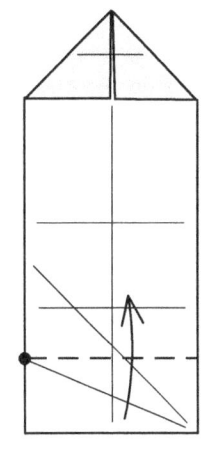

9

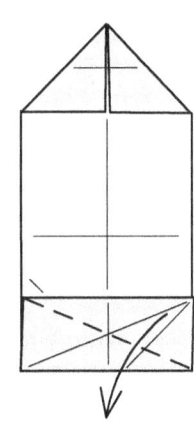

10

Squash-fold.

11

1. Kite-fold.
2. Squash-fold.

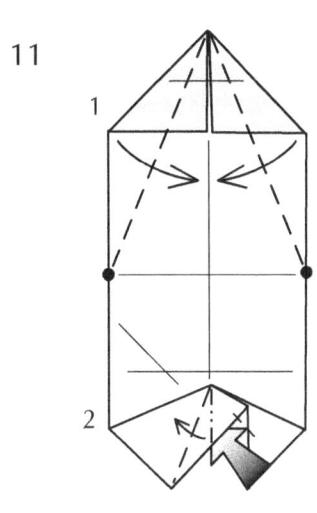

12

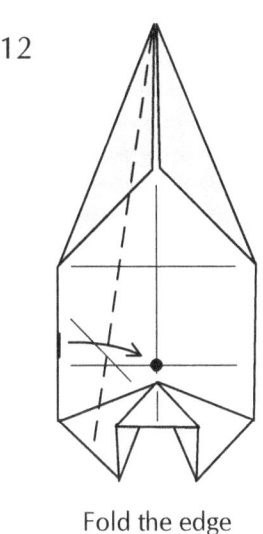

Fold the edge to the dot.

13

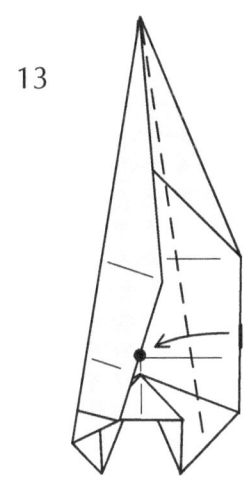

14

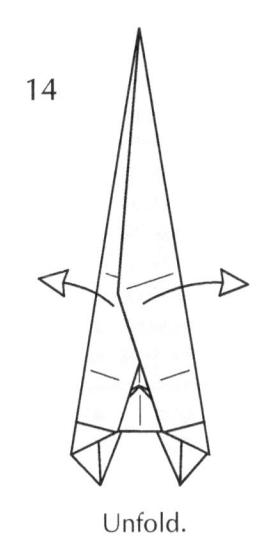

Unfold.

15

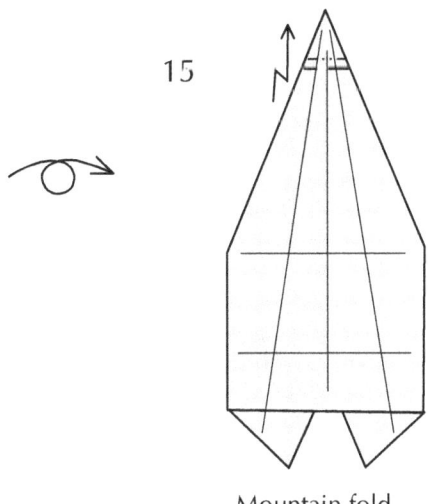

Mountain-fold along the crease.

Eiffel Tower 23

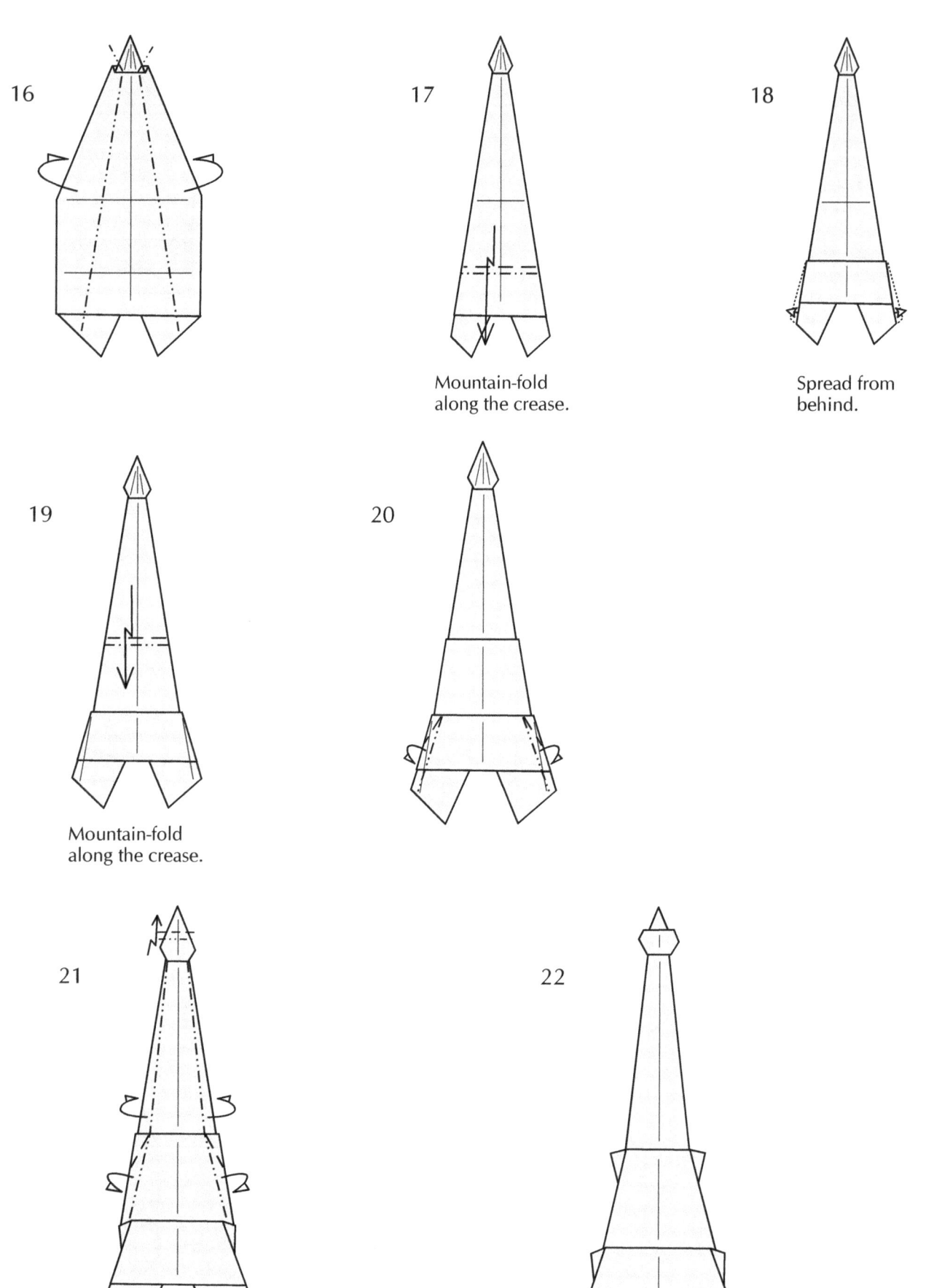

Eiffel Tower

24 *Dollar Origami Treasures*

Kimono

Variation of traditional Kimono by John Montroll

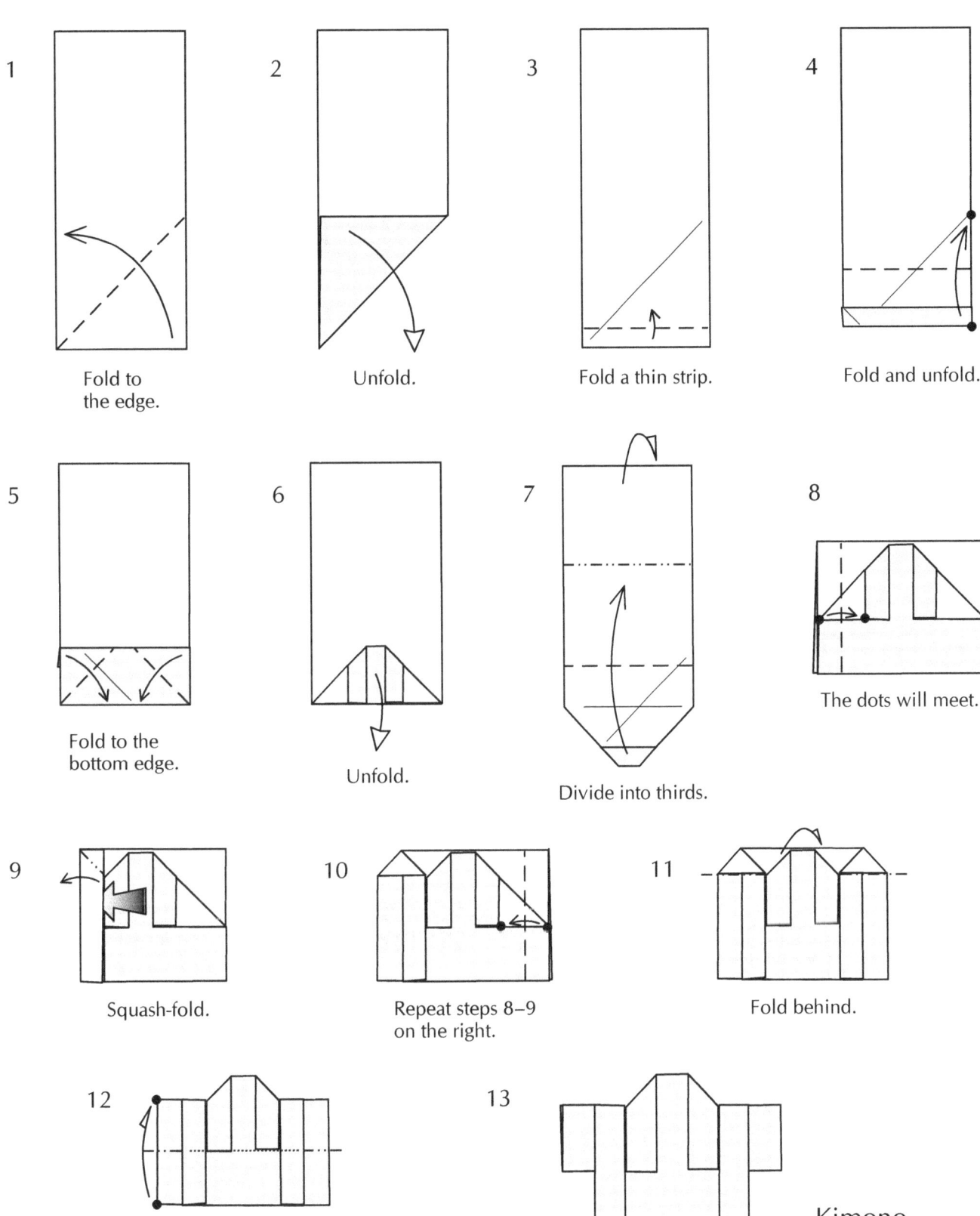

Boats & Hats

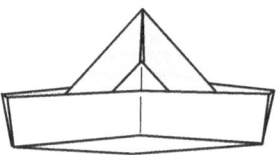

With this collection of eight models, you can fold several dollar boats and hats. Though these are all original designs, most are variations of traditional models folded from a square.

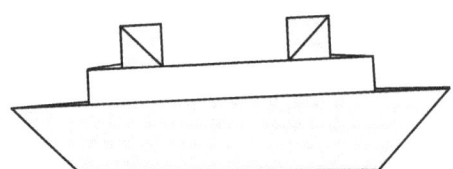

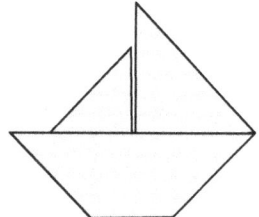

Navy Cap

1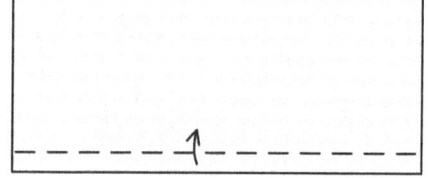

Fold a thin strip up.

2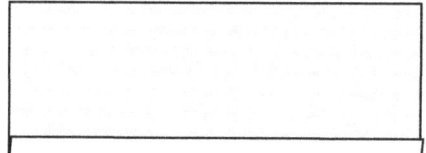

3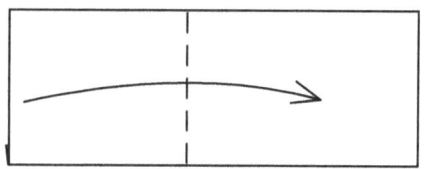

Fold to the right but leave a little space on the right.

4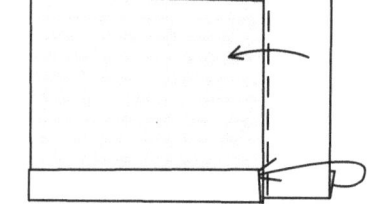

Tuck inside at the bottom.

5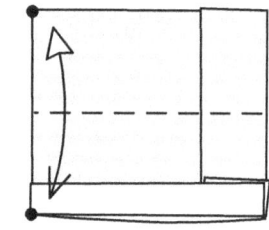

Fold in half and unfold.

6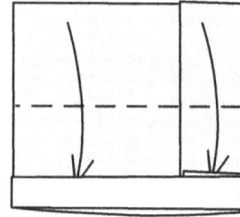

Tuck inside.

7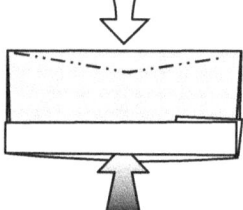

Push in at the top and open at the bottom.

8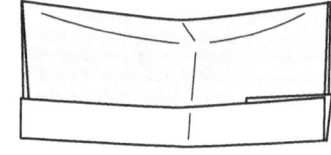

Navy Cap

26   *Dollar Origami Treasures*

Pirate Hat

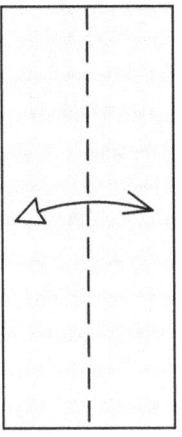

1 Fold and unfold.

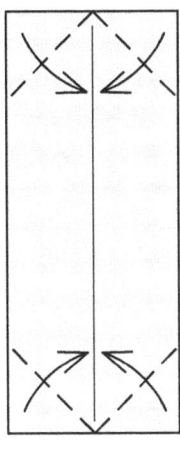

2 Fold to the center.

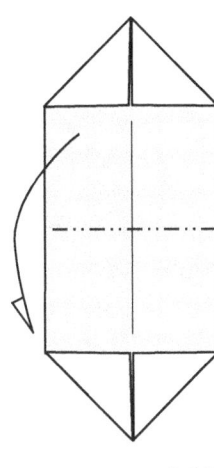

3 Mountain-fold in half.

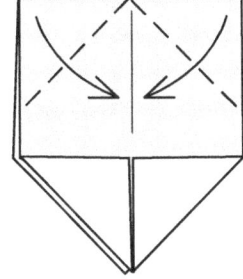

4 Fold to the center.

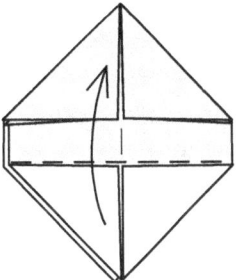

5 Fold the top layer up and repeat behind.

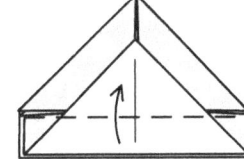

6 Fold the top layer up and repeat behind.

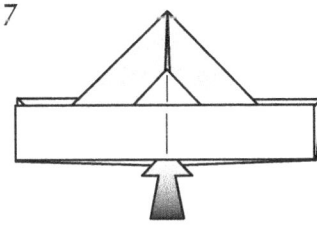

7 Open.

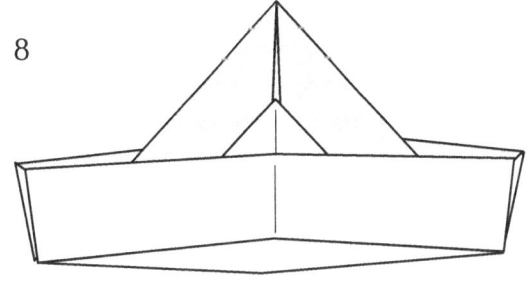

8 Pirate Hat

Samurai Hat

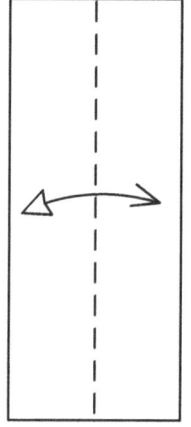

1. Fold and unfold.

2.

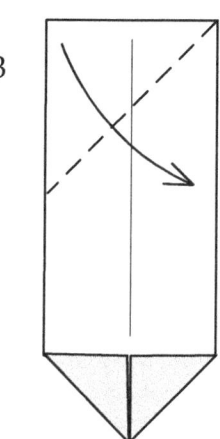

3.

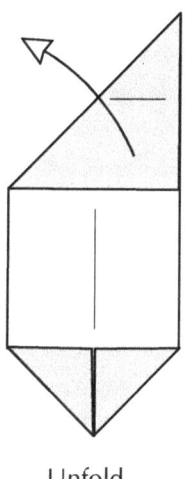

4. Unfold.

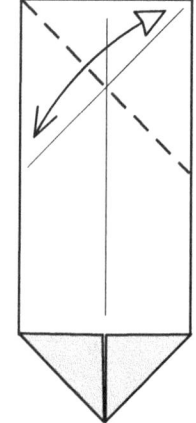

5. Fold and unfold.

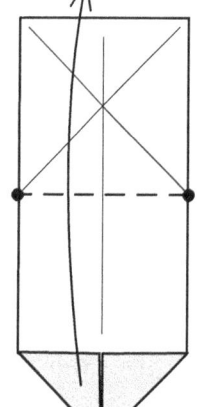

6.

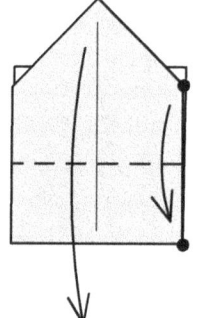

7.

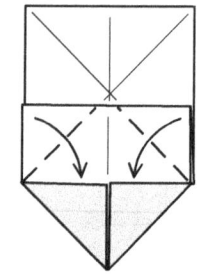

8.

28   *Dollar Origami Treasures*

9

Fold along the creases.

10

11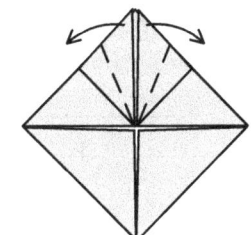

12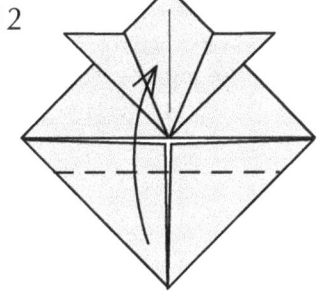

13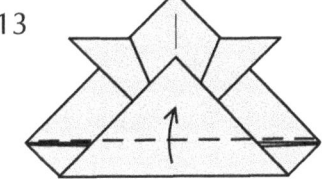

14

Place your finger inside to open the hat.

15

Samurai Hat

Party Hat

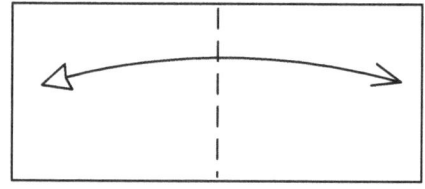
1 Fold and unfold.

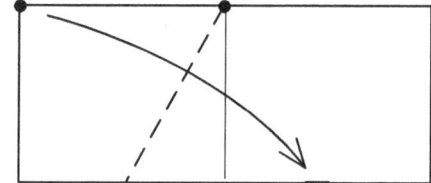
2 Bring the corner to the bottom edge.

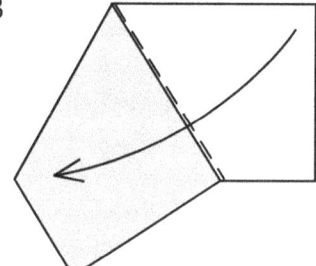
3

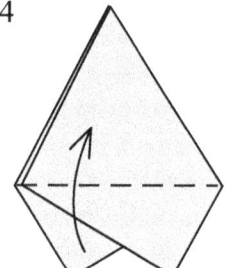
4

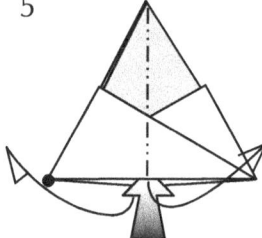
5 Open the hat and follow the dot into the next step.

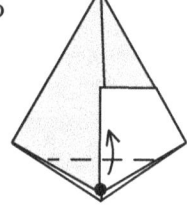
6 Fold the top layers and repeat behind.

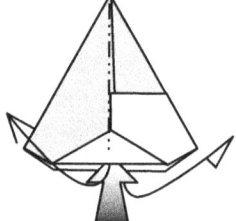
7 Open and flatten.

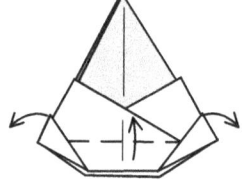
8 Stretch on both sides. Repeat behind.

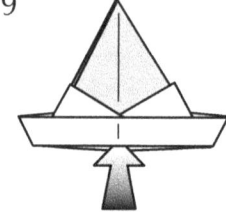
9 Open.

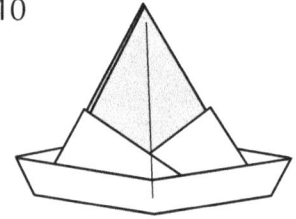
10 Party Hat

30 *Dollar Origami Treasures*

Yacht

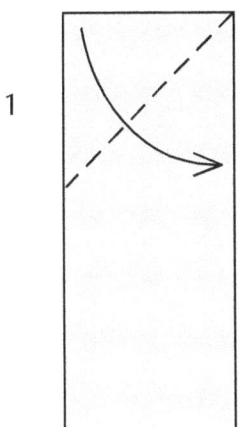

1

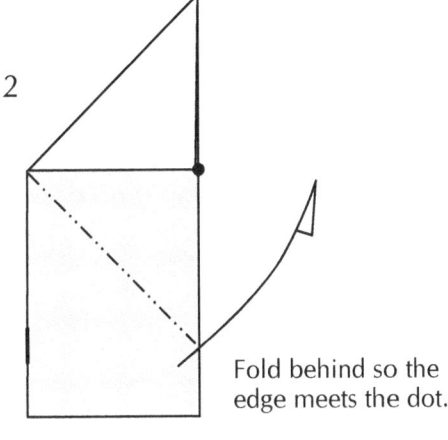

2

Fold behind so the edge meets the dot.

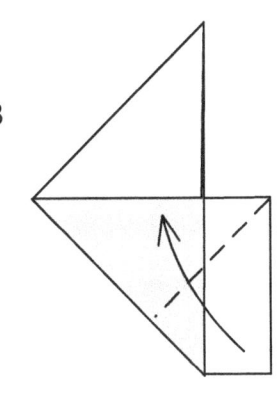

3

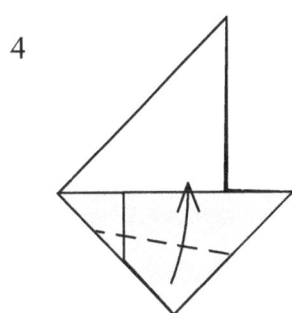

4

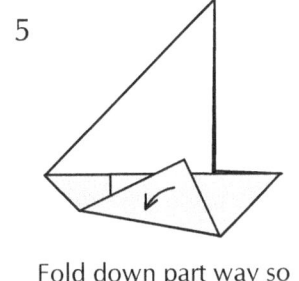

5

Fold down part way so the yacht can balance.

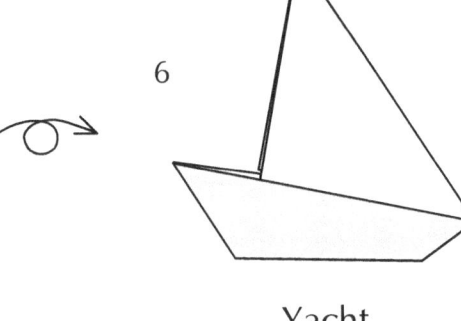

6

Yacht

Canoe

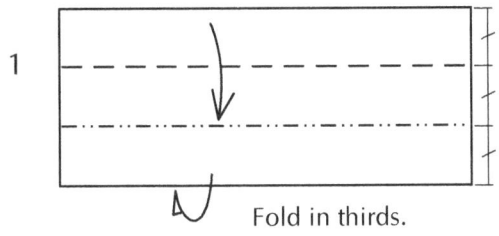

1

Fold in thirds.

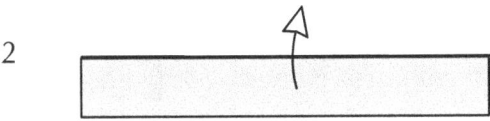

2

Unfold the top layer.

3

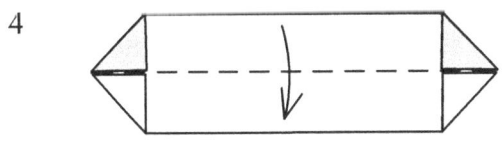

4

Fold along the crease.

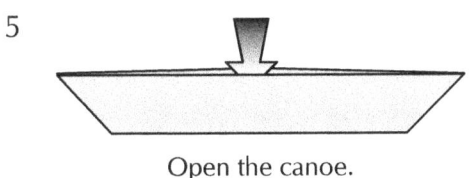

5

Open the canoe.

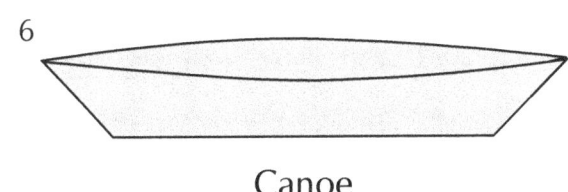

6

Canoe

Yacht 31

Ocean Liner

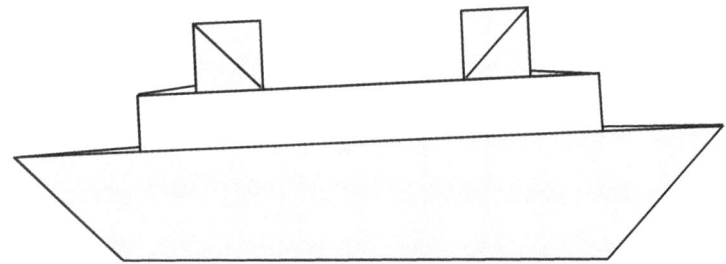

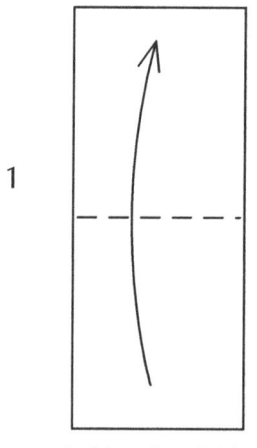

1. Fold and unfold.

2. Fold the top layer down and repeat behind.

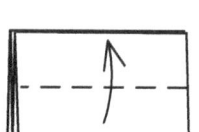

3. Fold the top layer up and repeat behind.

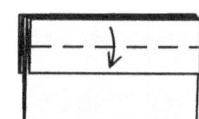

4. Fold the top layer down and repeat behind.

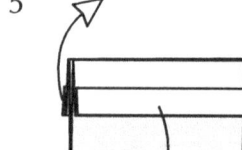

5. Spread and rotate. Keep some of the folds by the ends.

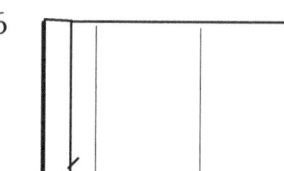

6. Fold behind.

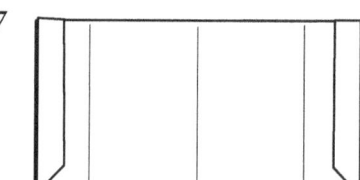

7.

32 *Dollar Origami Treasures*

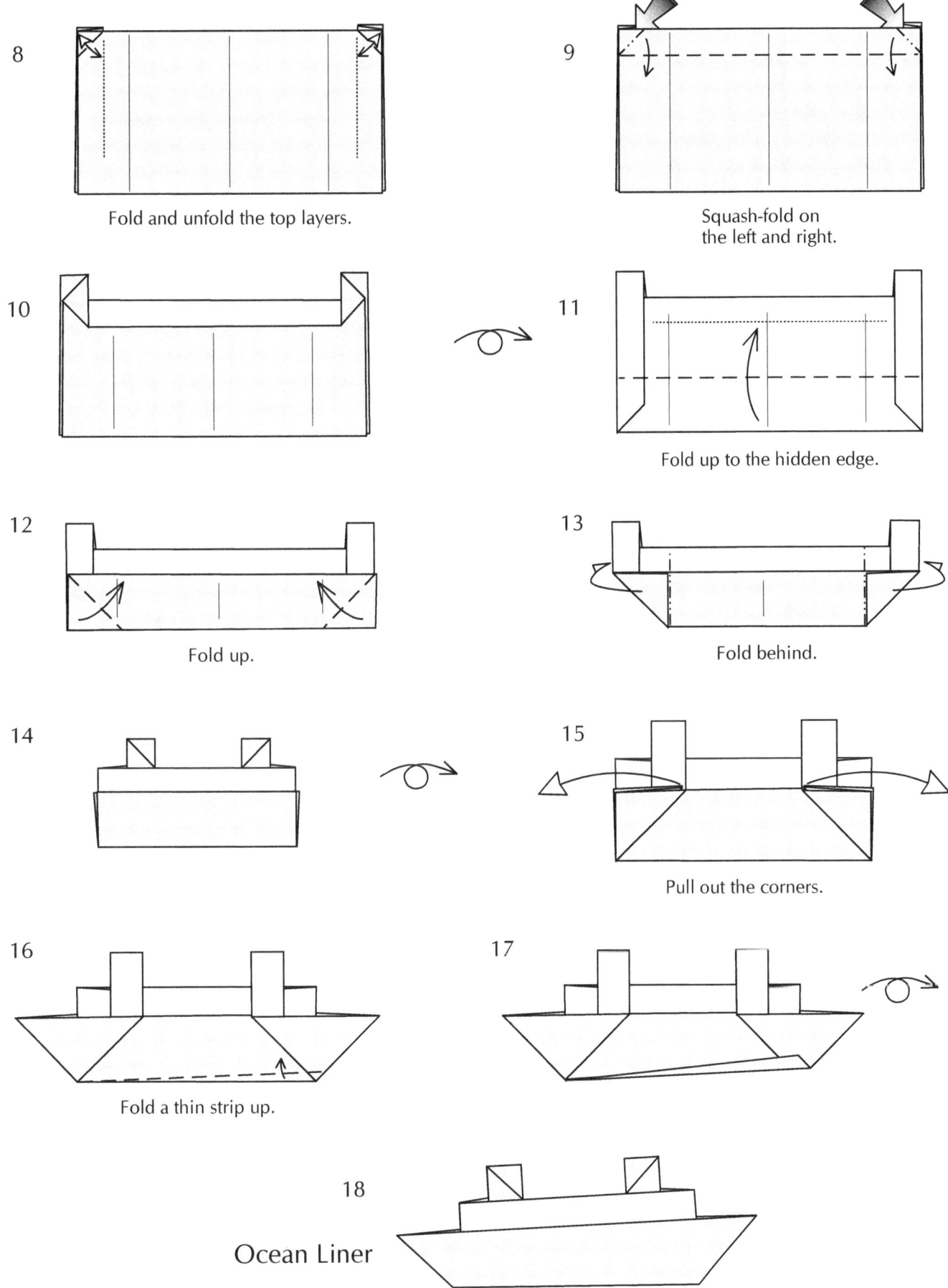

Sailboat

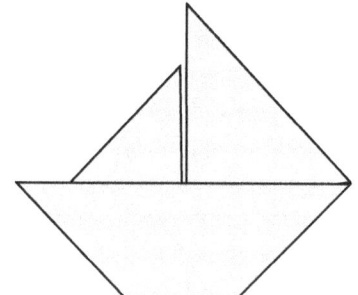

1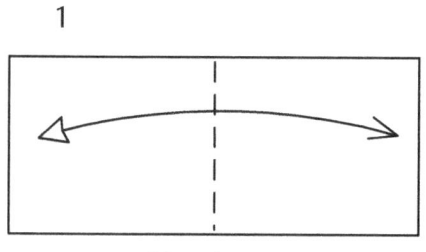
Fold and unfold.

2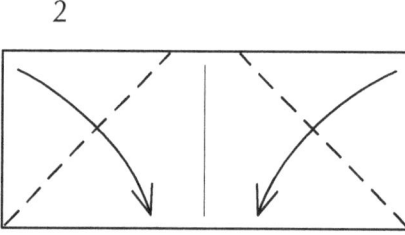

3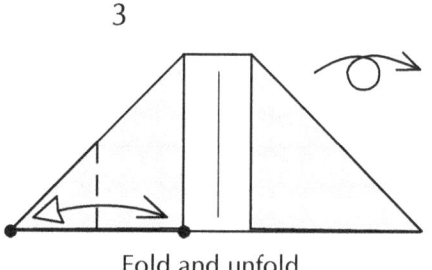
Fold and unfold.

4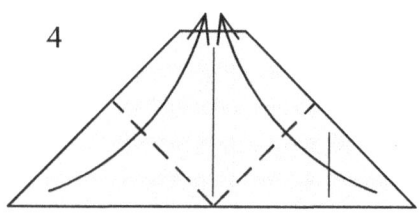

5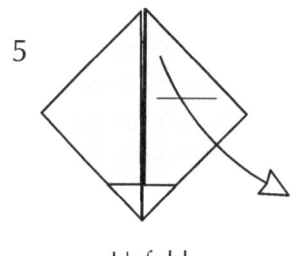
Unfold.

6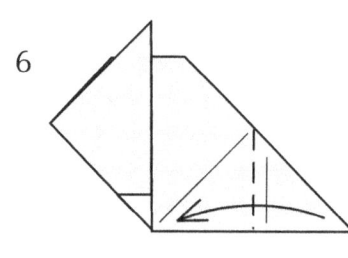

7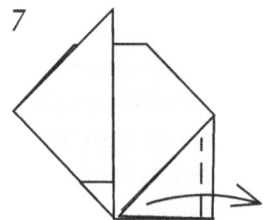

8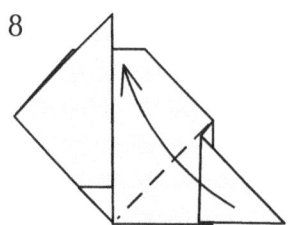

9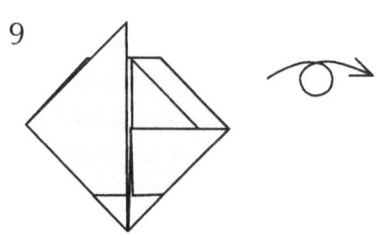

10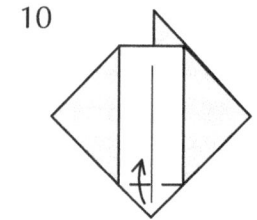

11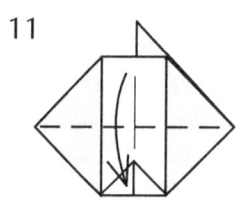

12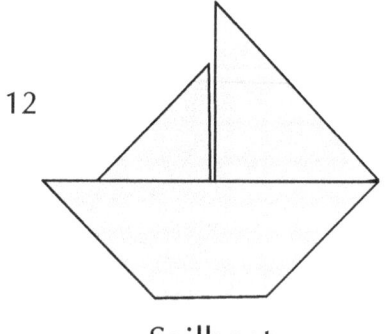
Sailboat

34 *Dollar Origami Treasures*

Bugs & Birds

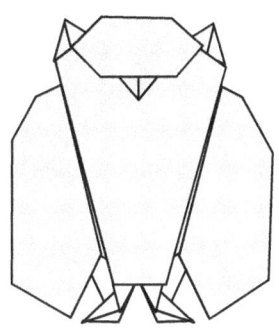
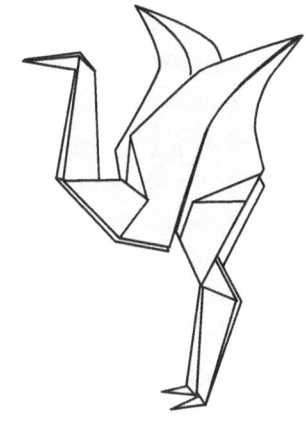
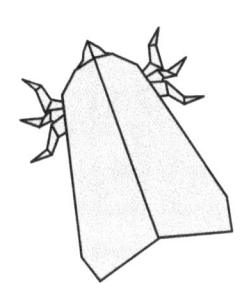

Here is a collection of over a dozen dollar models of bugs and birds. The birds are flying, standing, or wading. The pajarita was designed to resemble the Spanish version of their traditional "little bird". The dollar moth is not so difficult, even with its six legs.

Butterfly

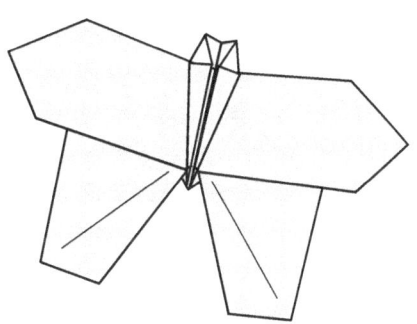

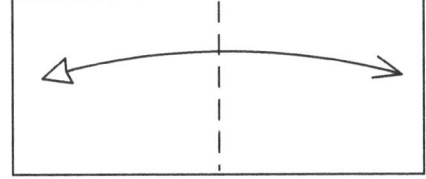

1. Fold and unfold.

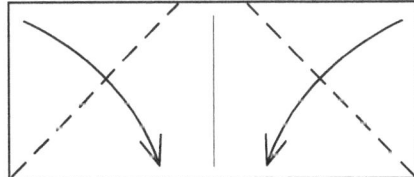

2.

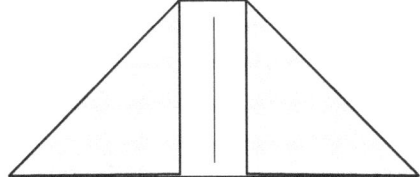

3.

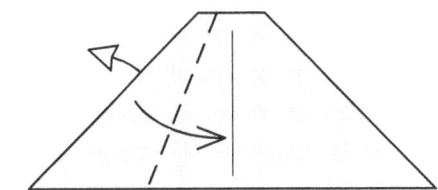

4. Fold to the center and swing out from behind.

Butterfly 35

5

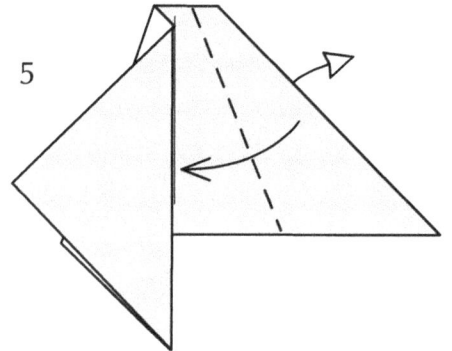

Fold to the center and swing out from behind.

6

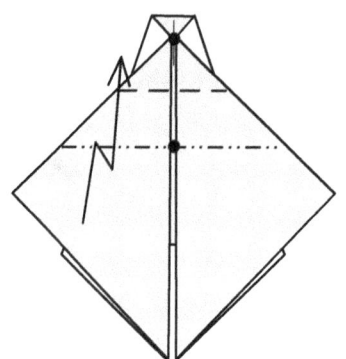

Fold back and forth so the dots meet.

7

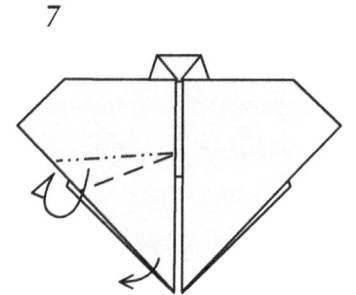

Push in and spread at the bottom.

8

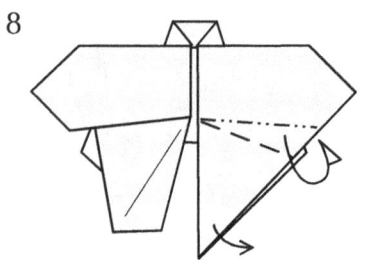

Push in and spread at the bottom.

9

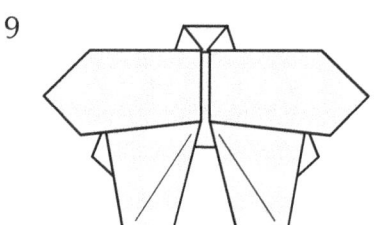 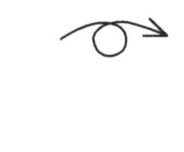

10

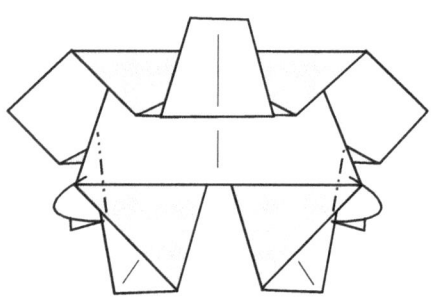

Tuck inside.

11

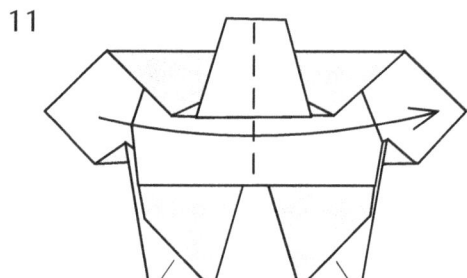

Fold in half.

12

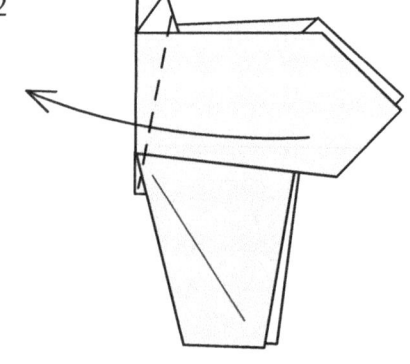

Repeat behind and spread.

13

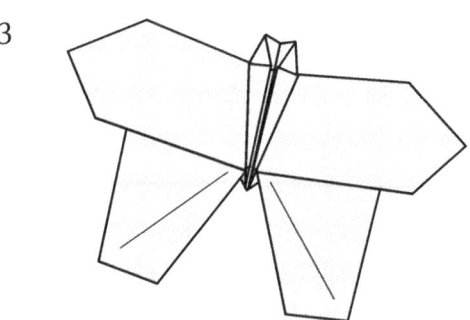

Butterfly

36 *Dollar Origami Treasures*

Flying Crane

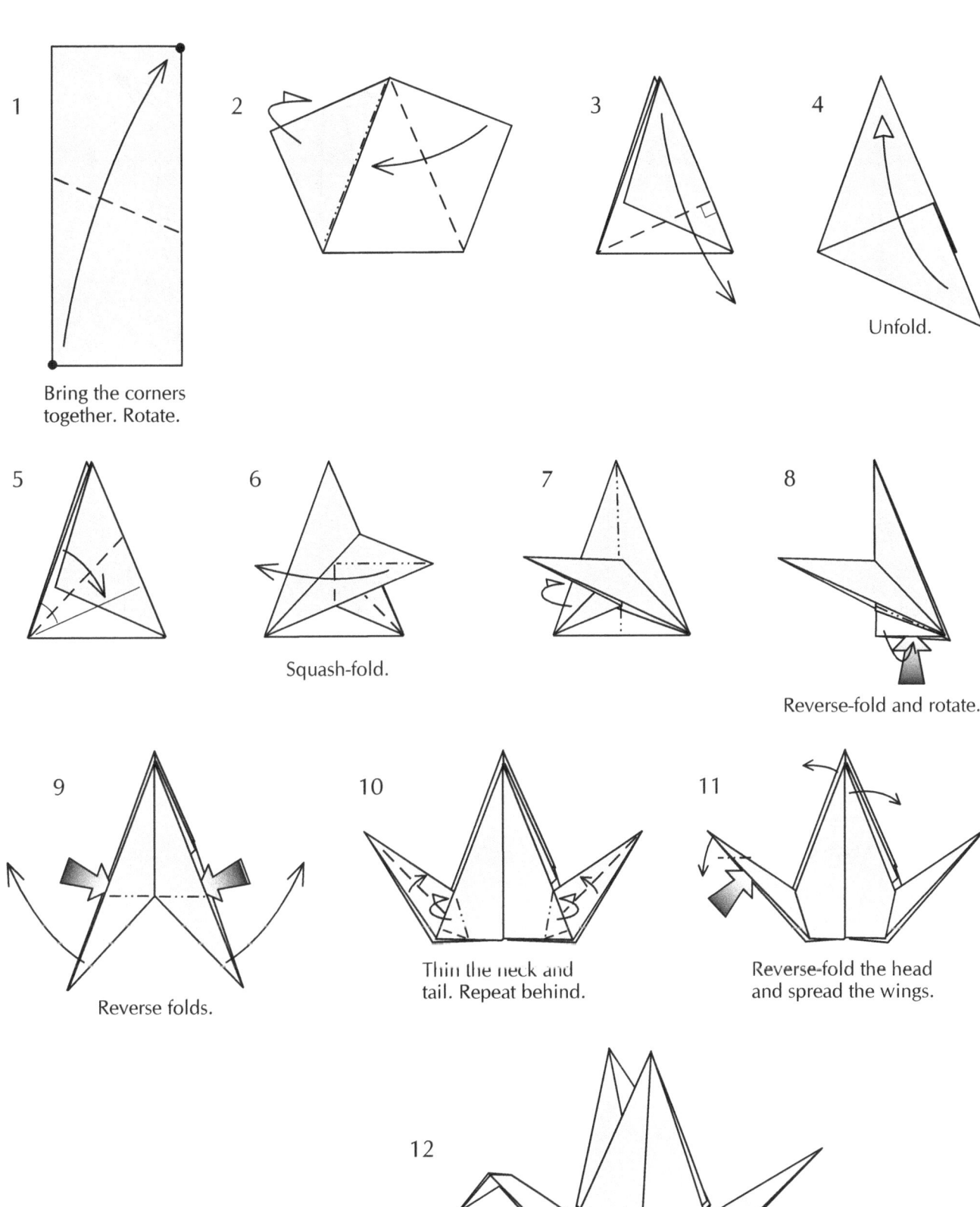

Standing Crane

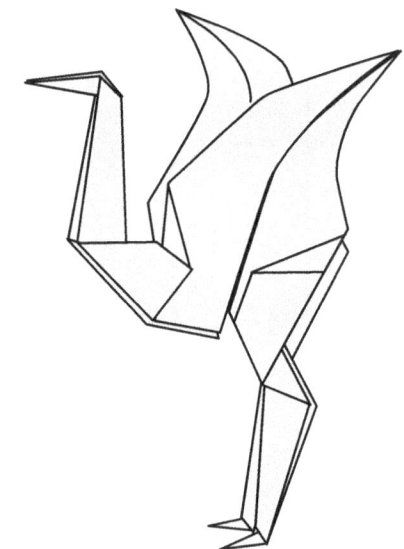

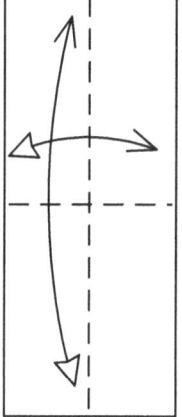

1

Fold and unfold.

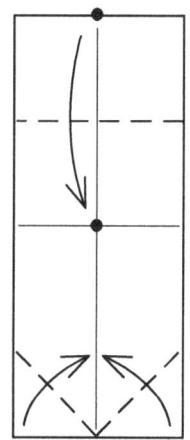

2

Fold to the center.

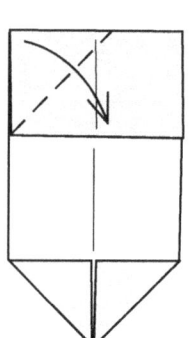

3

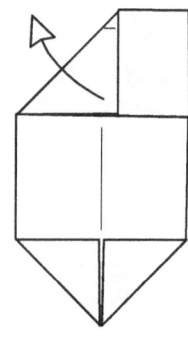

4

Unfold.

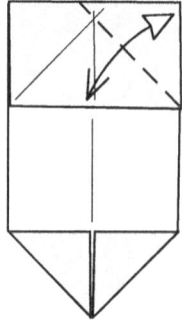

5

Fold and unfold.

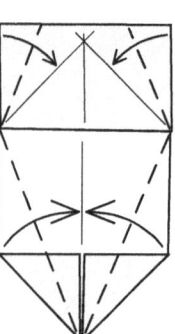

6

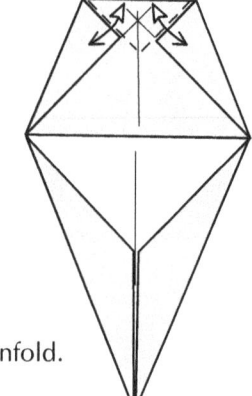

7

Fold and unfold.

38 *Dollar Origami Treasures*

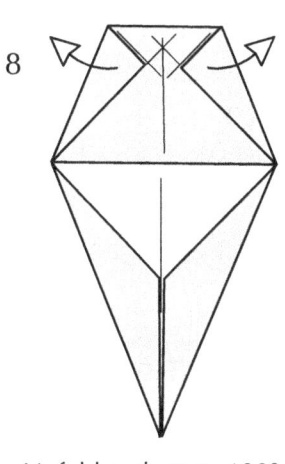

8

Unfold and rotate 180°.

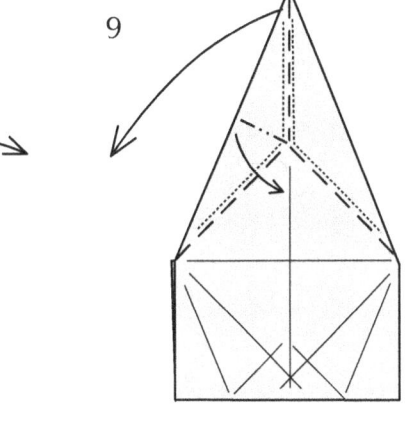

9

Rabbit-ear.

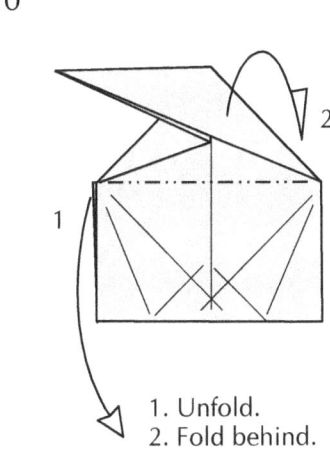

10

1. Unfold.
2. Fold behind.

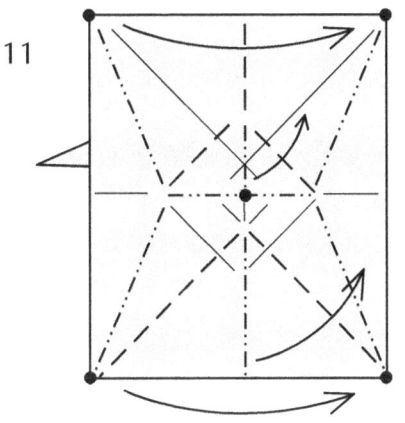

11

Push up at the center dot. The other pairs will meet.

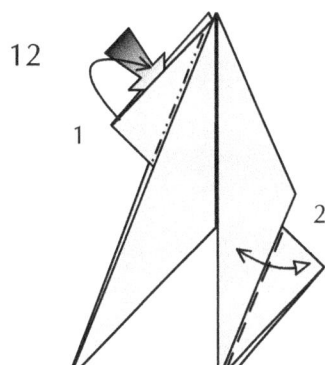

12

1. Reverse-fold.
2. Fold and unfold both layers.

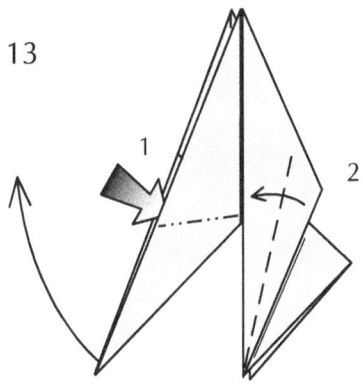

13

1. Push in.
2. Repeat behind.

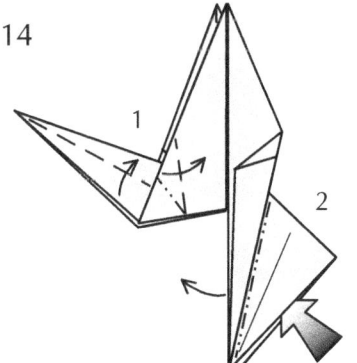

14

1. Thin the neck and repeat behind.
2. Reverse-fold.

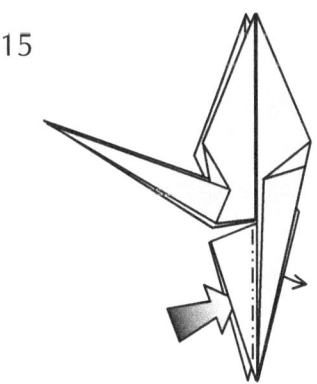

15

Reverse-fold along the crease.

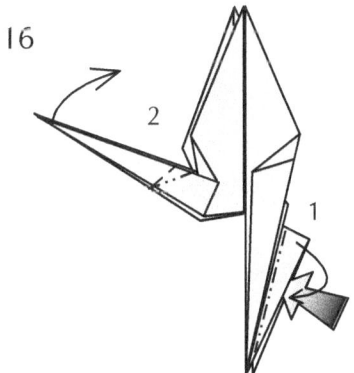

16

1. Reverse-fold.
2. Crimp-fold.

Standing Crane 39

17

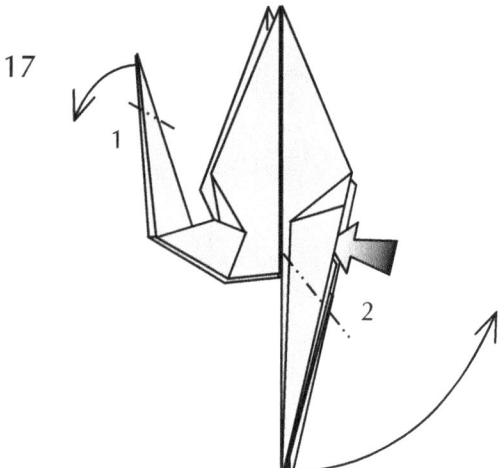

1. Reverse-fold.
2. Reverse-fold all the layers together.

18

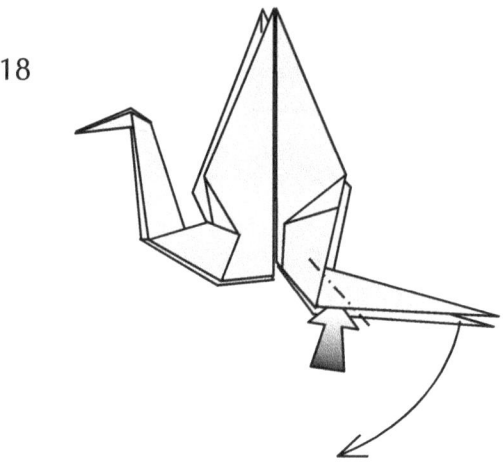

Reverse-fold all the layers together.

19

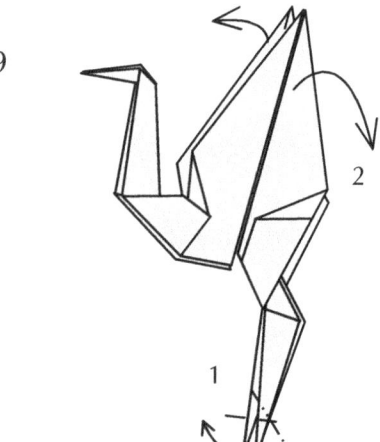

1. Crimp-fold.
2. Spread the wings.
Repeat behind.

20

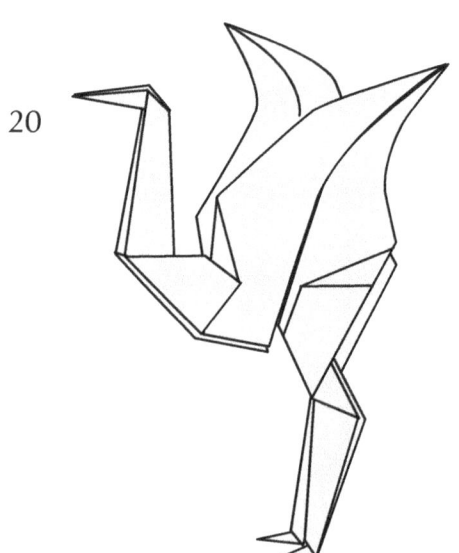

Standing Crane

Parakeet

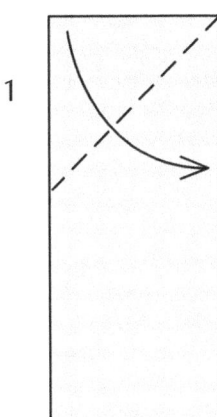

1.

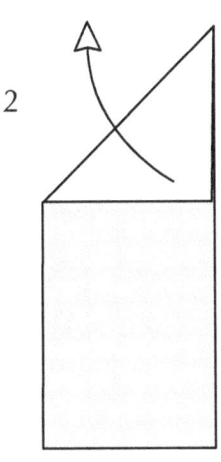

2. Unfold.

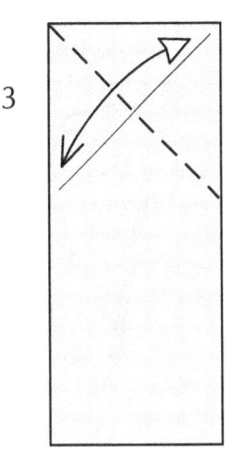

3. Fold and unfold.

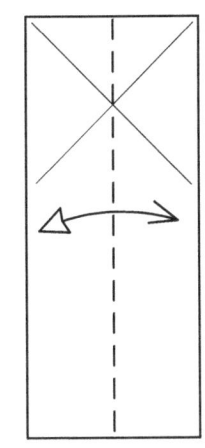

4. Fold and unfold.

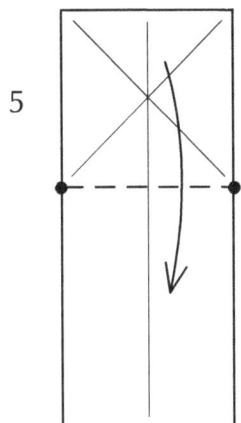

5.

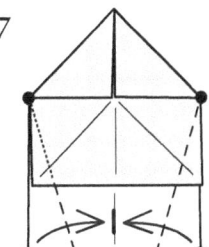

6. Fold to the center.

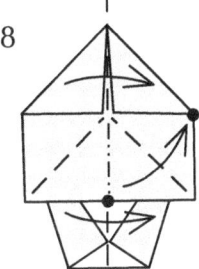

7. Fold the corners to the center crease.

8. Fold the dots together while folding in half.

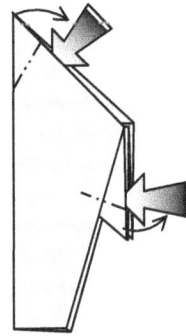

9. Reverse-fold the beak and feet. Repeat behind. Rotate.

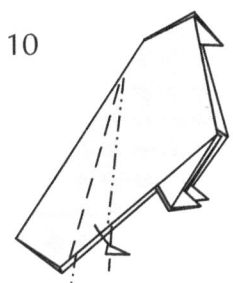

10. Crimp-fold.

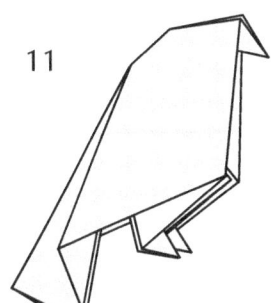

11. Parakeet

Parakeet 41

Swan

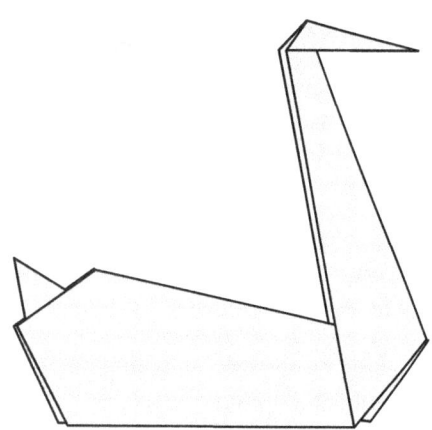

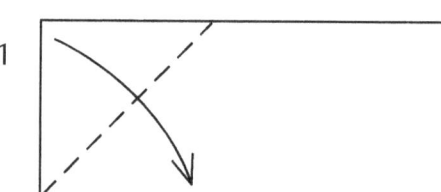
1

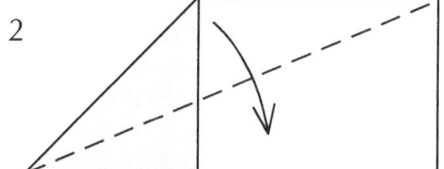
2

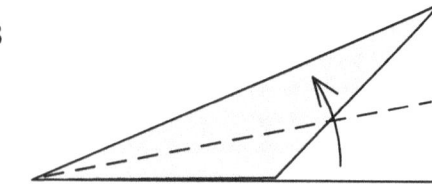
3

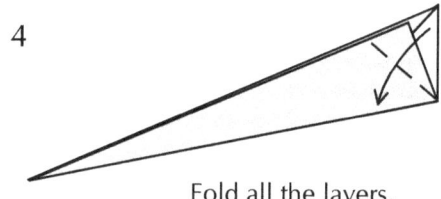
4

Fold all the layers.

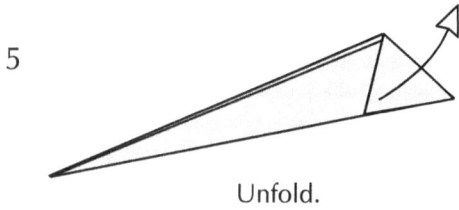
5

Unfold.

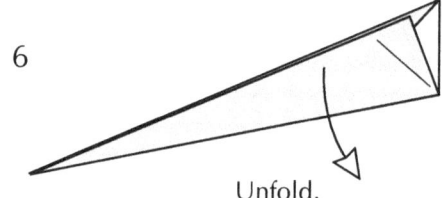
6

Unfold.

42   Dollar Origami Treasures

7
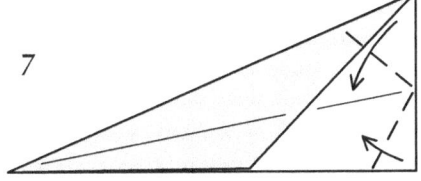
Fold along the creases.

8
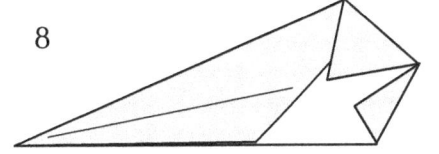
Turn over and rotate.

9
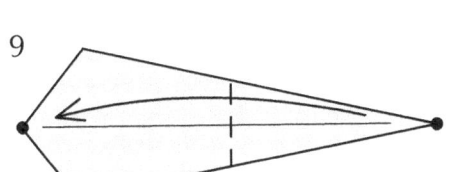

10
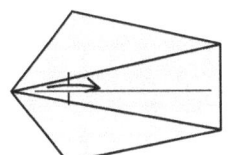

11
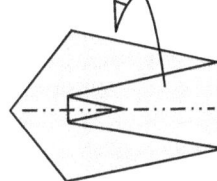

12
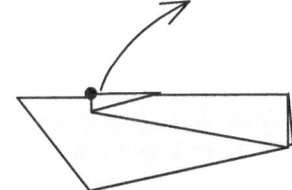
Slide the neck up.

13

Slide the head up.

14
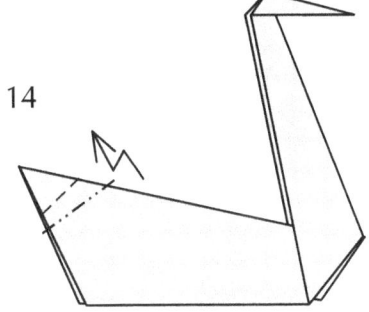
Crimp-fold.

15
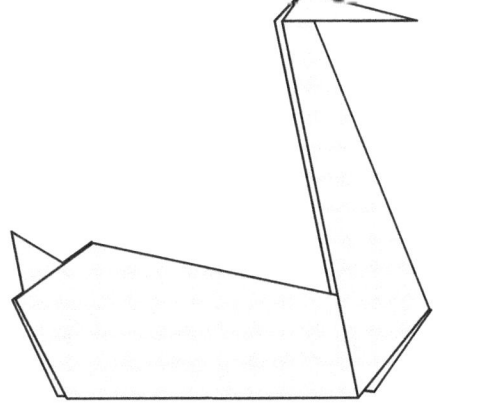
Swan

Eagle

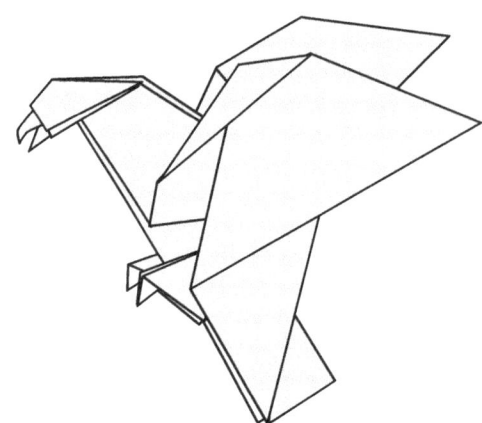

1.

2.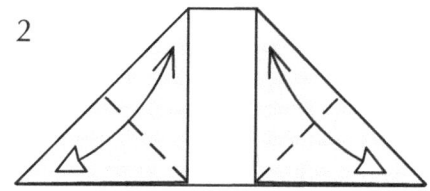
Fold and unfold.

3. Fold and unfold.

4.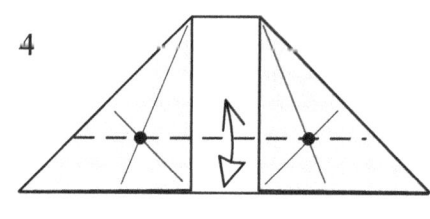
Fold and unfold.

5.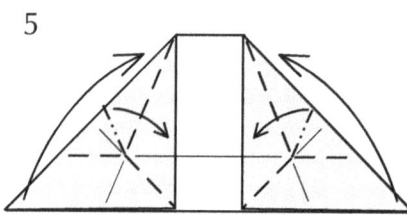
Make two rabbit ears. Valley-fold along the creases.

6.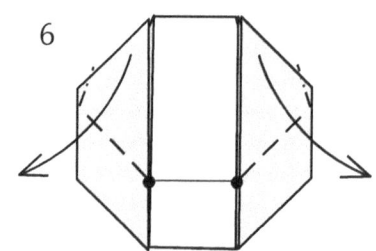
Make squash folds.

7.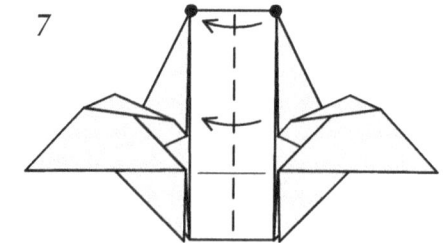

44   Dollar Origami Treasures

8

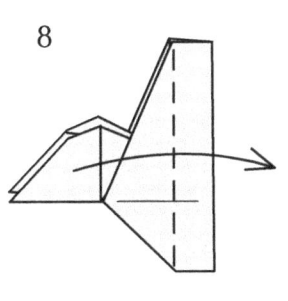

9

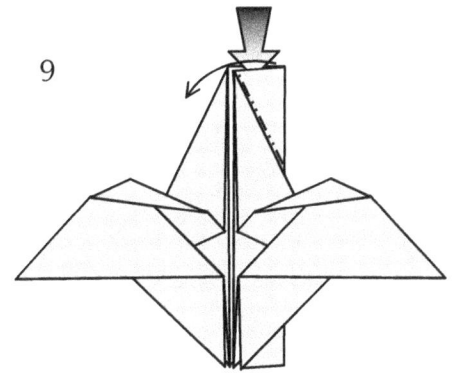

Reverse-fold.

10

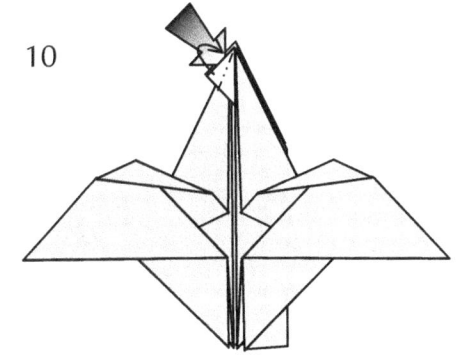

Reverse-fold.

11

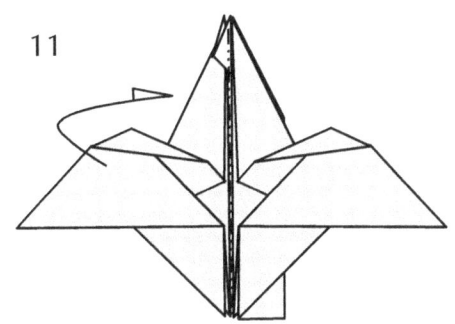

12

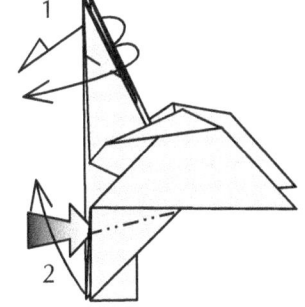

1. Outside-reverse-fold the head.
2. Reverse-fold and repeat behind.

13

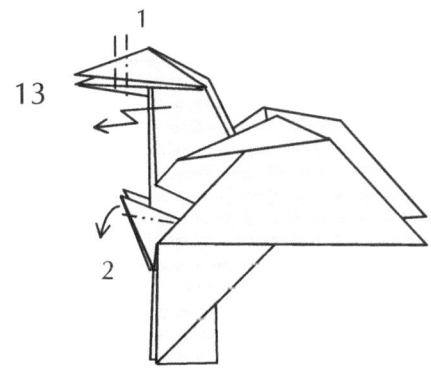

1. Crimp-fold, separate, and curl the beak.
2. Reverse-fold and repeat behind.

14

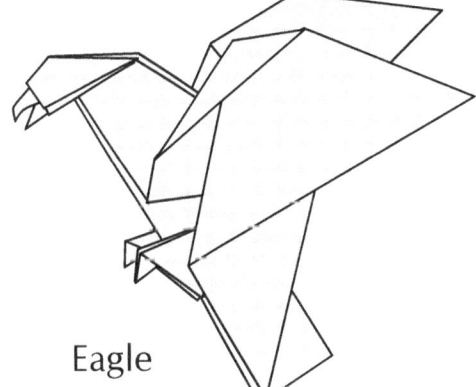

Eagle

Owl

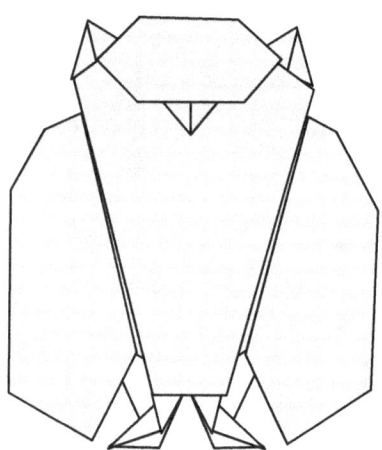

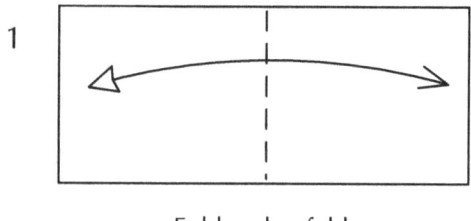
1 Fold and unfold.

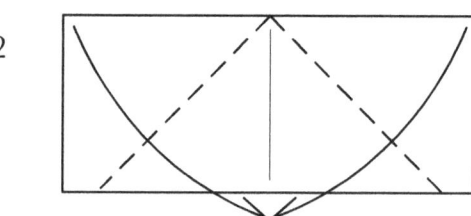
2

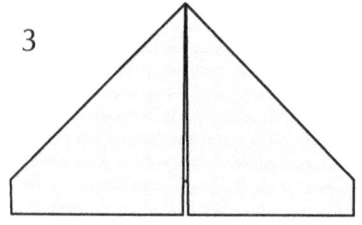
3

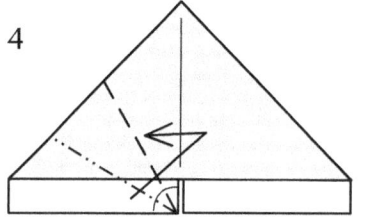
4 Fold in thirds.

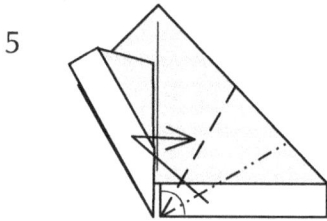
5 Fold in thirds.

46 *Dollar Origami Treasures*

6

7

Fold to the center and swing out from behind.

8

Fold to the center and swing out from behind.

9

10

11

12

Squash folds.

13

14

15

1. Reverse folds.
2. Pleat-fold the beak and ears.

16

Owl

Hummingbird

1 Fold and unfold.

2

3

4 Squash folds.

5

6

48 *Dollar Origami Treasures*

7
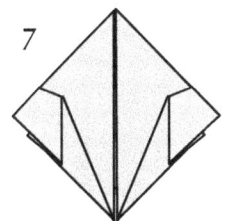

8
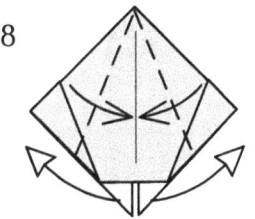

Fold to the center and swing out the flaps.

9

10
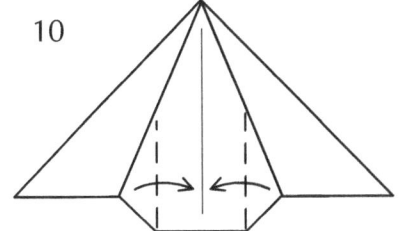

11
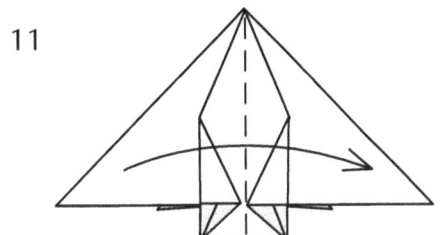

12
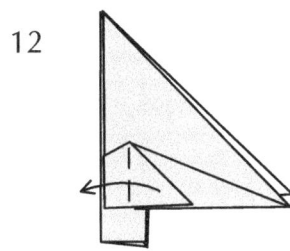

Repeat behind. Rotate.

13
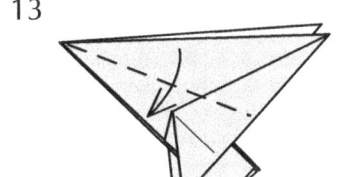

Repeat behind.

14
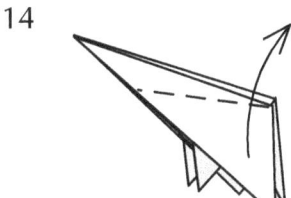

Repeat behind.

15
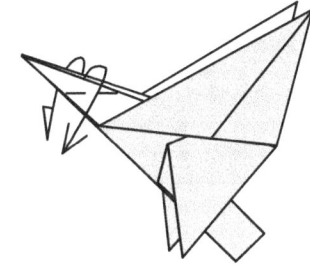

Outside-reverse-fold.

16
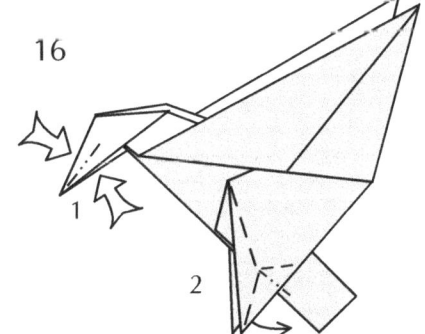

1. Squeeze the beak.
2. Rabbit-ear and repeat behind.

17
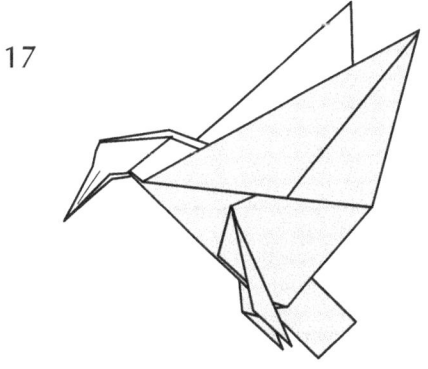

Hummingbird

Pigeon

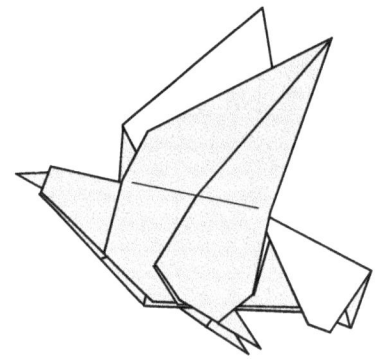

1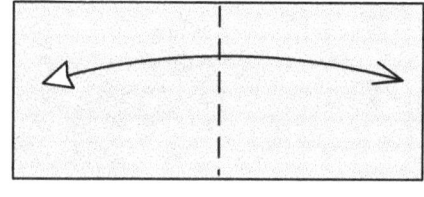

Fold and unfold.

2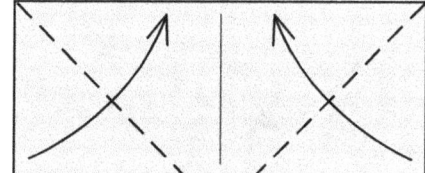

3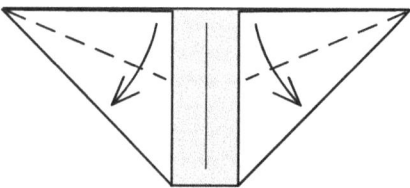

4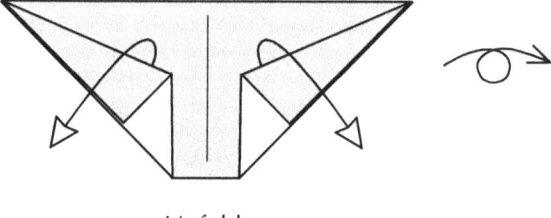

Unfold.

5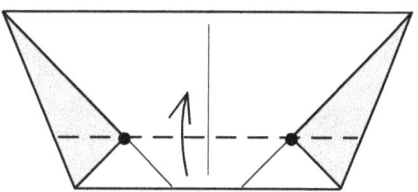

6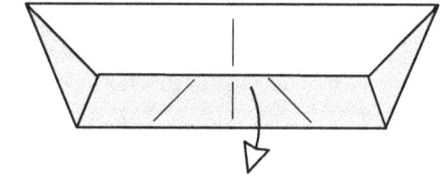

Unfold.

50 *Dollar Origami Treasures*

7

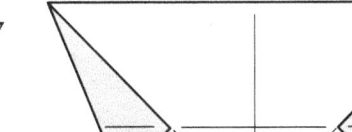

Unfold.

8

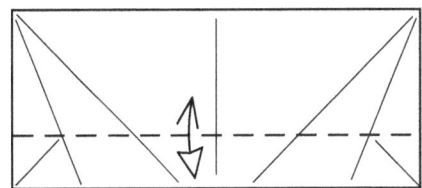

Fold and unfold along the crease.

9

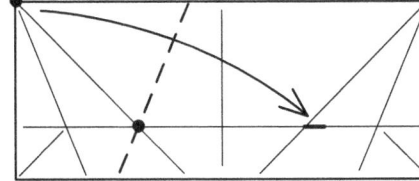

10

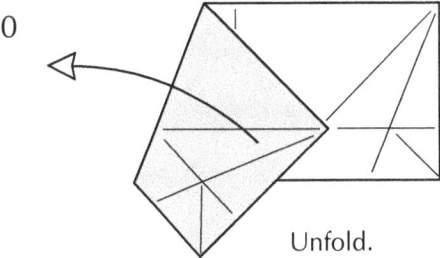

Unfold.

11

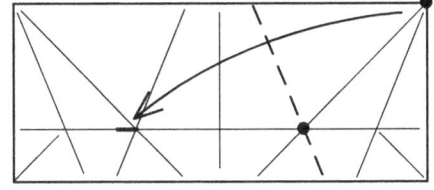

Repeat steps 9–10 on the right.

12

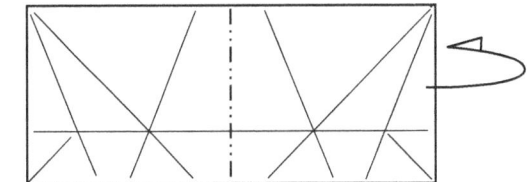

Fold behind and rotate 90°.

13

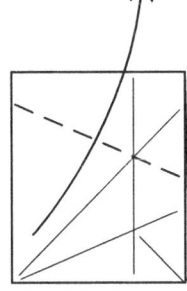

Fold along the crease and repeat behind.

14

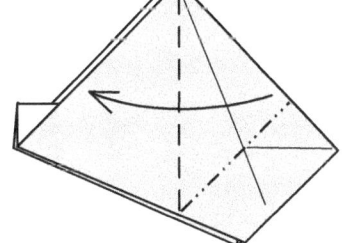

Squash-fold along the creases and repeat behind.

15

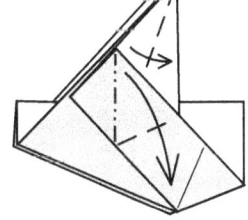

Squash-fold along the creases and repeat behind.

Pigeon 51

16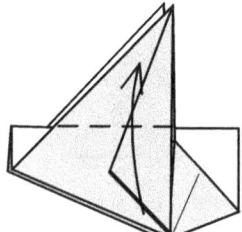

17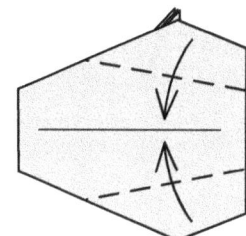

18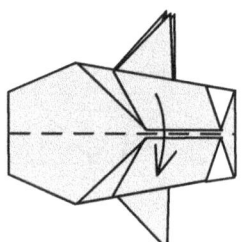

19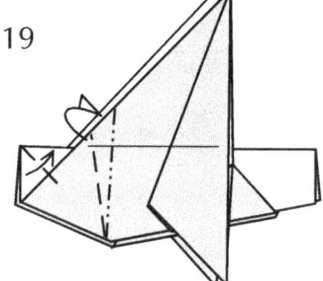

Repeat behind.

20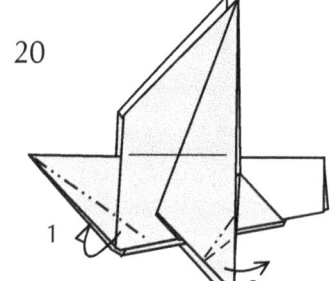

1. Fold behind.
2. Pleat-fold.
Repeat behind.

21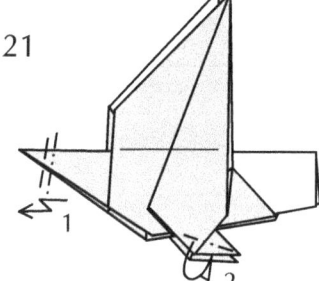

1. Crimp-fold.
2. Fold behind and repeat behind.

22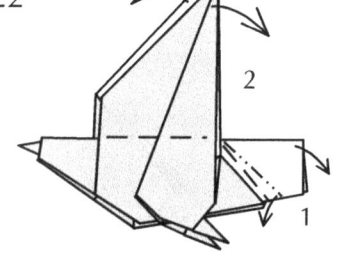

1. Crimp-fold the tail.
2. Spread the wings.

23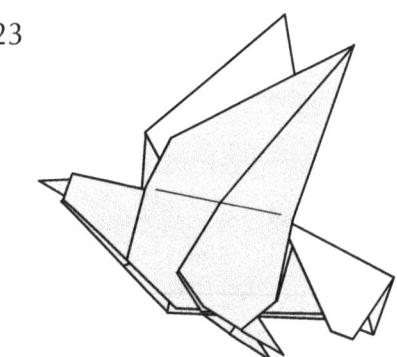

Pigeon

52   *Dollar Origami Treasures*

Pajarita

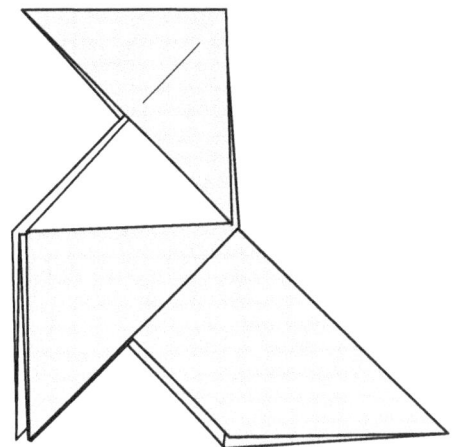

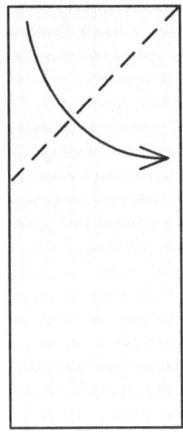

1

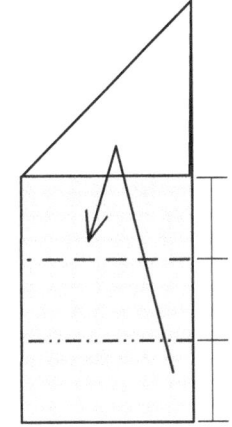

2

Fold in thirds.

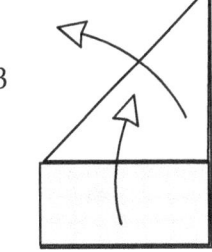

3

Unfold.

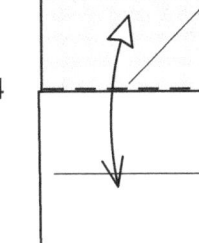

4

Fold and unfold along the edge.

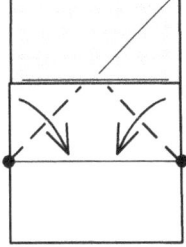

5

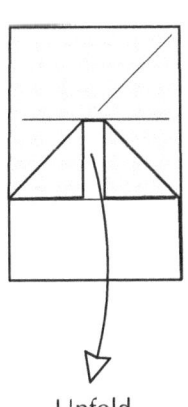

6

Unfold.

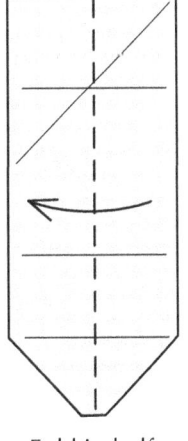

7

Fold in half.

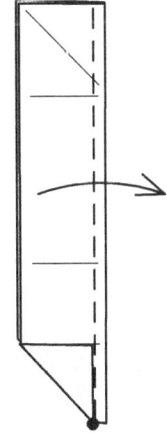

8

Pajarita   53

9

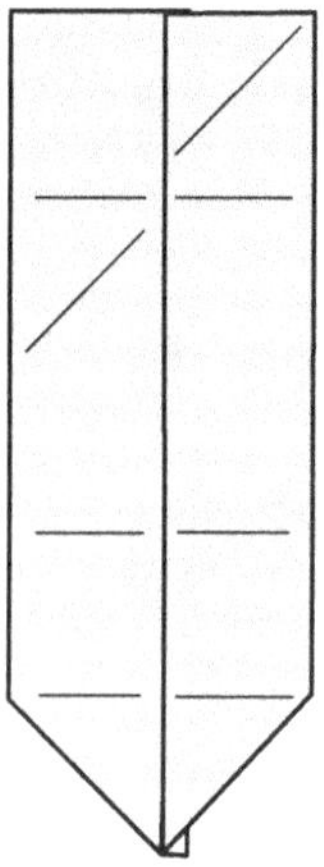

10

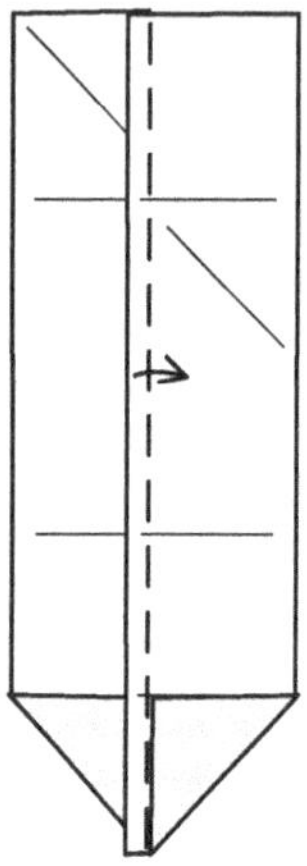

Fold a thin strip.

11

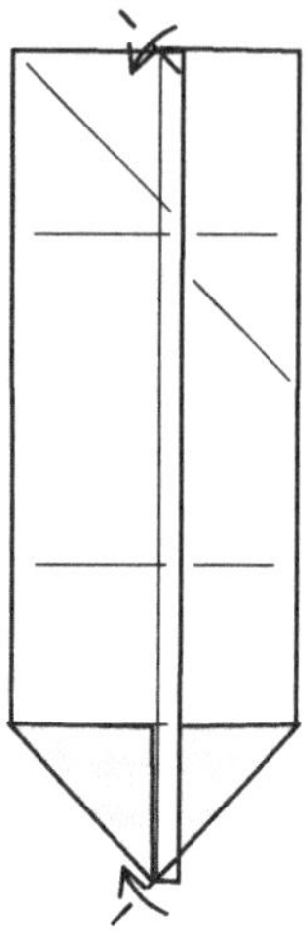

Fold the tips.

12

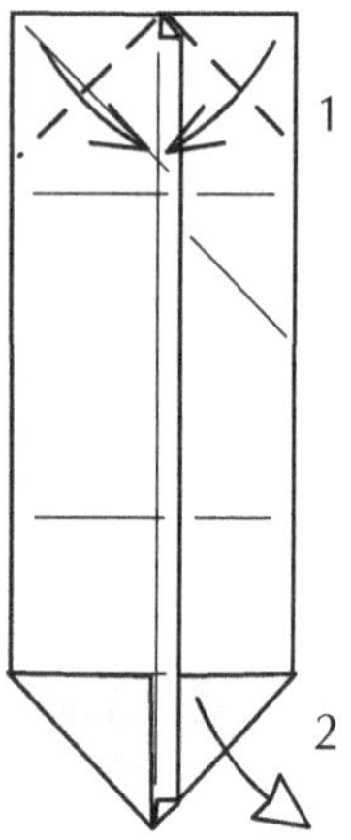

1. Fold to the center.
2. Unfold.

13

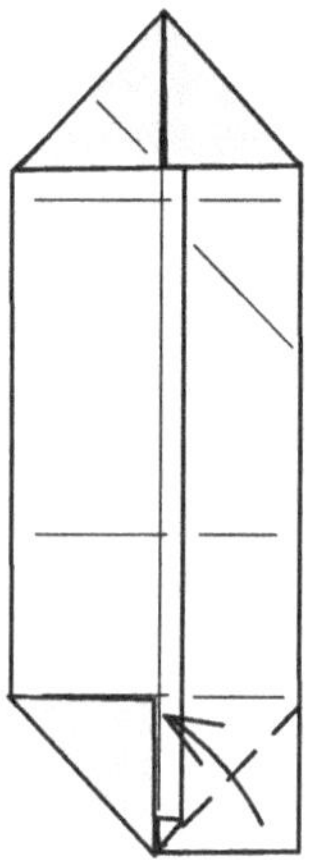

Fold along the crease.

14

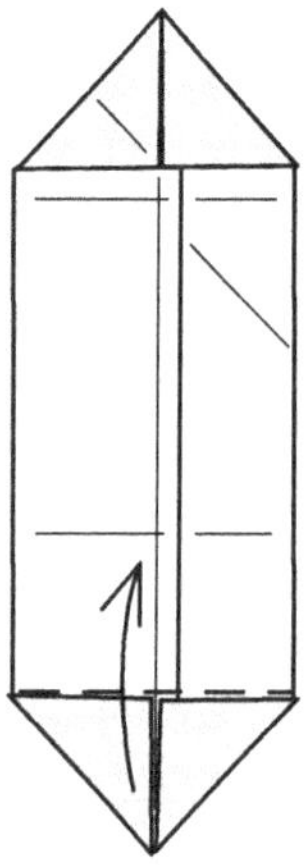

Fold along the crease.

15

16

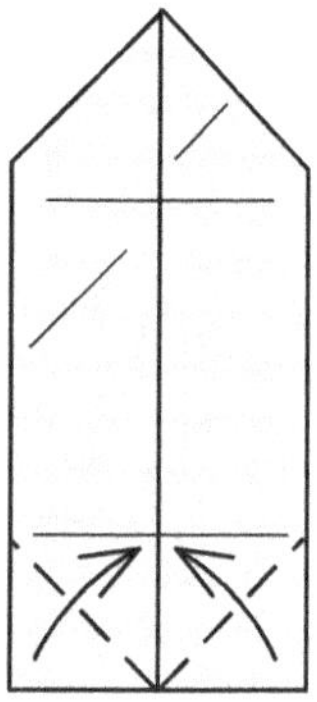

17

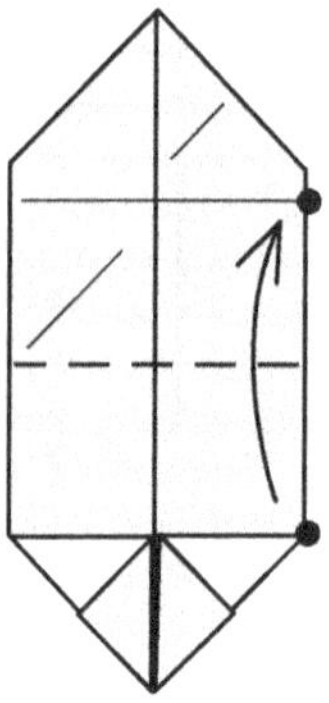

18

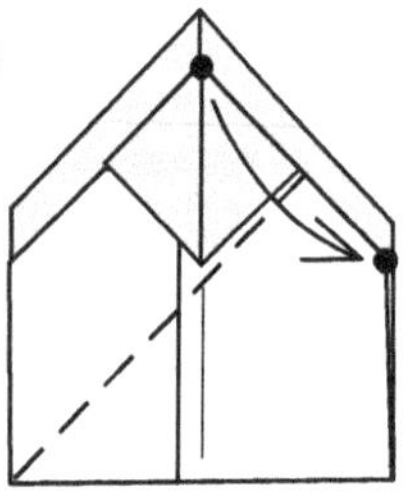

19

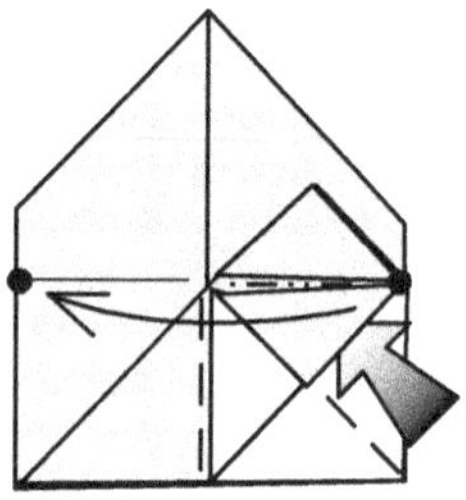

Squash-fold.

20

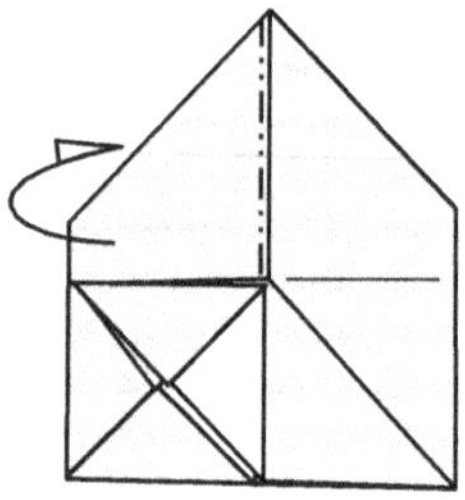

Fold behind and rotate.

54 *Dollar Origami Treasures*

21

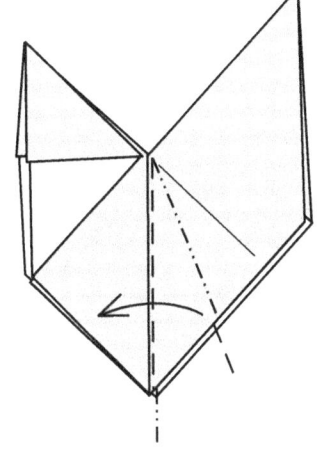

Crimp-fold.

22

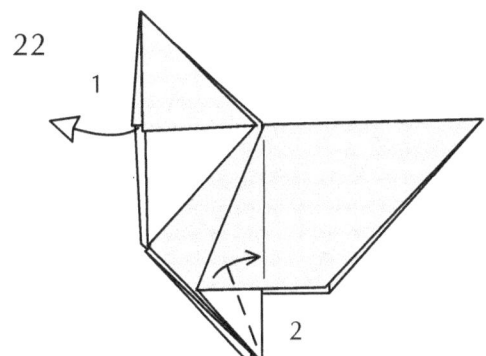

1. Pull out the head.
2. Repeat behind.

23

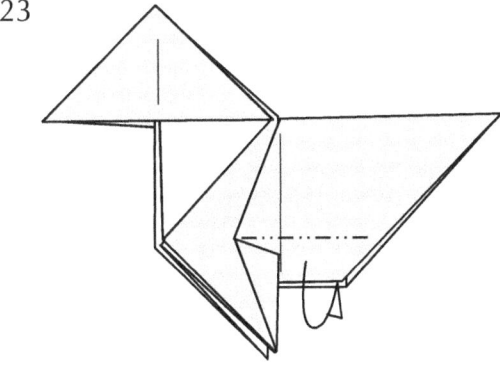

Fold inside and repeat behind.

24

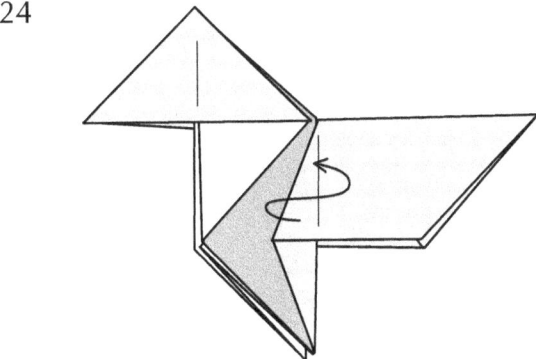

Tuck under the darker layer.
Repeat behind and rotate so
the pajarita can stand.

25

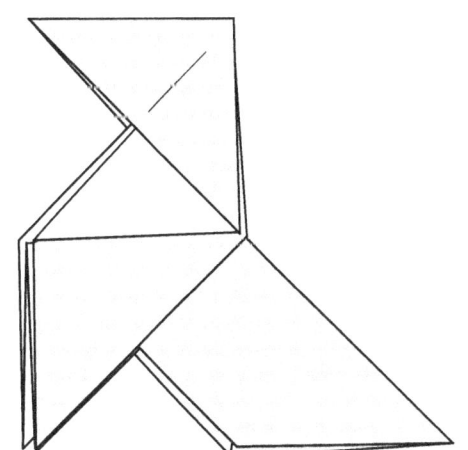

Pajarita
"Little Bird" in Spanish.

Ostrich

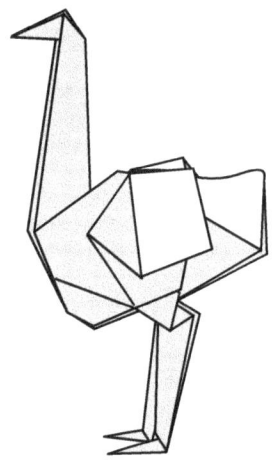

1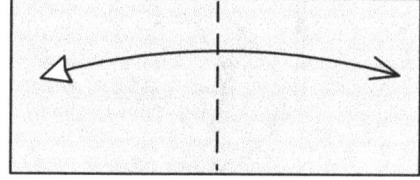

Fold and unfold.

2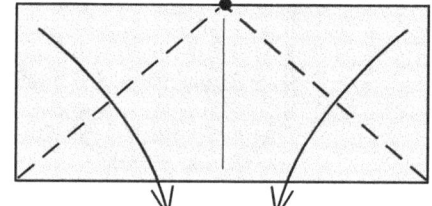

3

4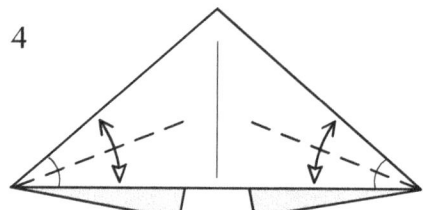

Fold and unfold the top layer to bisect the angle.

5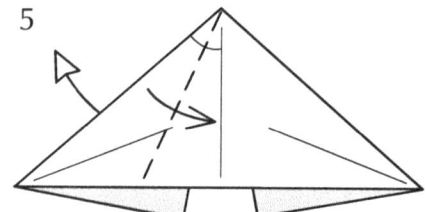

Bisect the angle and swing out the paper from behind.

6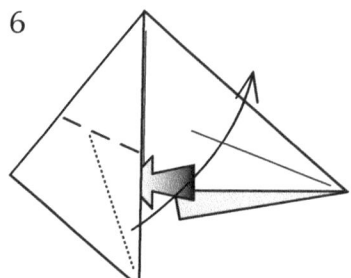

Squash-fold. Fold along the hidden crease shown as a dotted line.

7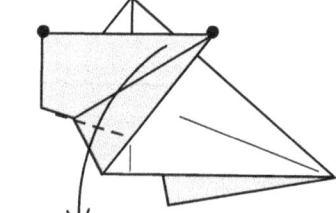

Note the horizontal line between the dots. Fold down.

56 *Dollar Origami Treasures*

8

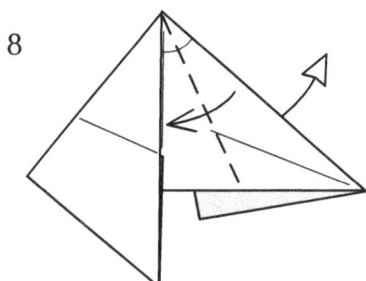

Repeat steps 5–7 on the right.

9

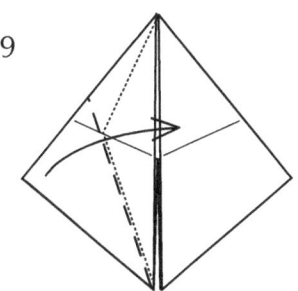

Fold along a hidden edge.

10

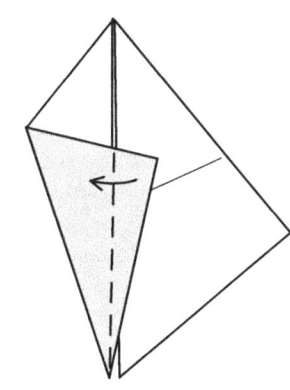

Fold along a hidden edge.

11

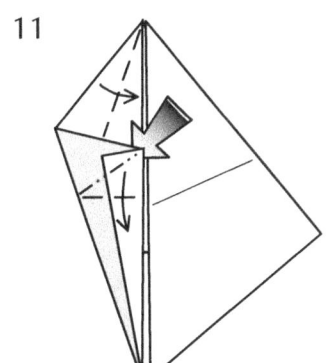

Squash-fold.

12

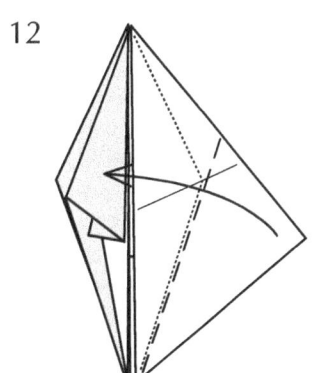

Repeat steps 9–11 on the right.

13

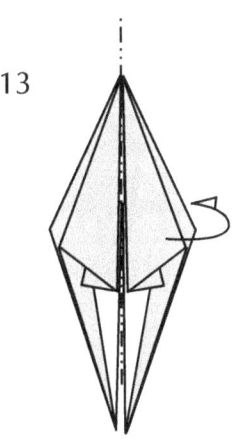

Fold in half. Rotate.

14

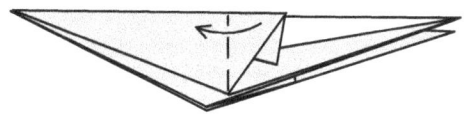

Repeat behind.

15

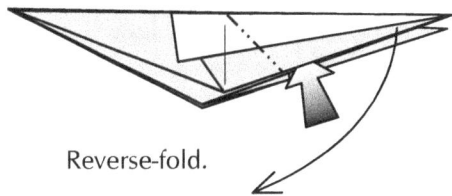

Reverse-fold.

16

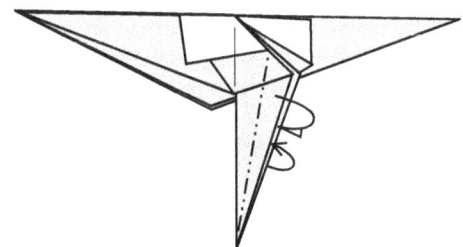

Fold inside on both sides.

17

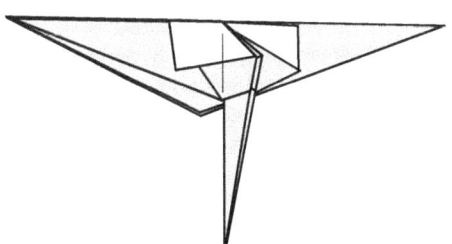

Repeat steps 15–16 behind.

Ostrich 57

18

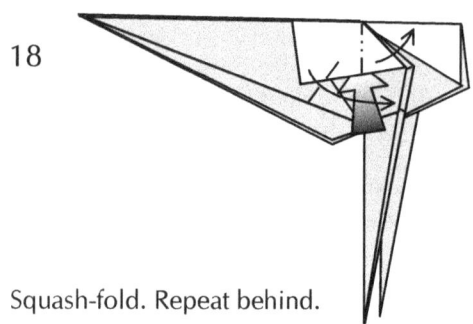

Squash-fold. Repeat behind.

19

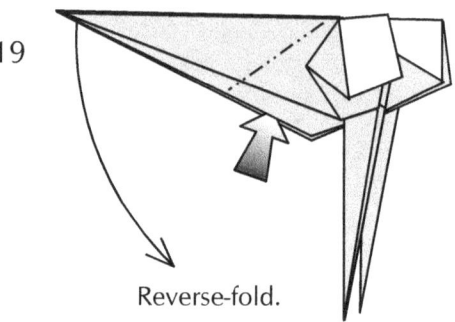

Reverse-fold.

20

1. Squash-fold.
2. Crimp-fold.
Repeat behind.

21

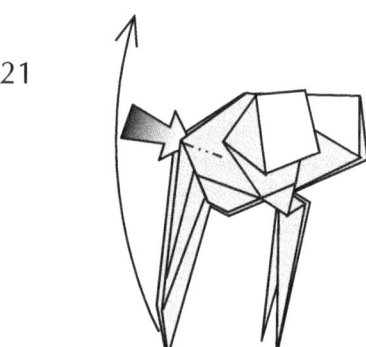

Reverse-fold.

22

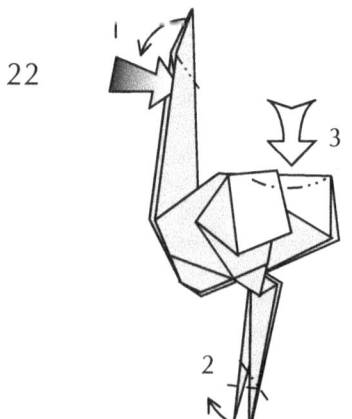

1. Reverse-fold.
2. Crimp-fold and repeat behind.
3. Shape the tail.
The bird can stand.

23

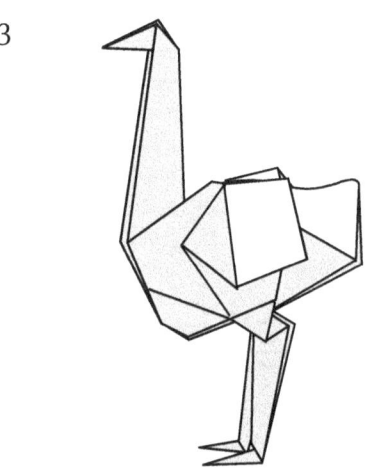

Ostrich

Heron

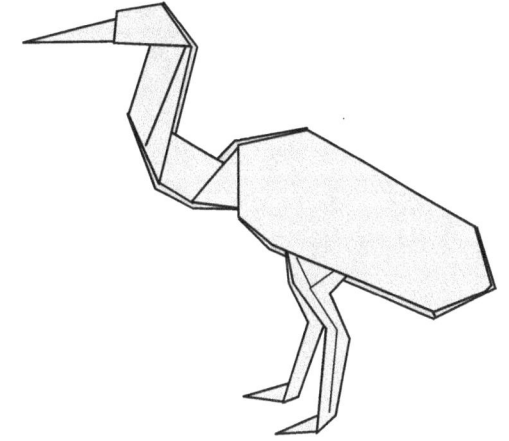

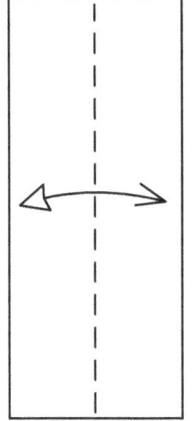
1

Fold and unfold.

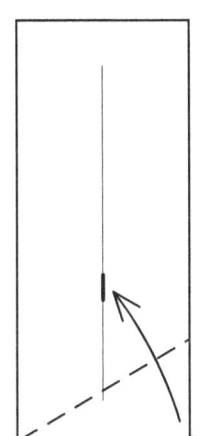
2

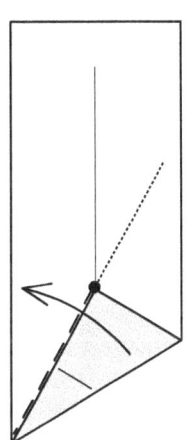
3

Crease below the dot.

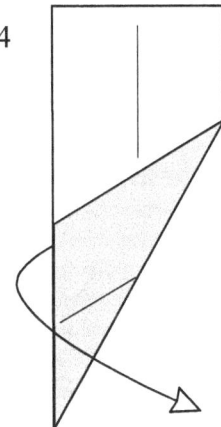
4

Unfold.

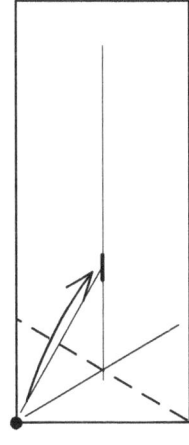
5

Repeat steps 2–4 on the right.

6

Fold and unfold.

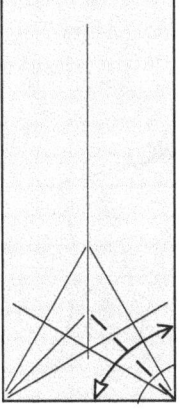
7

Fold and unfold.

Heron 59

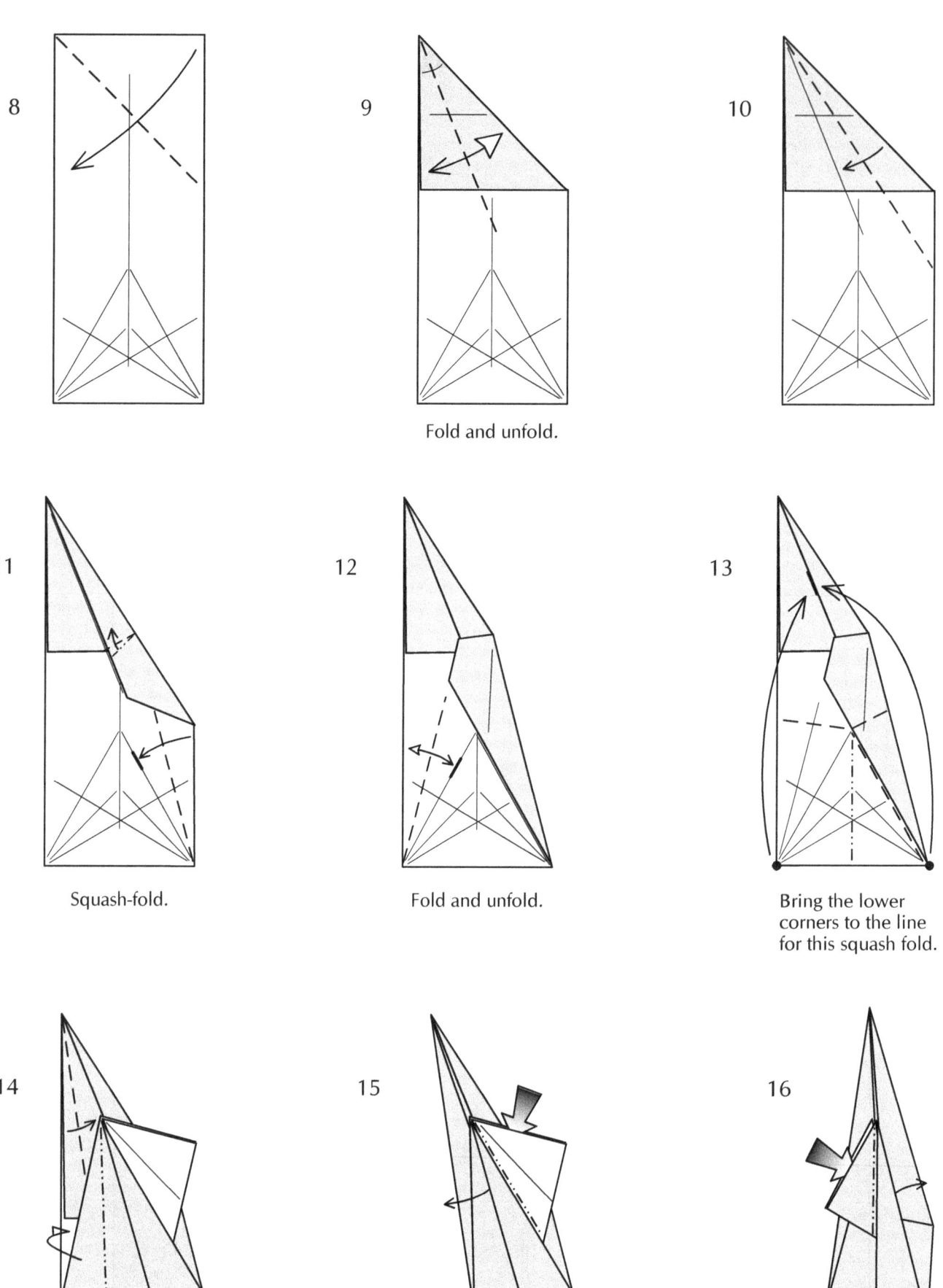

8

9 Fold and unfold.

10

11 Squash-fold.

12 Fold and unfold.

13 Bring the lower corners to the line for this squash fold.

14 Mountain-fold along the crease.

15 Reverse-fold.

16 Reverse-fold.

60   *Dollar Origami Treasures*

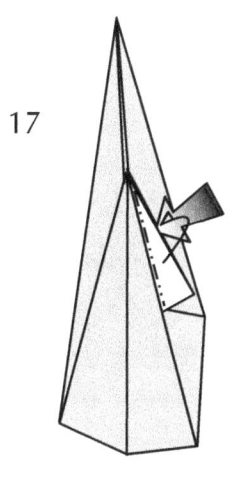

17

Reverse-fold.

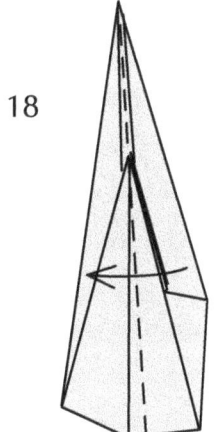

18

Bisect at the top.

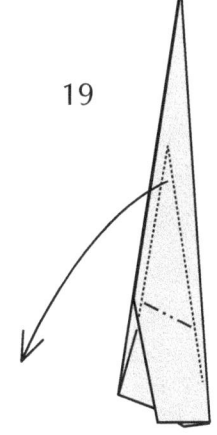

19

Reverse-fold and rotate.

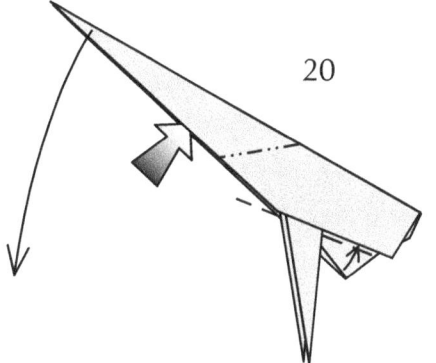

20

Reverse-fold the neck.

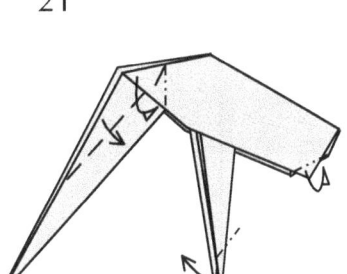

21

Reverse-fold the feet. Repeat behind at the neck and feet.

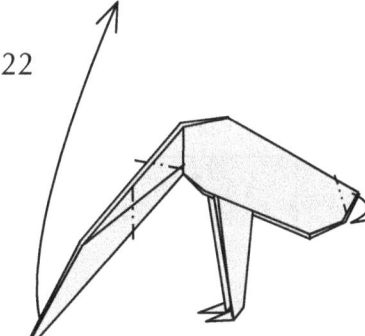

22

Make reverse folds for the neck and back.

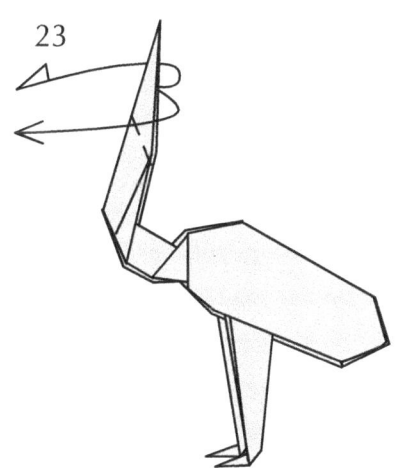

23

Outside-reverse-fold.

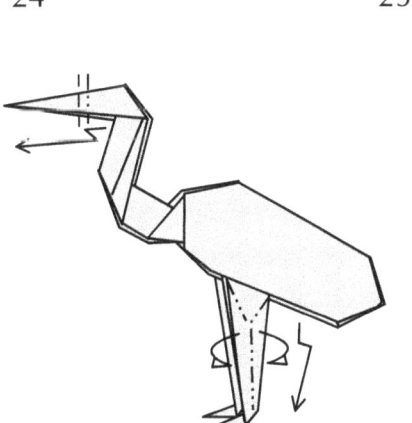

24

Crimp-fold the beak. Fold all the layer together to thin the leg and bend at the knee. Repeat behind. The heron can stand.

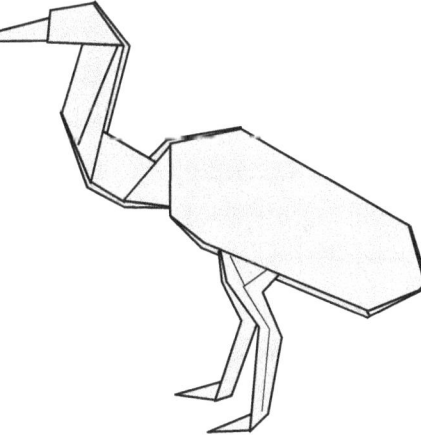

25

Heron

Heron 61

Moth

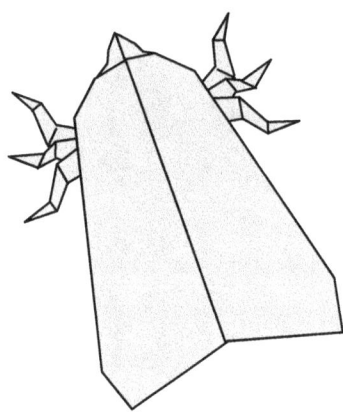

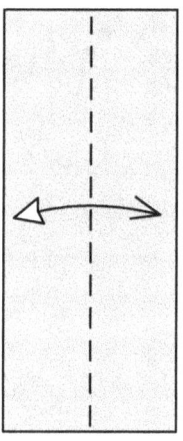

1

Fold and unfold.

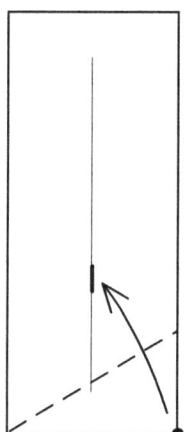

2

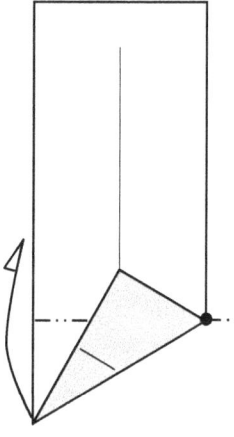

3

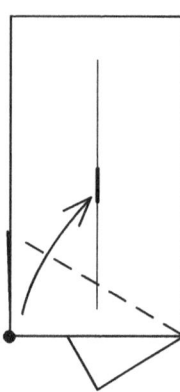

4

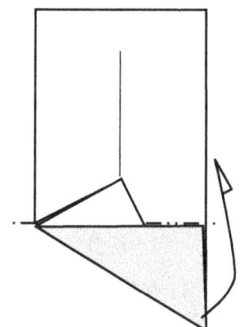

5

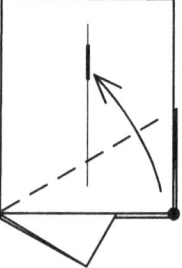

6

7

Unfold.

8

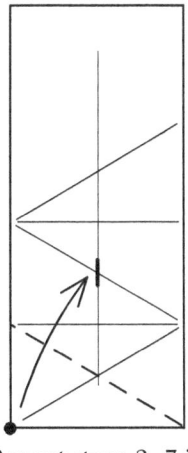

Repeat steps 2–7 in the other direction.

9

Push in at the dot.

10

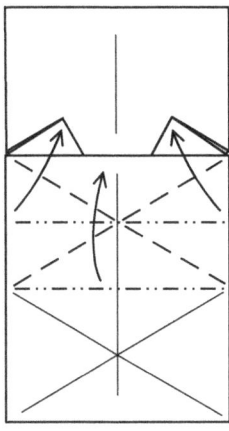

11

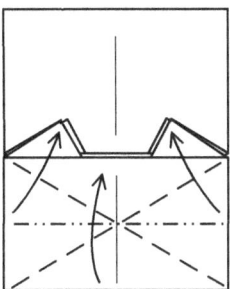

12

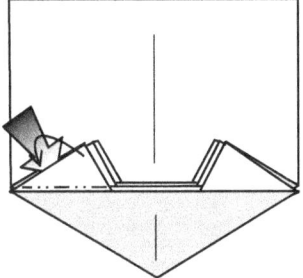

Reverse-fold.

13

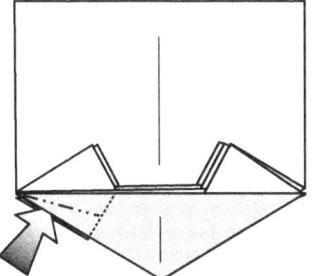

Reverse-fold the inside layers.

14

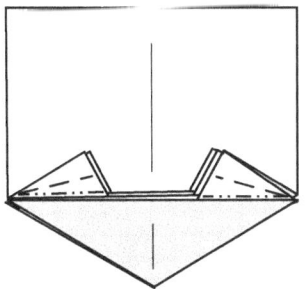

Repeat steps 12–13 five more times.

15

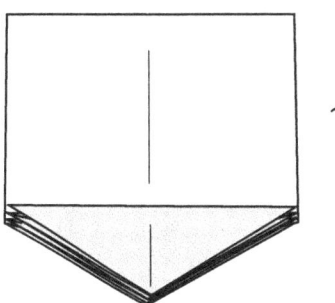

Turn over and rotate.

Moth   63

16
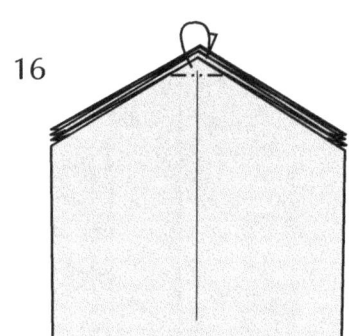

17
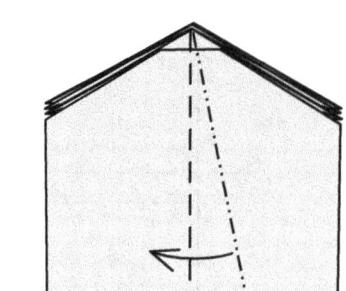

18
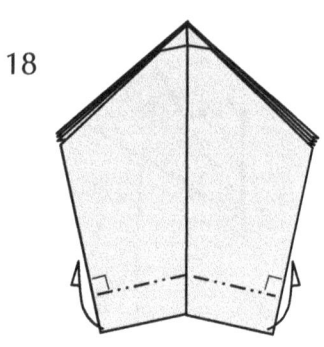

19
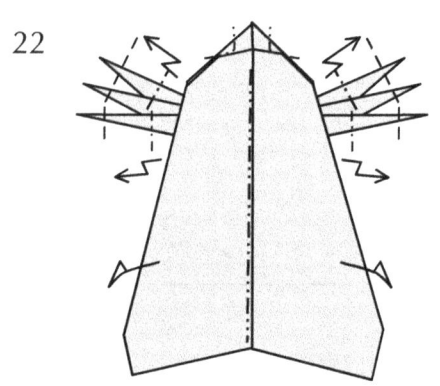

20
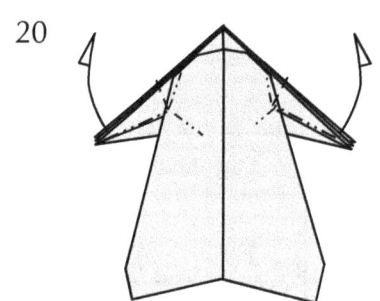

Rabbit-ear all the layers together on each side.

21
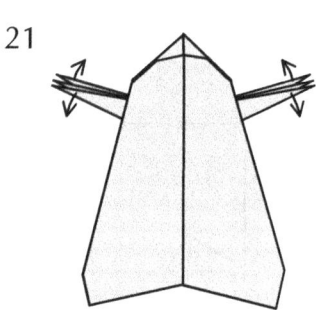

Spread the legs.

22
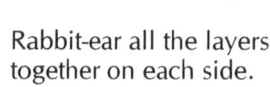

23
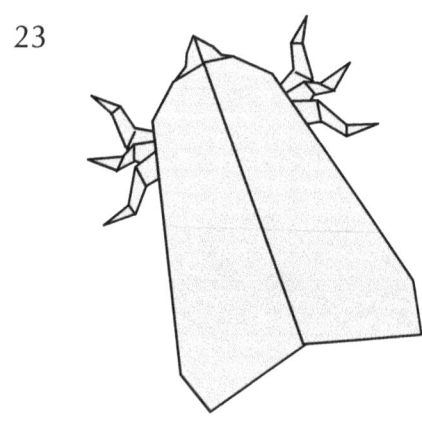

Moth

64 *Dollar Origami Treasures*

Sea Creatures

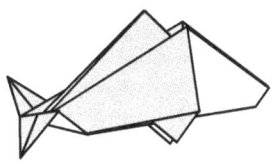
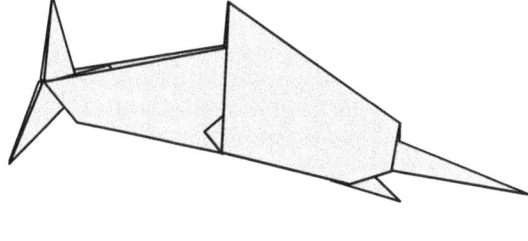
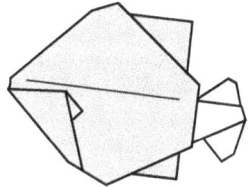

Sea creatures add an interesting variety to dollar bill folds. Though all original, the frog is taken from the traditional version. These models range from the simple angelfish to the challenging crab.

Angelfish

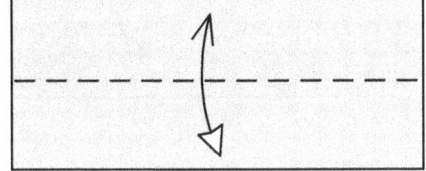

1 Fold and unfold.

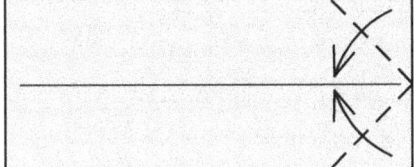

2

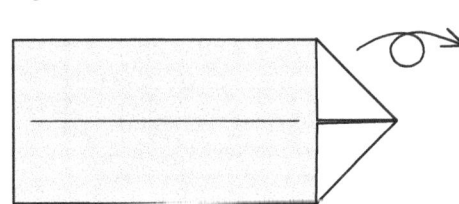

3

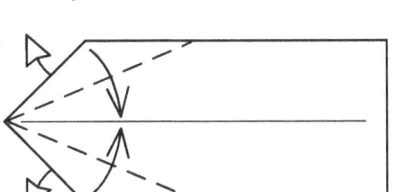

4 Fold to the center and swing out the corners.

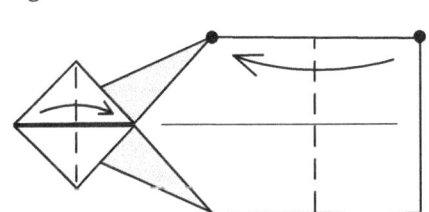

5

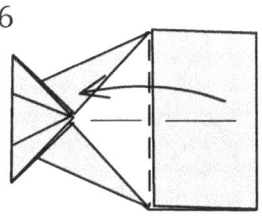

6

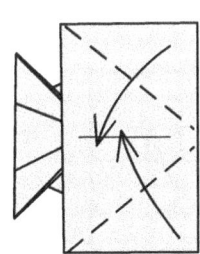

7

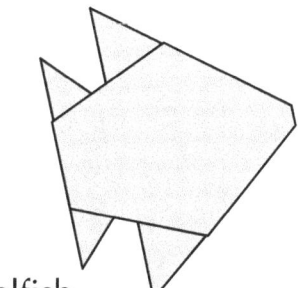

8 Angelfish

Angelfish 65

Tropical Fish

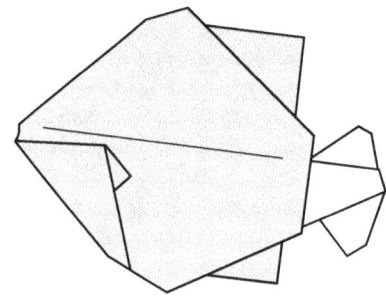

1.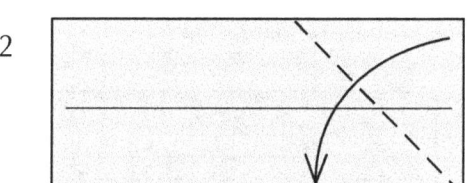
Fold and unfold.

2.
Fold.

3.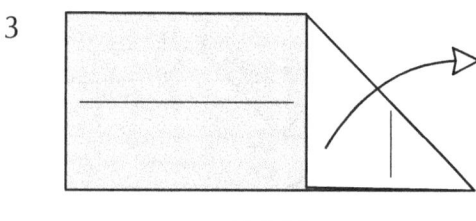
Unfold.

4.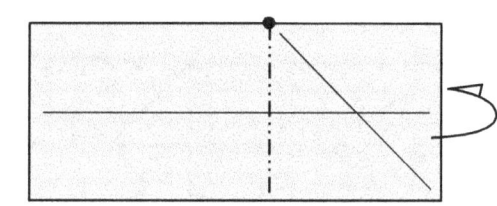
Fold behind.

5.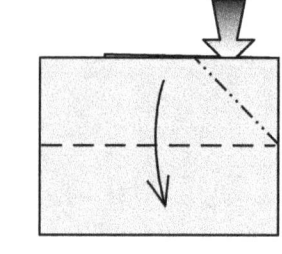
Squash-fold.

6.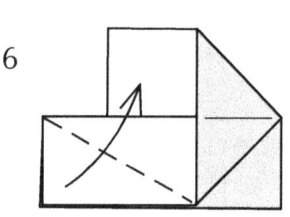
Fold the top layer.

7.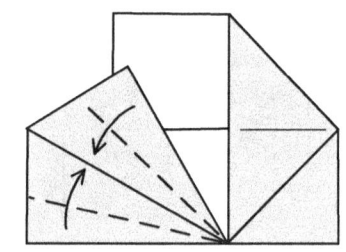

66 *Dollar Origami Treasures*

8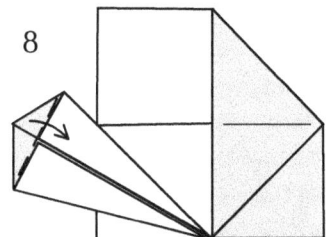

9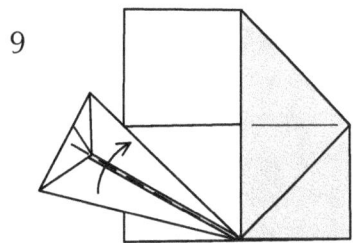

10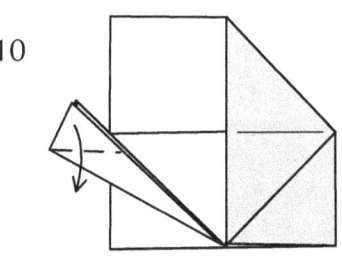
Fold the top layer.

11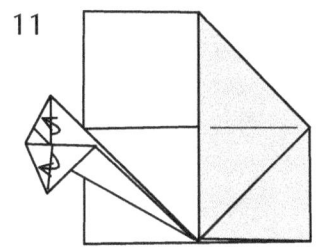
Spread the tip.

12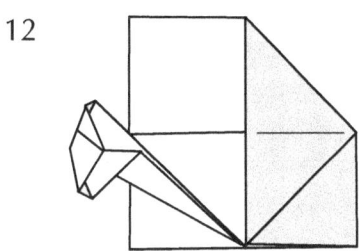

13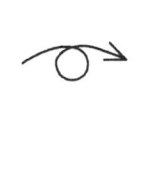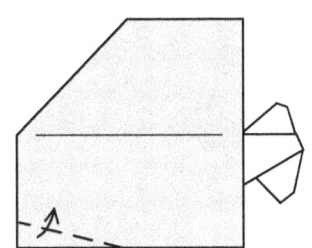

14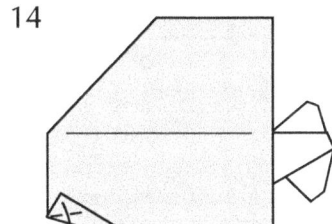

15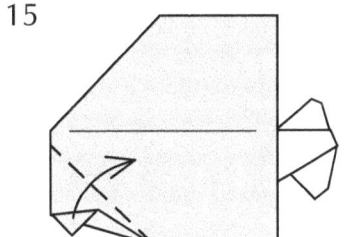

16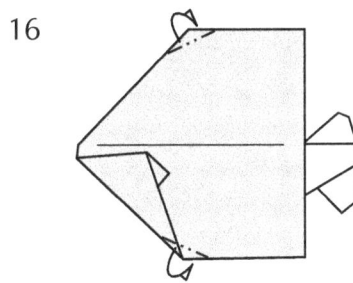

17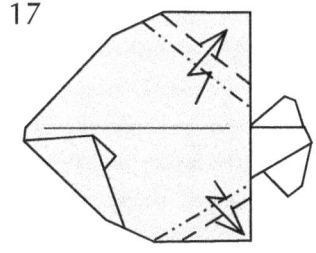
Pleat folds.

18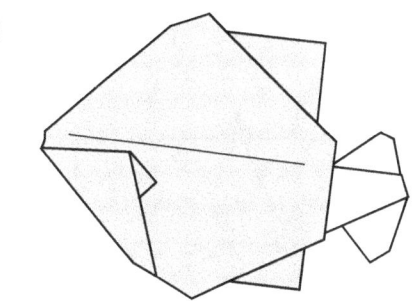
Tropical Fish

Tropical Fish 67

Swordfish

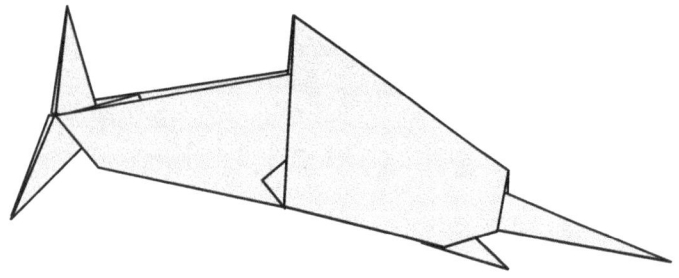

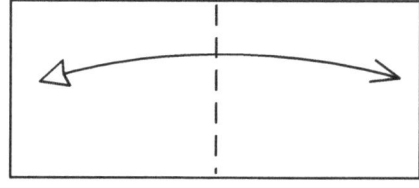

1

Fold and unfold.

2

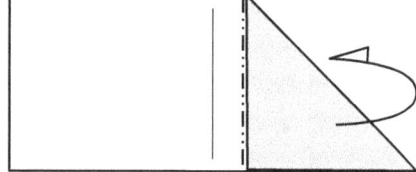

3

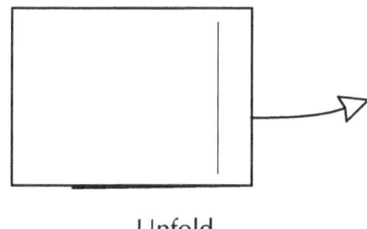

4

Unfold.

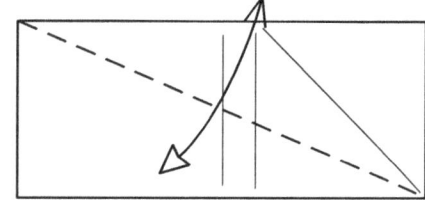

5

Fold and unfold.

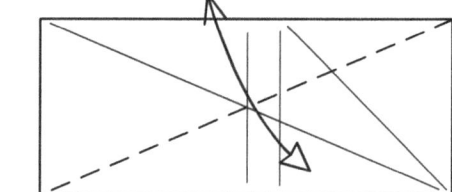

6

Fold and unfold.

68   *Dollar Origami Treasures*

7

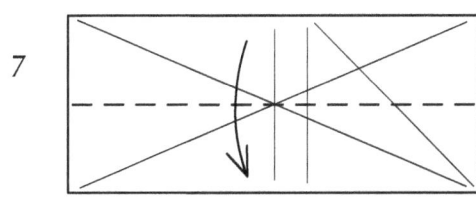

8

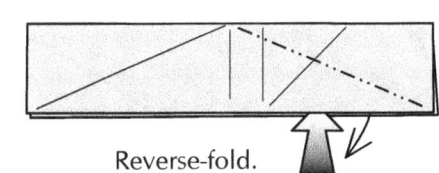

Reverse-fold.

9

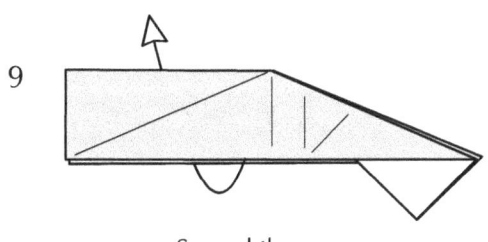

Spread the paper.

10

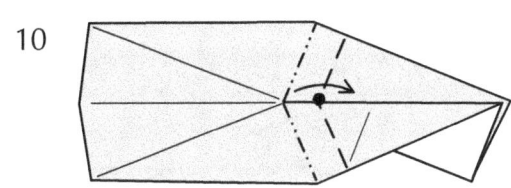

The model is 3D. Fold along the creases and push in at the dot.

11

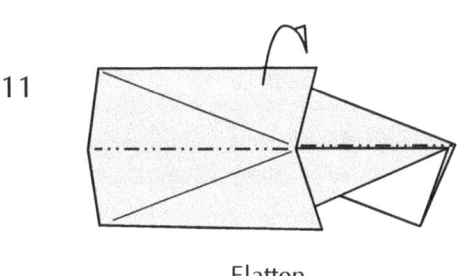

Flatten.

12

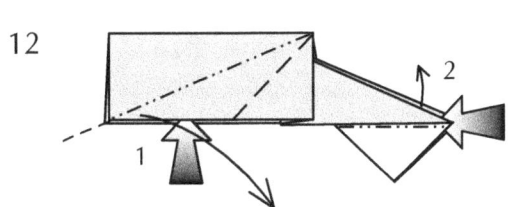

1. Squash-fold. Mountain-fold along the crease.
2. Reverse-fold.

13

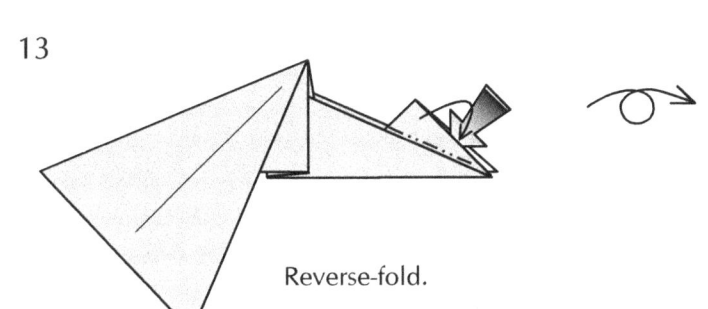

Reverse-fold.

14

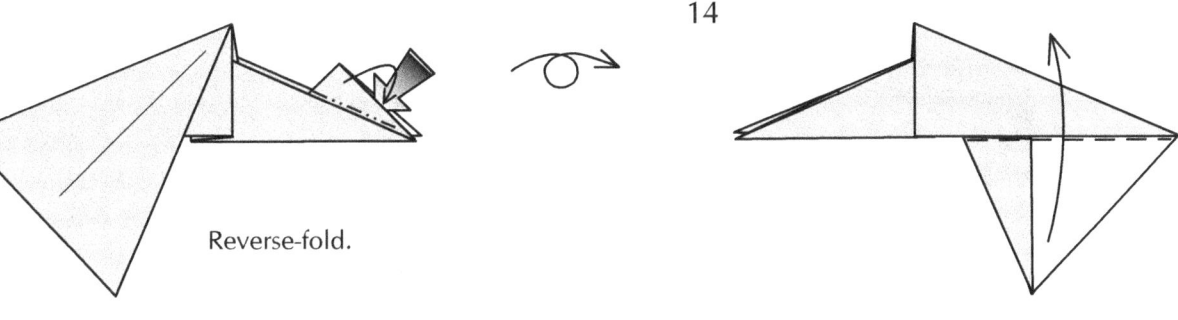

15

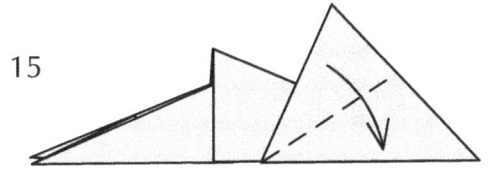

16

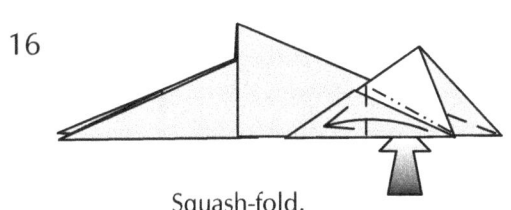

Squash-fold.

Swordfish 69

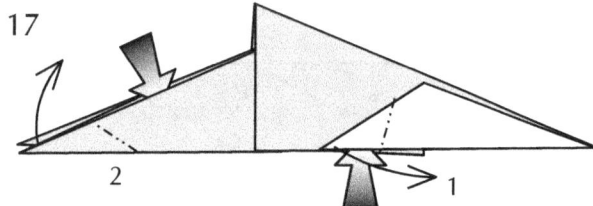

1. Reverse-fold.
2. Reverse-fold and repeat behind.

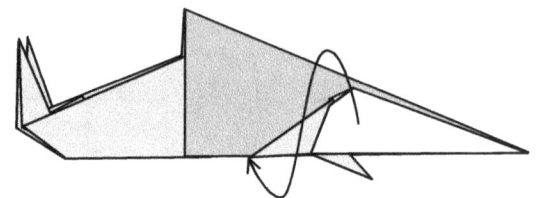

Tuck the paper under the darker region.

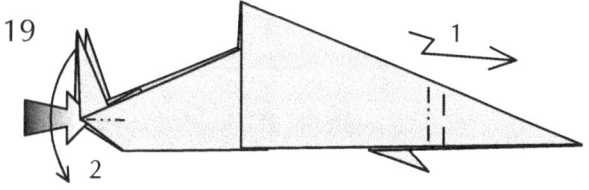

1. Crimp-fold.
2. Reverse-fold.

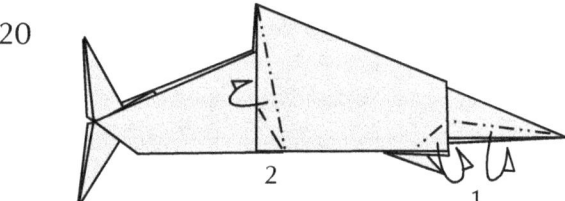

1. Fold inside to thin the sword.
2. Pleat-fold to make a fin. Repeat behind.

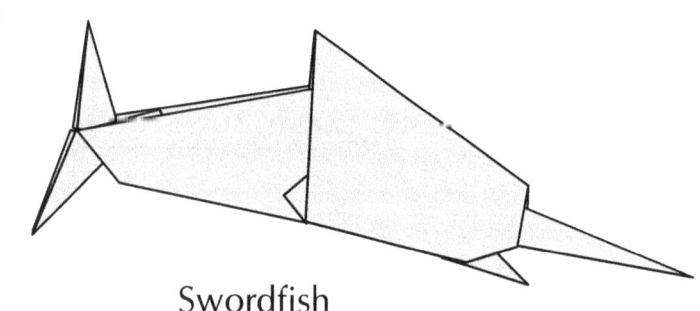

Swordfish

Carp

1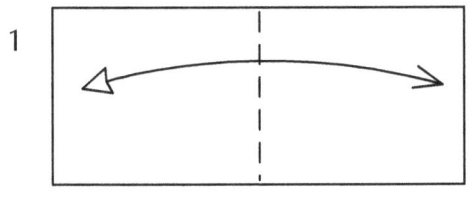
Fold and unfold.

2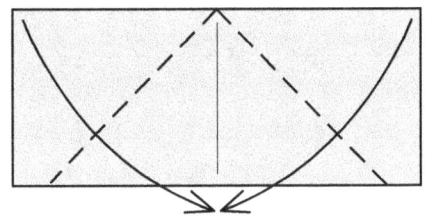

3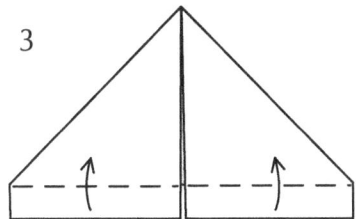

4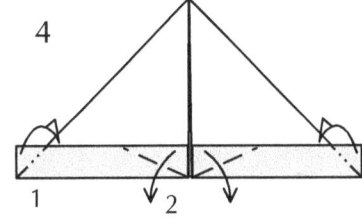
1. Fold inside.
2. Fold down.

5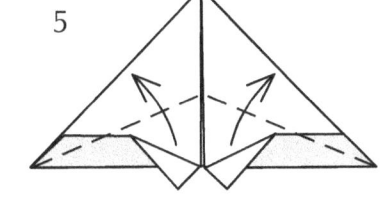

6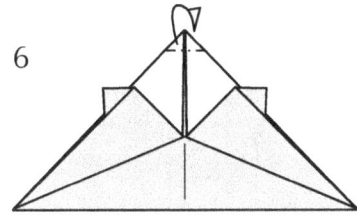
Fold behind.

7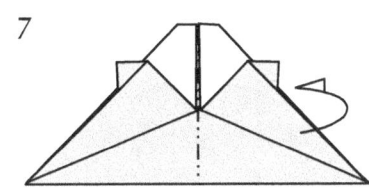
Fold in half and rotate.

8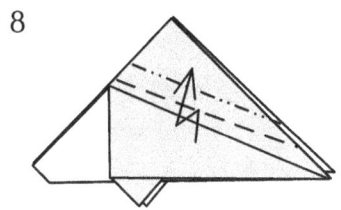
Pleat-fold both layers.

9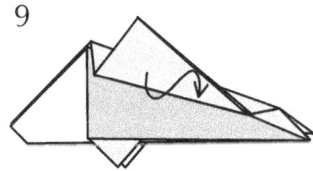
Tuck under the darker paper.

10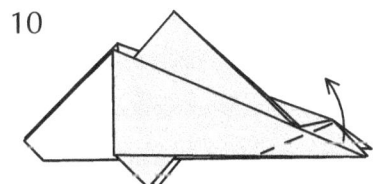
Fold the top layer and repeat behind.

11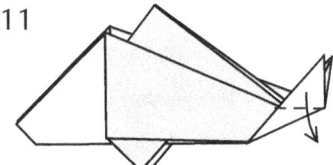
Fold the top layer.

12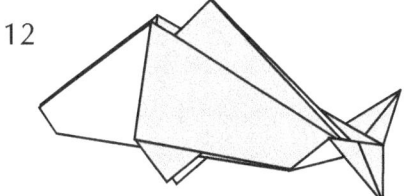
Carp

Carp 71

Frog

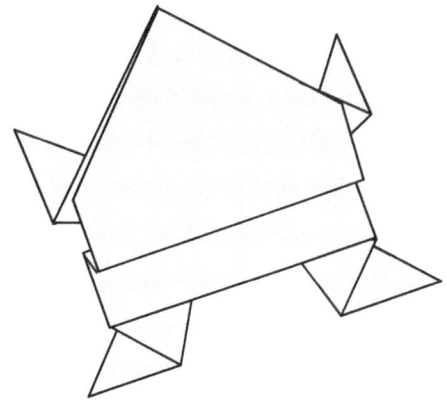

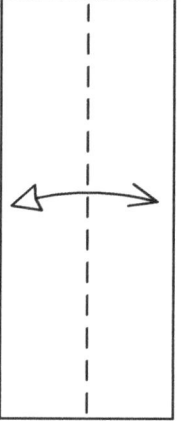

1

Fold and unfold.

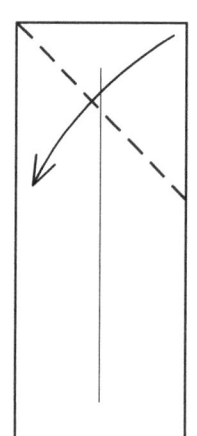

2

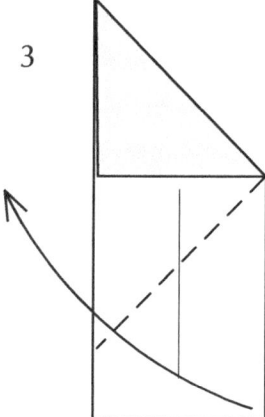

3

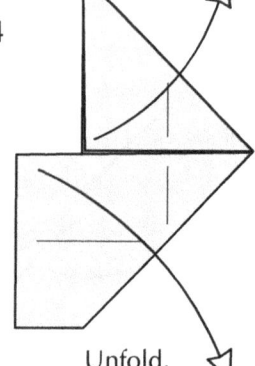

4

Unfold.

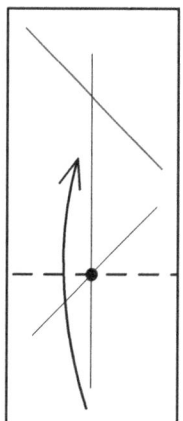

5

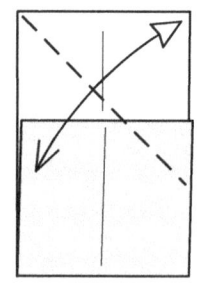

6

Fold and unfold.

72 Dollar Origami Treasures

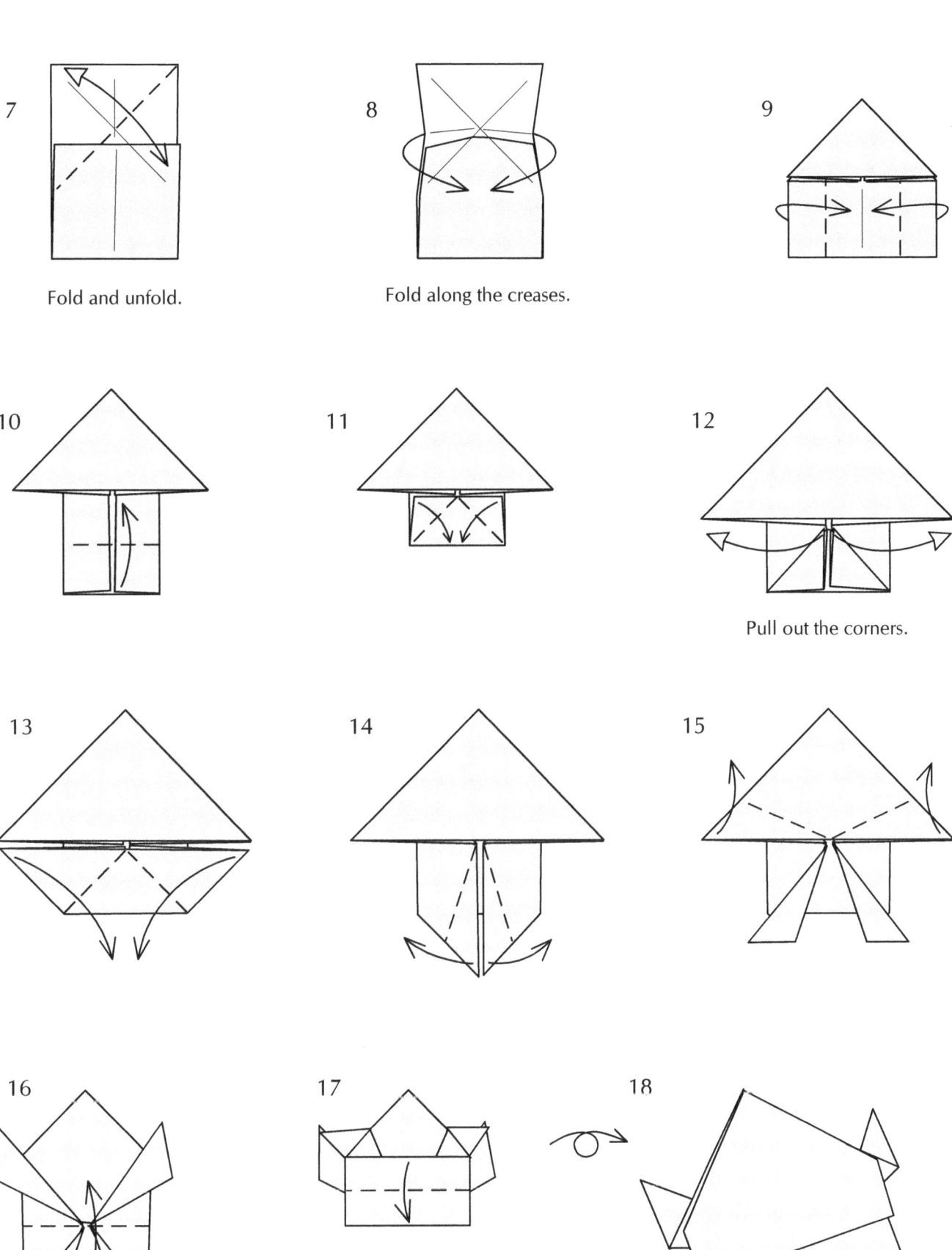

Frog 73

Whale

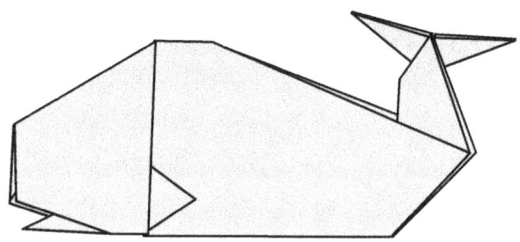

1.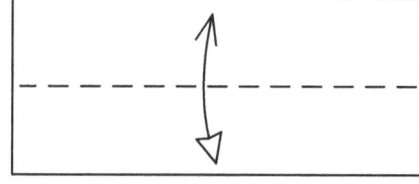

   Fold and unfold.

2.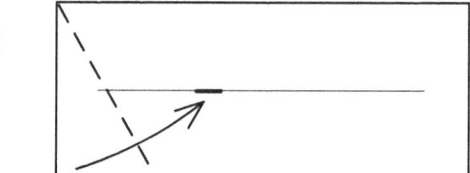

3.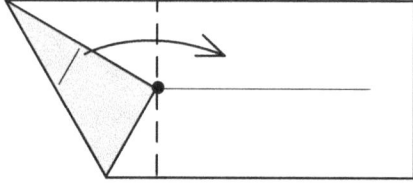

   Fold by the dot.

4.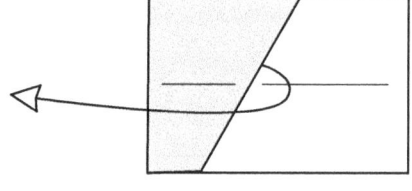

   Unfold.

5.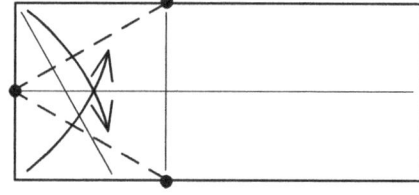

6.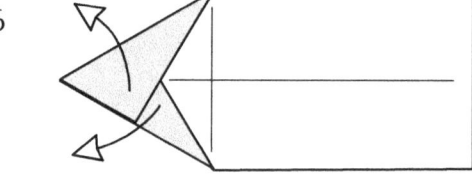

   Unfold.

74 *Dollar Origami Treasures*

7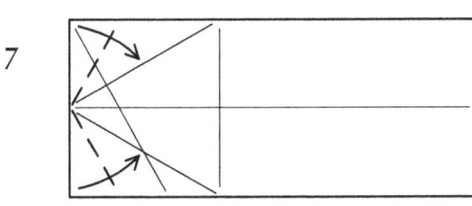

Fold to the crease.

8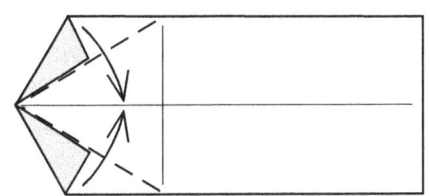

9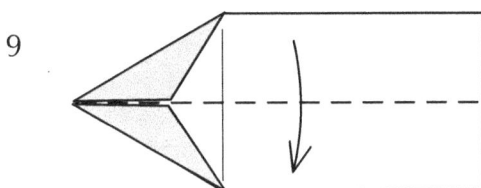

10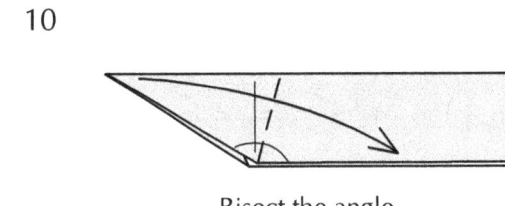

Bisect the angle.

11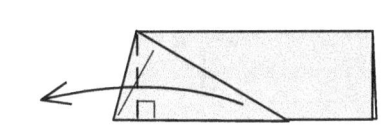

12

Unfold.

13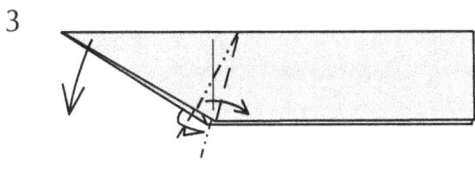

Crimp-fold along the creases.

14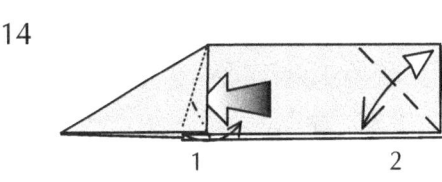

1. Reverse-fold and repeat behind.
2. Fold and unfold.

15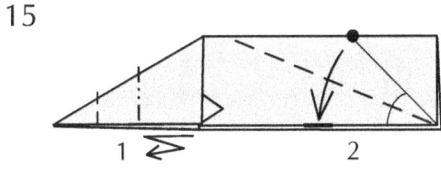

1. Make reverse folds.
2. Bring the dot to the bottom edge.

16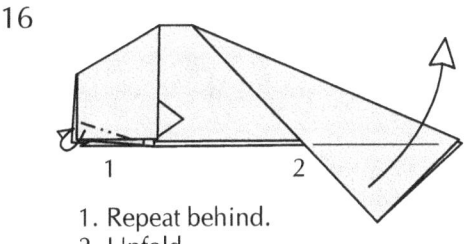

1. Repeat behind.
2. Unfold.

Whale 75

17
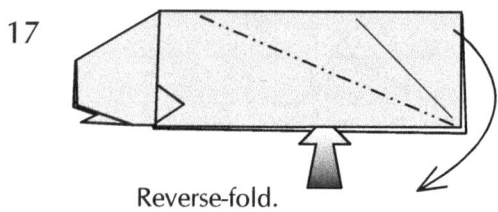
Reverse-fold.

18
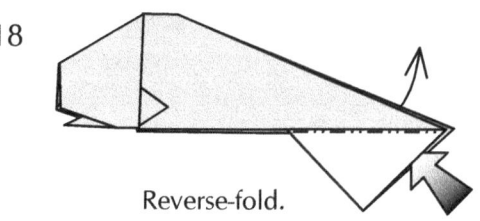
Reverse-fold.

19
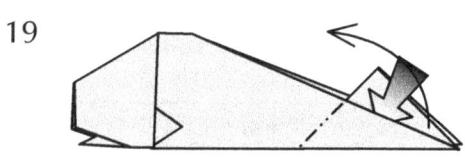
Reverse-fold.

20
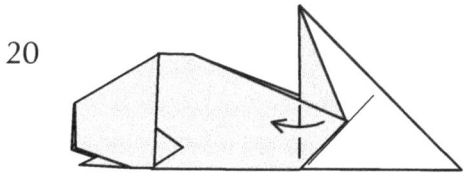

21
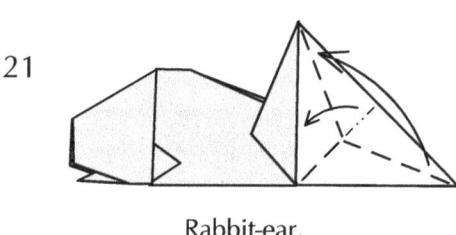
Rabbit-ear.

22
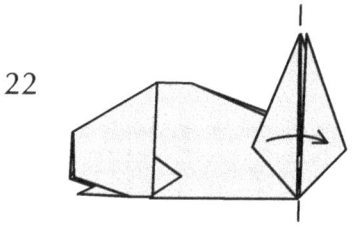

23
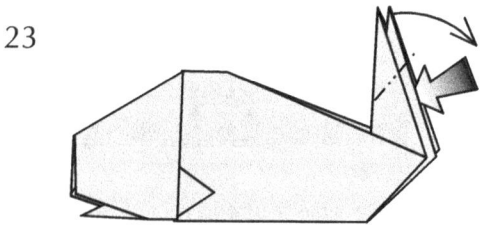
Place your finger into the center layer for this reverse fold.

24
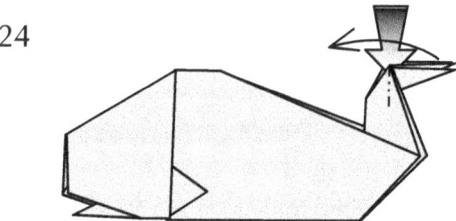
Reverse-fold the inner layer.

25
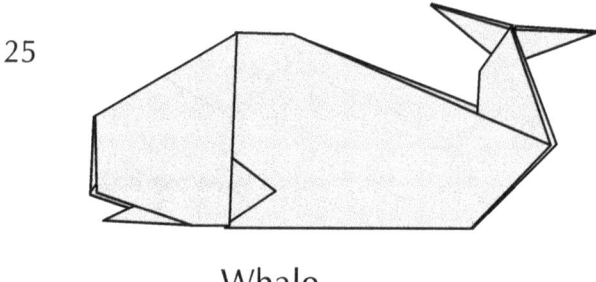
Whale

Crab

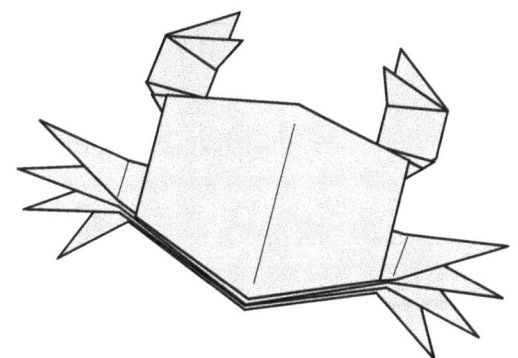

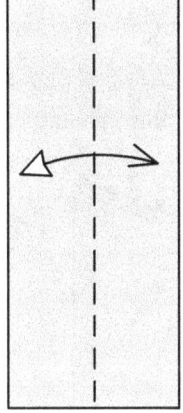

1. Fold and unfold.

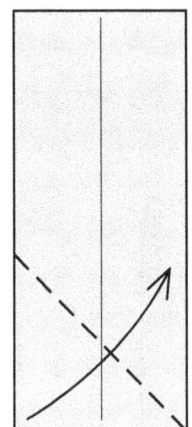

2.

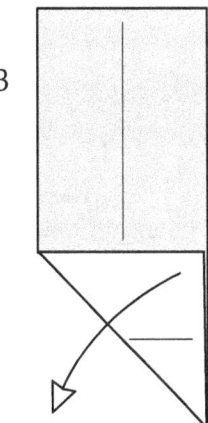

3. Unfold.

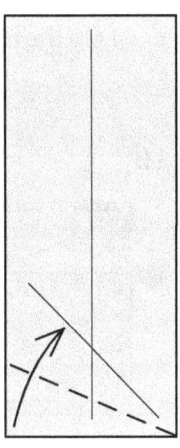

4.

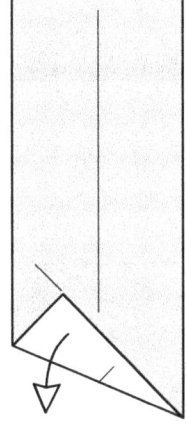

5. Unfold.

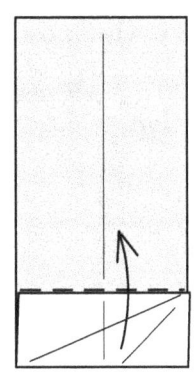

6.

7.

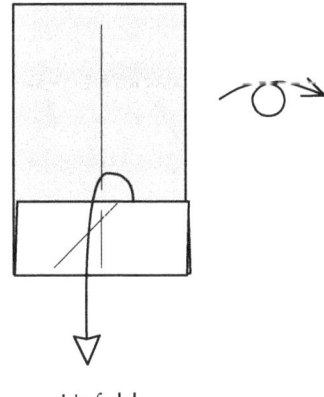

8. Unfold.

Crab 77

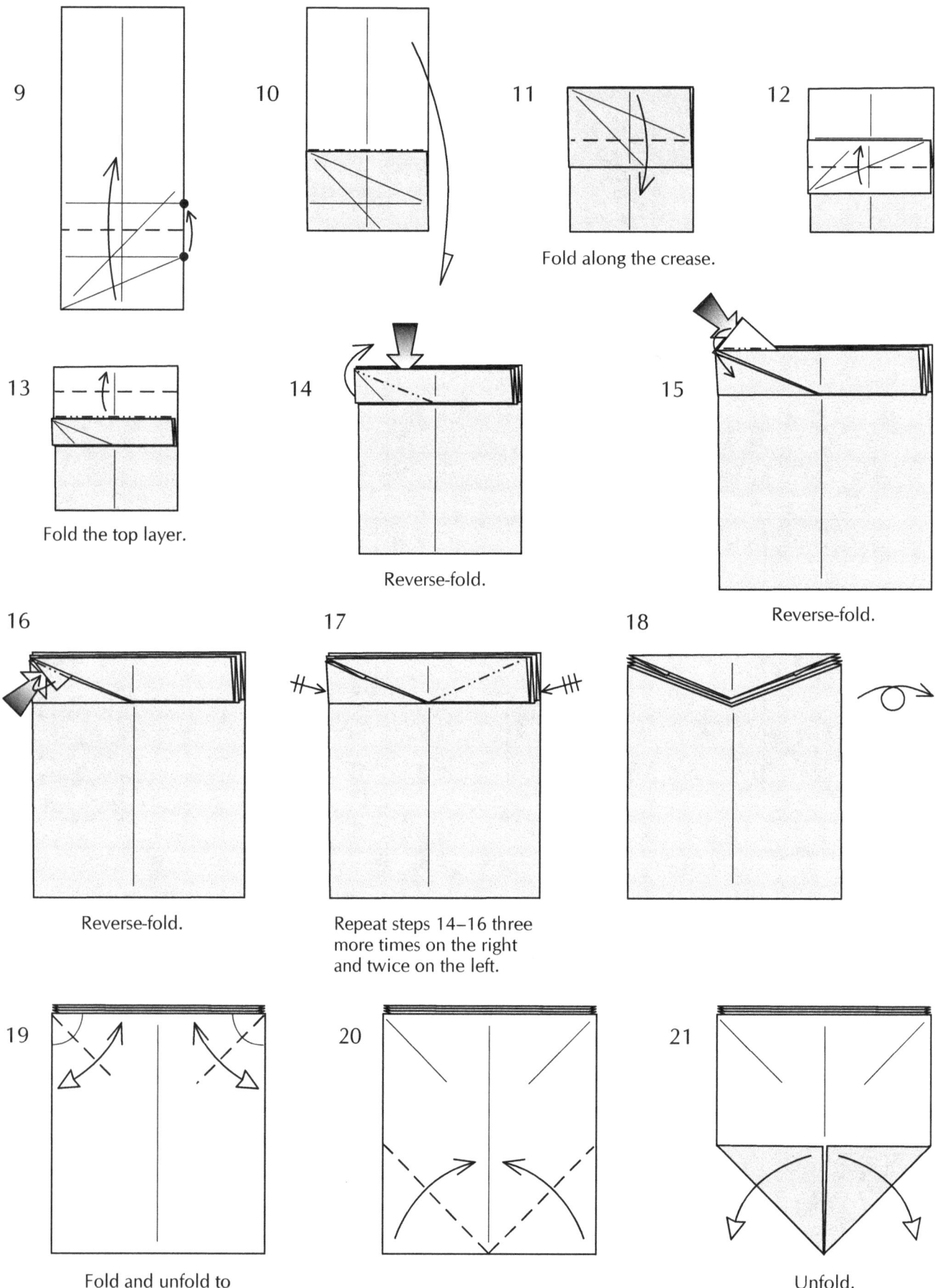

78 *Dollar Origami Treasures*

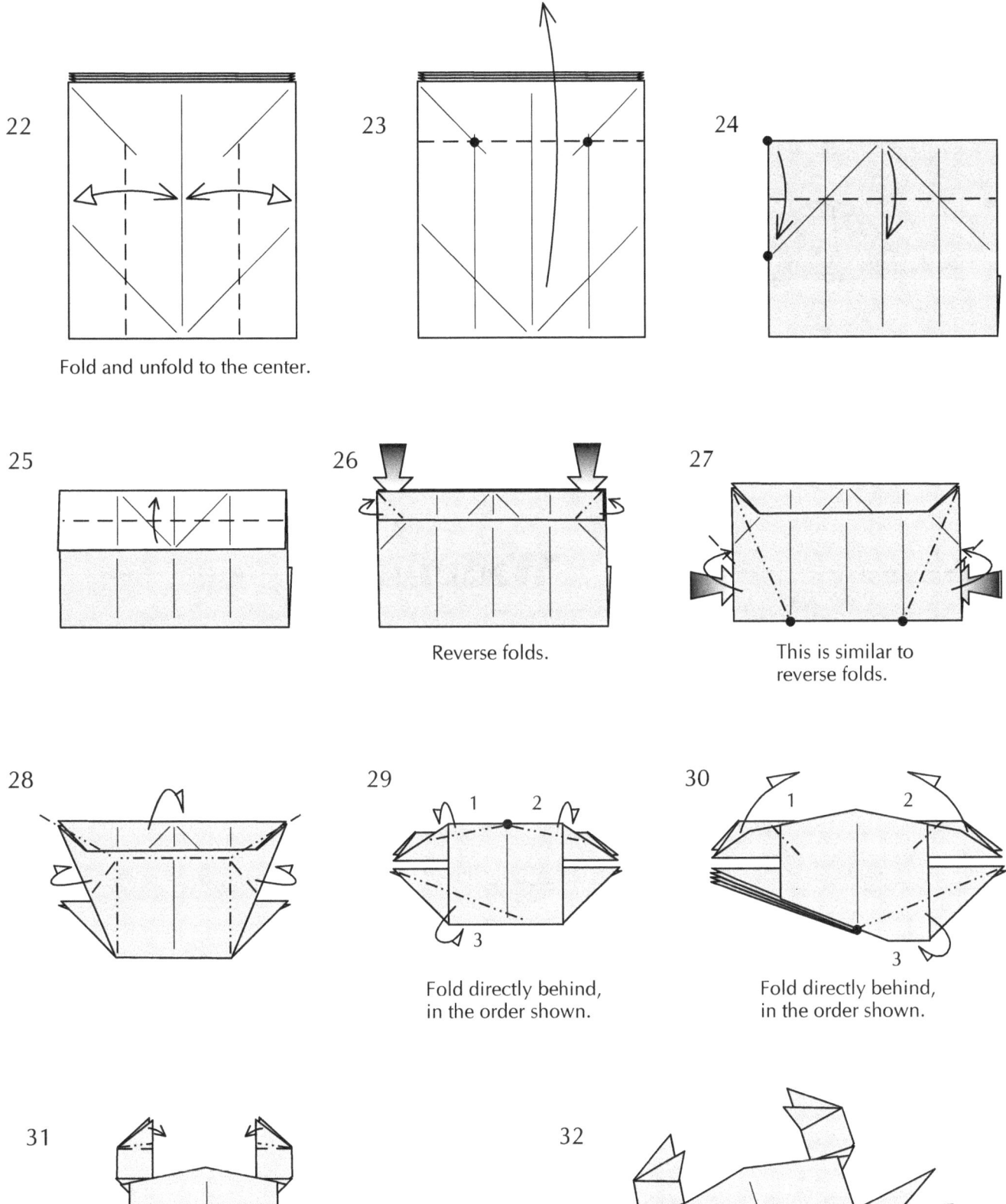

Crab

Mammals

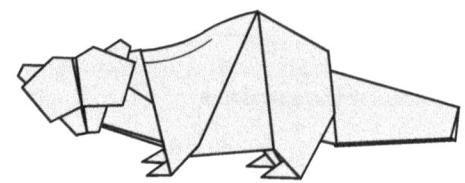

Mammals make for challenging dollar bill folds. The four legs and head detail demand more interesting folding methods. Here is a collection of nine models, showing a range of techniques.

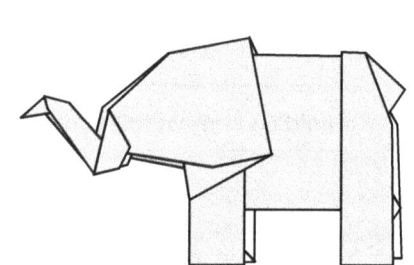

Walrus

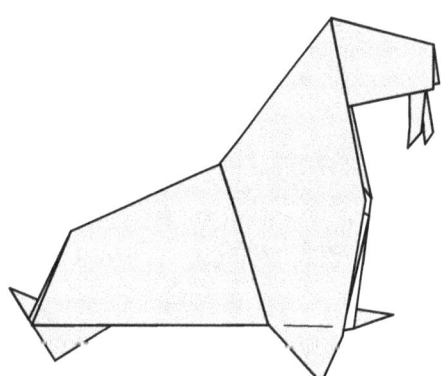

1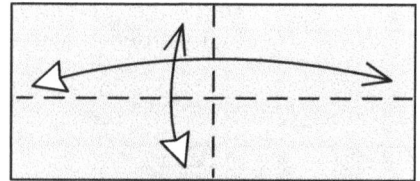

Fold and unfold.

2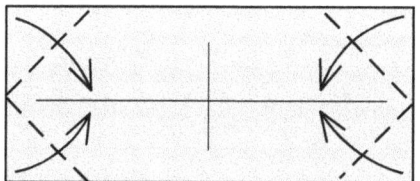

3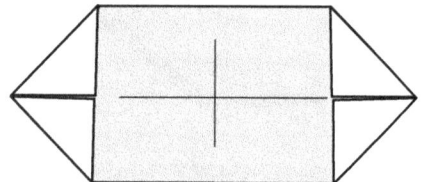

4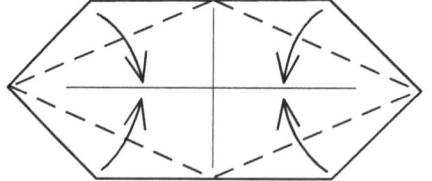

80 *Dollar Origami Treasures*

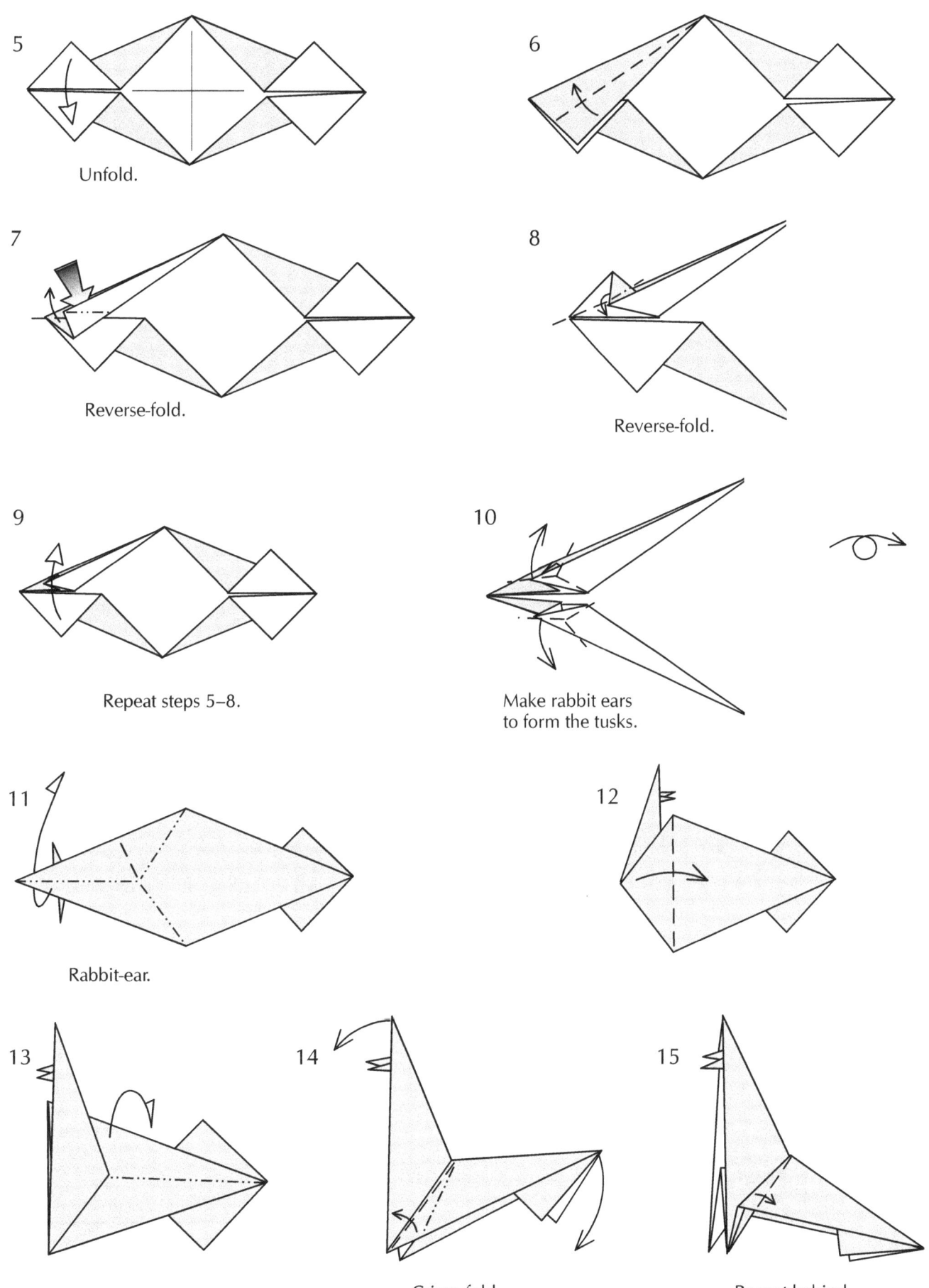

16

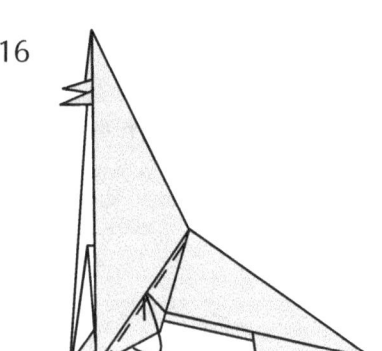

Tuck inside. Repeat behind.

17

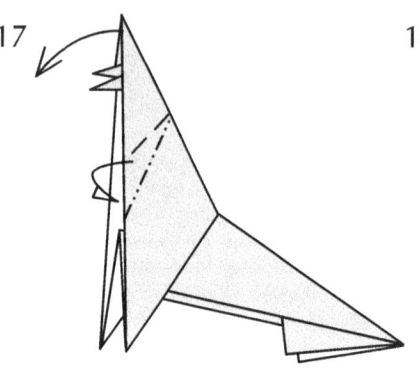

Crimp-fold.

18

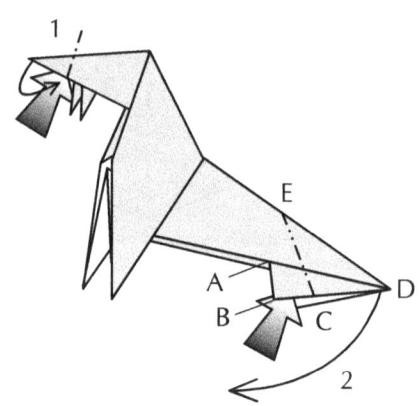

1. Reverse-fold the tip inside.
2. Reverse-fold so that
   a. Line C–D touches B and
   b. Line E–D meets A.

19

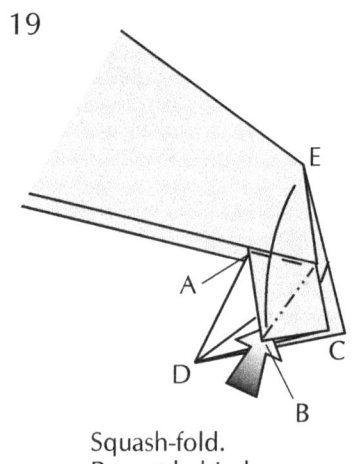

Squash-fold. Repeat behind.

20

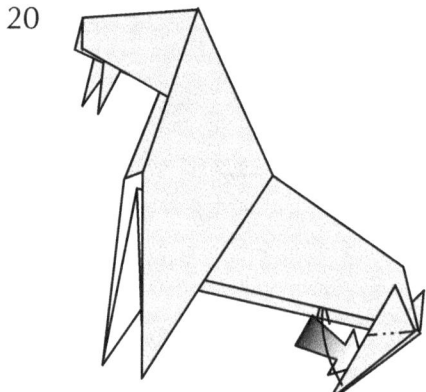

Reverse-fold the tip and tuck it inside to lock it.

21

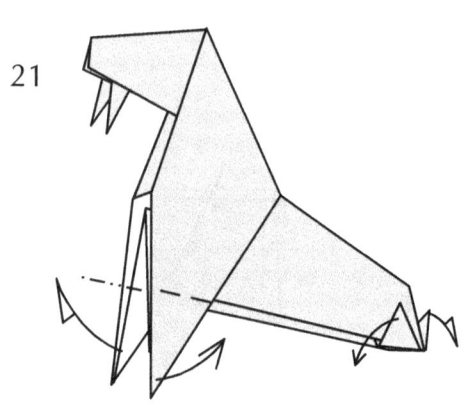

22

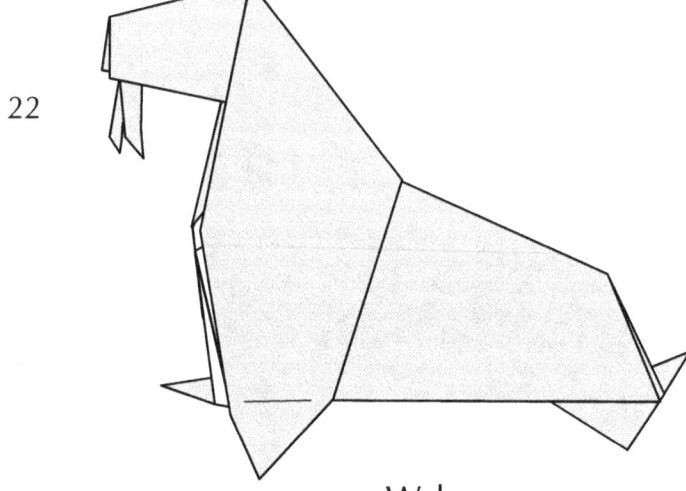

Walrus

Sheep

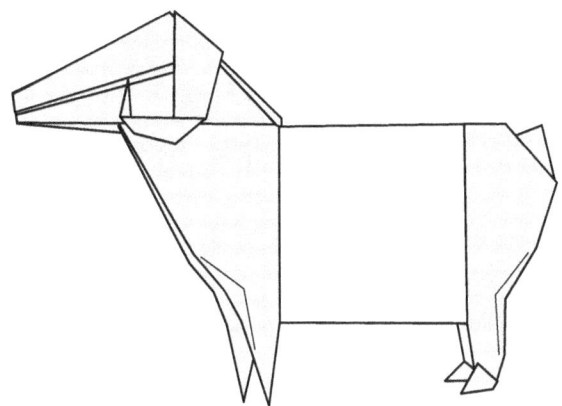

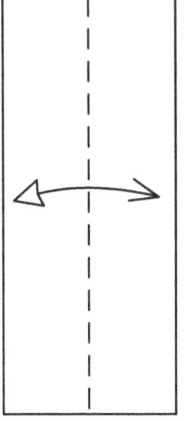
1
Fold and unfold.

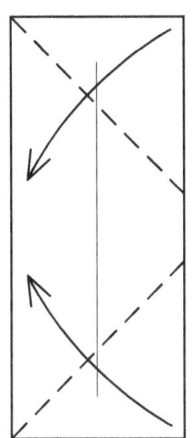
2

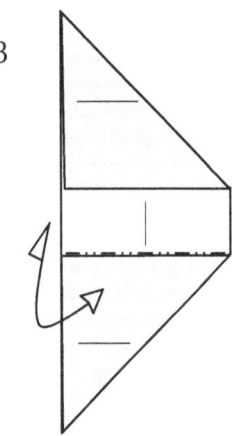
3
Fold and unfold.

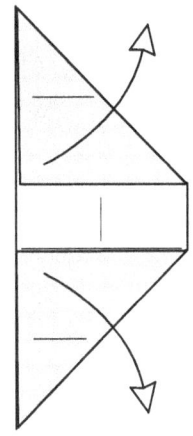
4
Unfold.

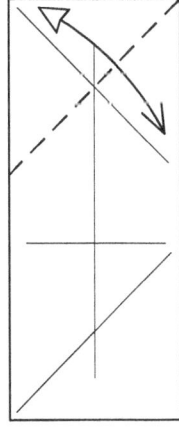
5
Fold and unfold.

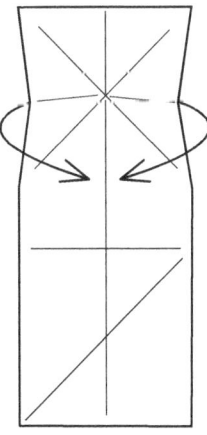
6
Collapse along the creases.

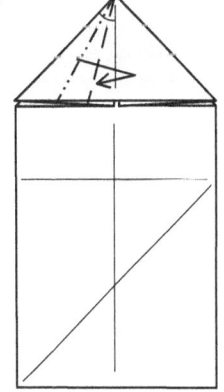
7
Divide in thirds.

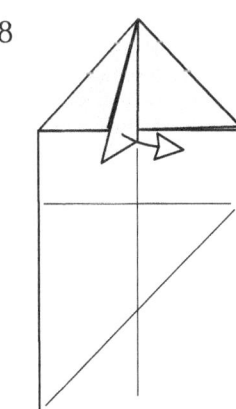
8
Unfold.

Sheep 83

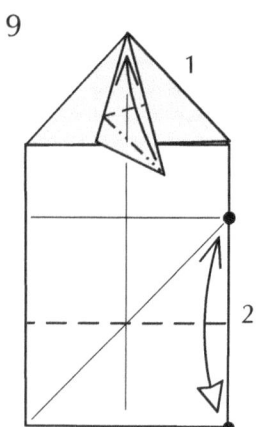

1. Squash-fold.
2. Fold and unfold.

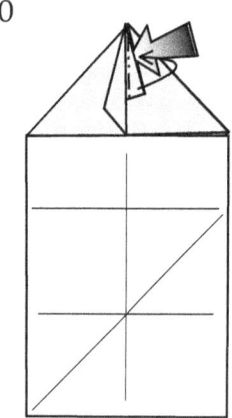

Reverse-fold.

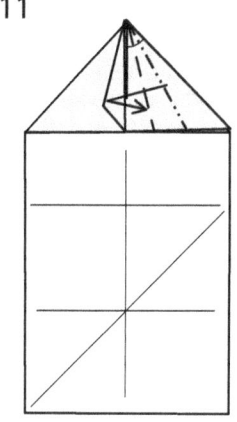

Repeat steps 7–10 on the right, at the top.

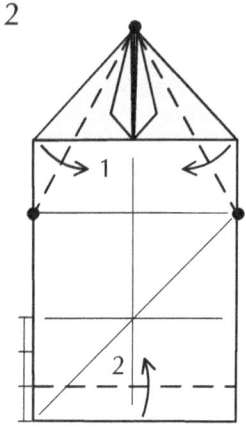

1. Fold by the dots.
2. Fold up by about 1/3.

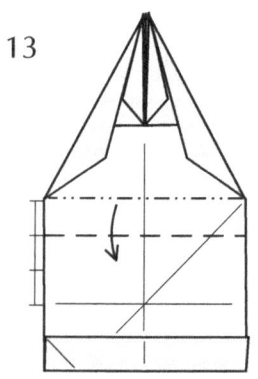

Divide in thirds.

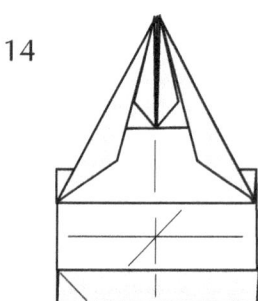

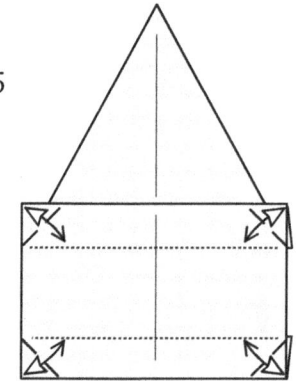

Fold and unfold.

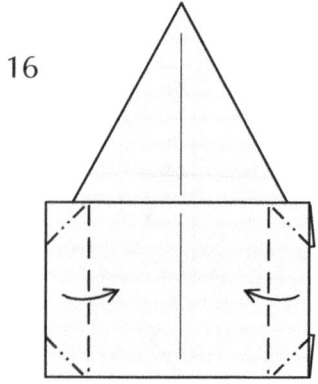

Petal folds.

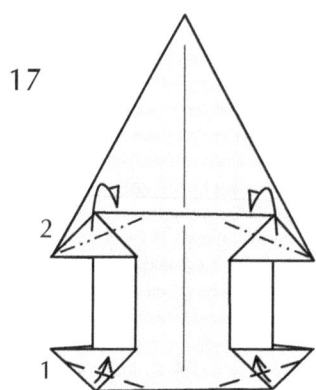

1. Do not fold to a point.
2. Fold behind.

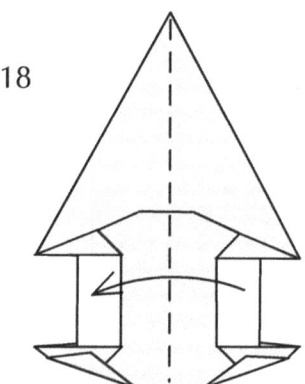

Fold in half and rotate 90°.

84 *Dollar Origami Treasures*

19

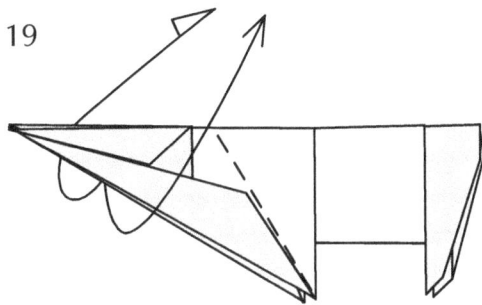

Outside-reverse-fold.

20

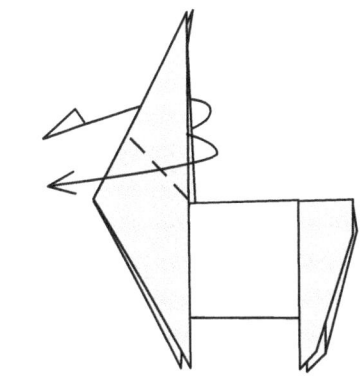

Outside-reverse-fold.

21

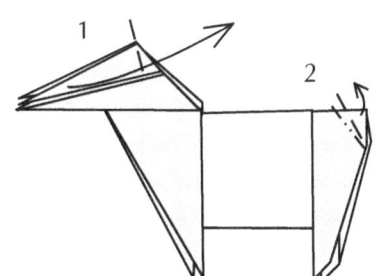

1. Repeat behind.
2. Crimp-fold.

22

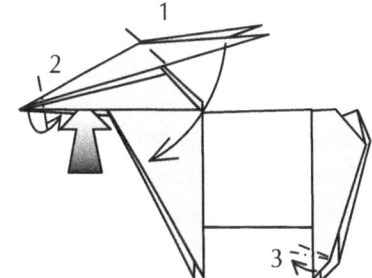

1. Fold down.
2. Reverse-fold.
3. Make little feet.
Repeat behind.

23

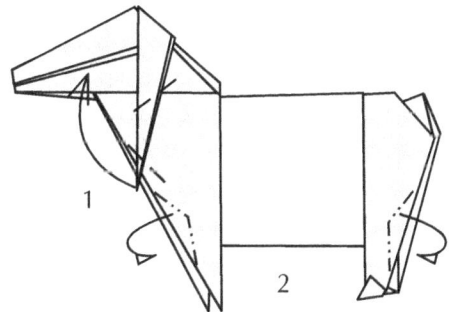

1. Shape the horns with reverse folds.
2. Thin and shape the legs.
Repeat behind.

24

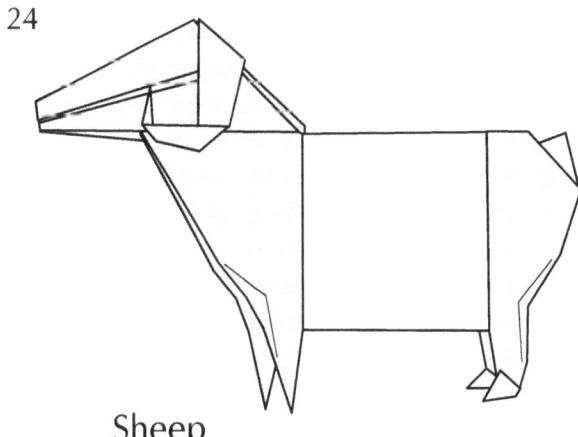

Sheep

Bear

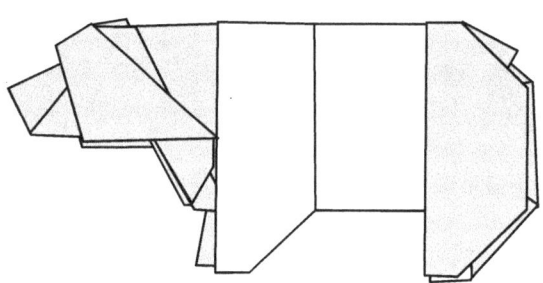

1

2

Unfold.

3

Fold to the crease.

4

Unfold.

5

6

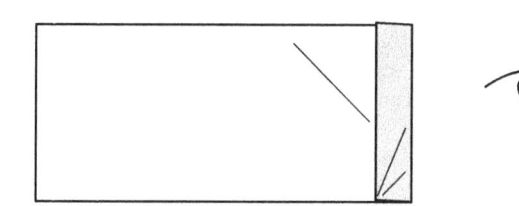

86 *Dollar Origami Treasures*

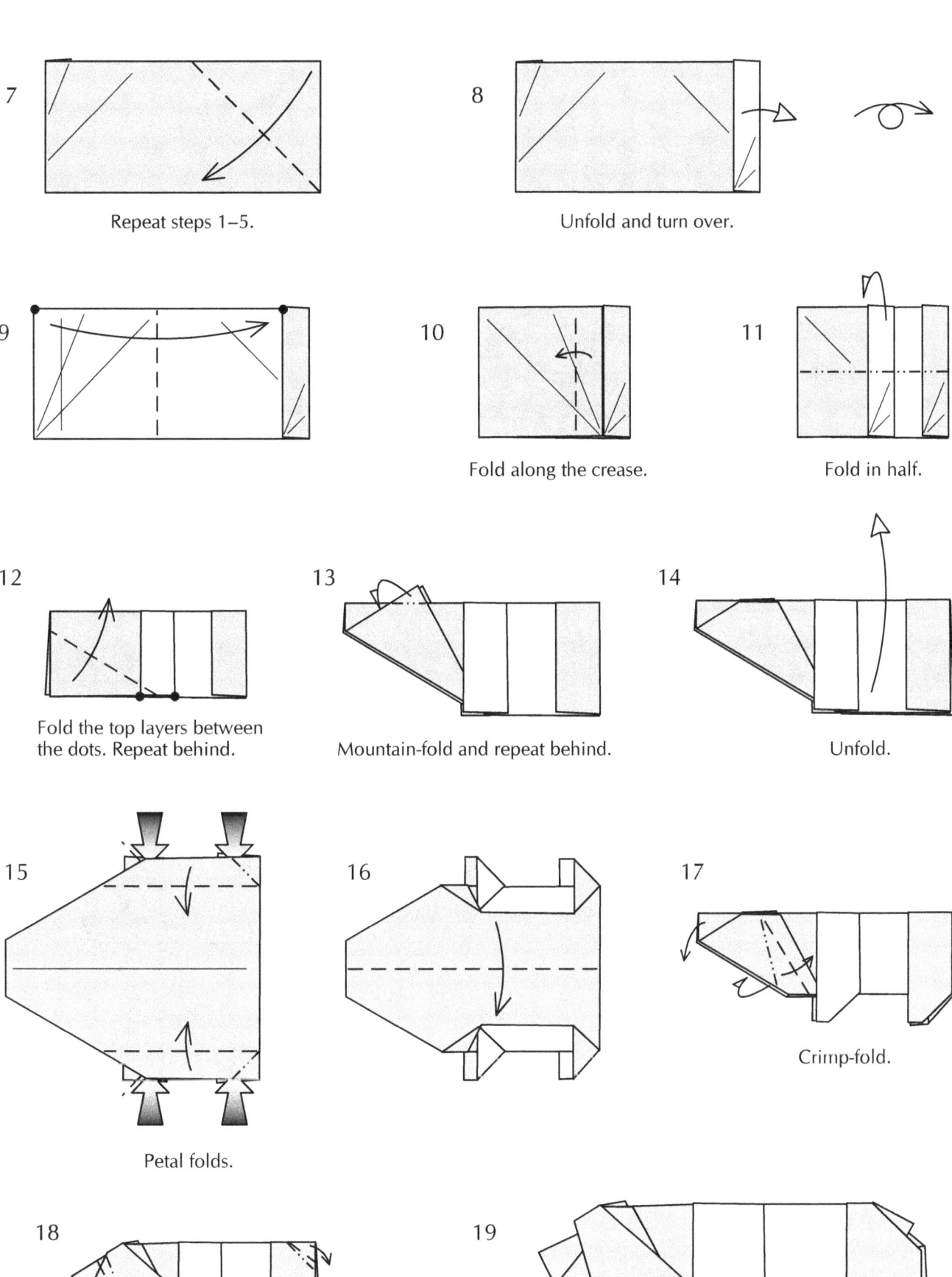

Mouse

1

2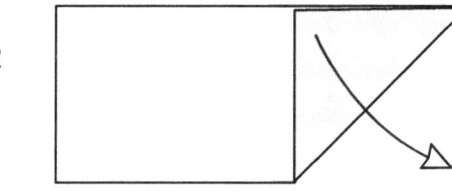
Unfold.

3
Fold to the crease.

4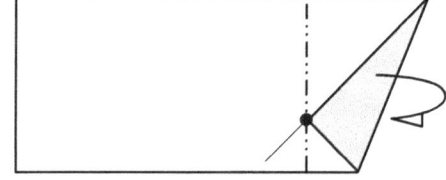

5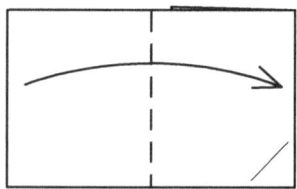

6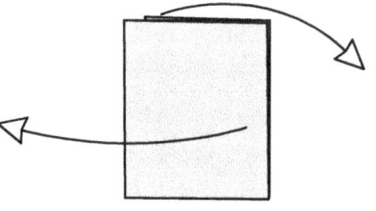
Unfold.

7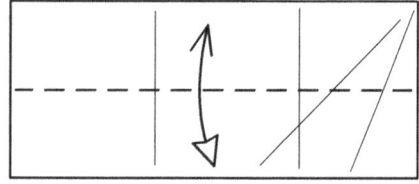
Fold and unfold.

8

88   *Dollar Origami Treasures*

9

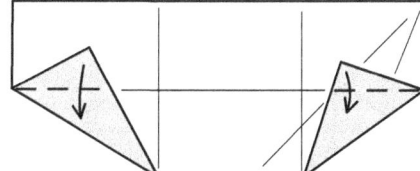

Fold along the horizontal crease.

10

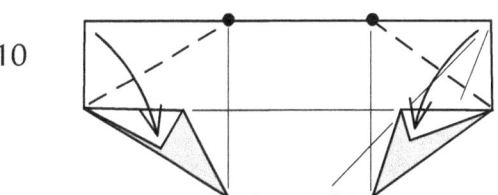

Repeat steps 8–9 on the upper half.

11

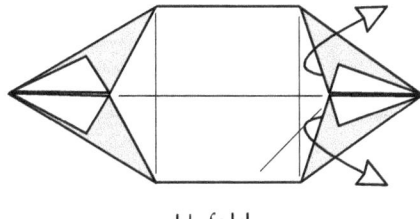

Unfold.

12

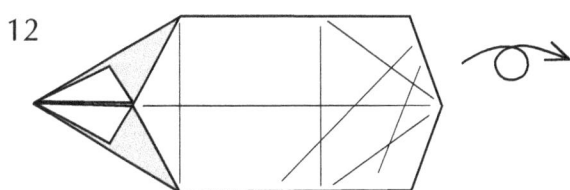

13

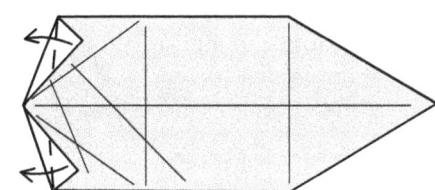

14

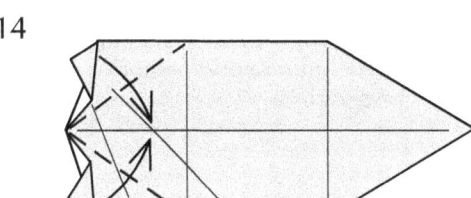

15

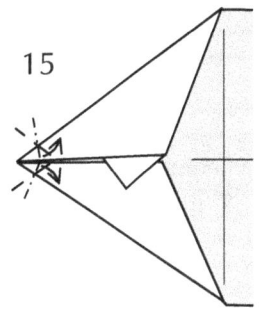

Only the left side is drawn.
Petal fold the nose.

16

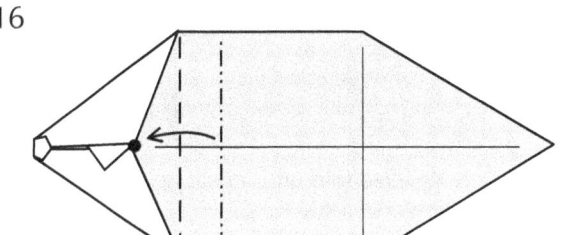

Pleat-fold to the dot.
Valley-fold along the crease.

17

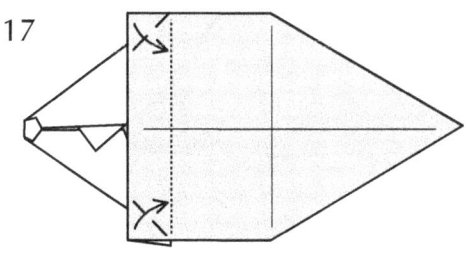

18

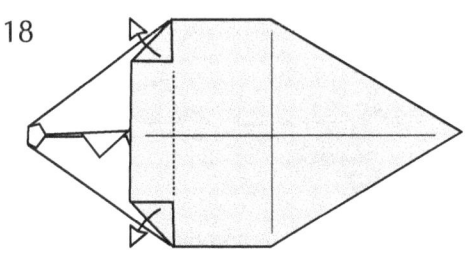

Unfold.

Mouse 89

19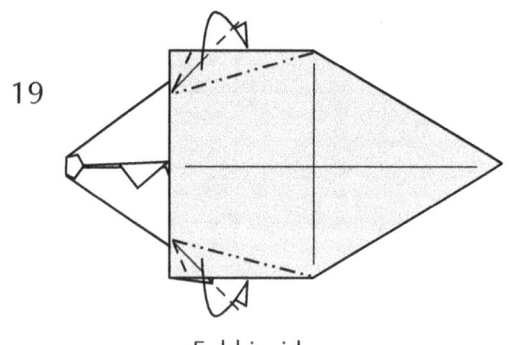
Fold inside.

20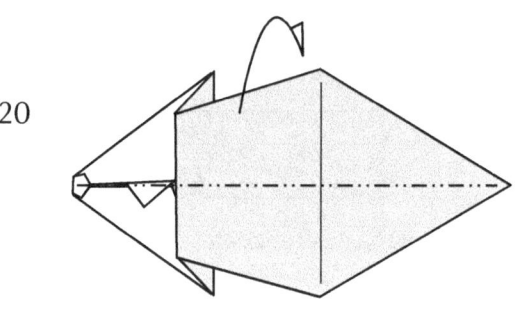

21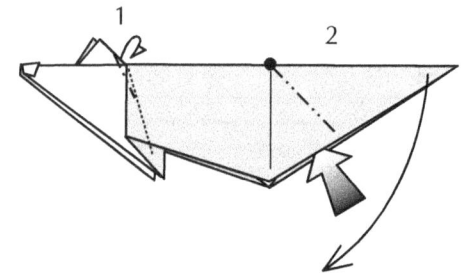
1. Be sure to show both ears. Fold a thin edge behind. Repeat behind.
2. Reverse-fold.

22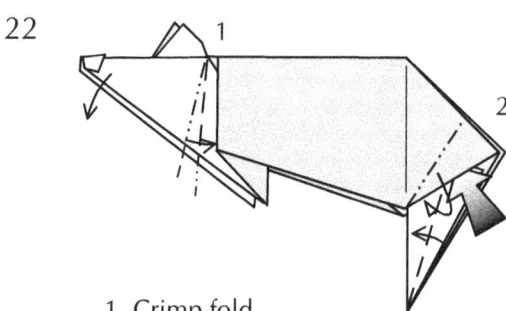
1. Crimp-fold.
2. Reverse-fold and repeat behind.

23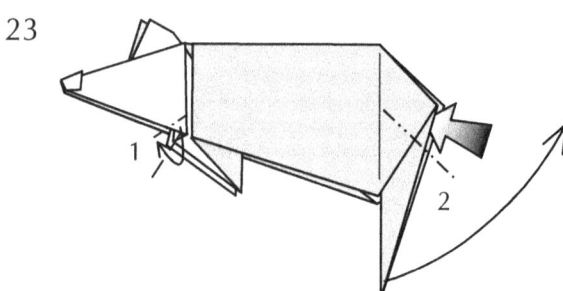
1. Reverse-fold and repeat behind.
2. Reverse-fold.

24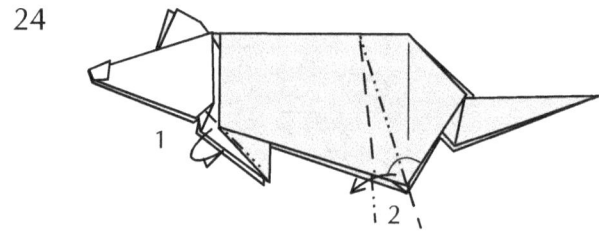
1. Repeat behind.
2. Crimp-fold.

25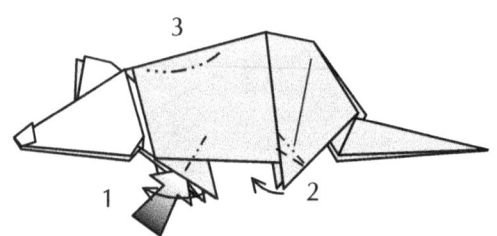
1. Reverse-fold and repeat behind.
2. Crimp-fold and repeat behind.
3. Shape the back.

26
Mouse

Raccoon

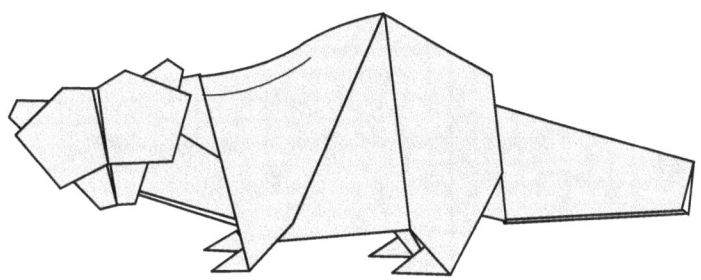

1.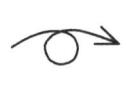

Fold and unfold.

2.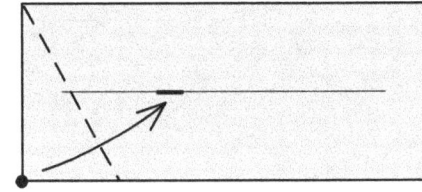

3.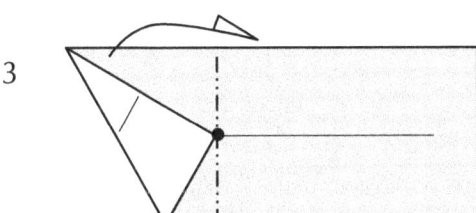

4.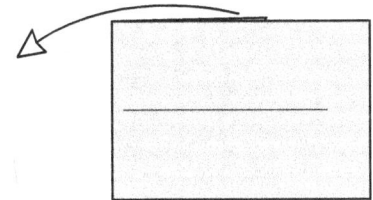

Unfold everything.

5.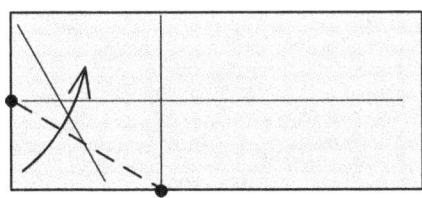

6.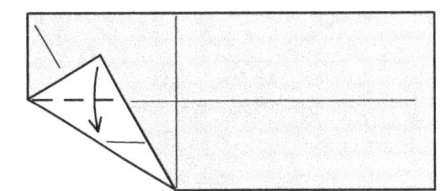

Raccoon 91

7

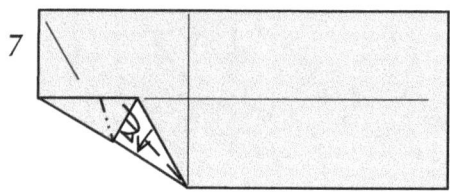

This is similar to a reverse fold.

8

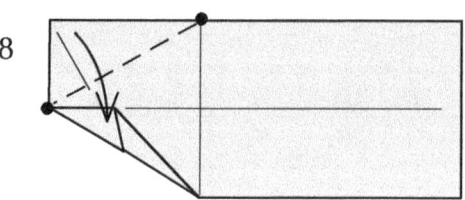

Repeat steps 4–7.

9

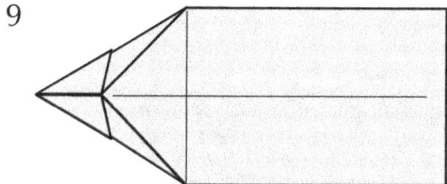

10

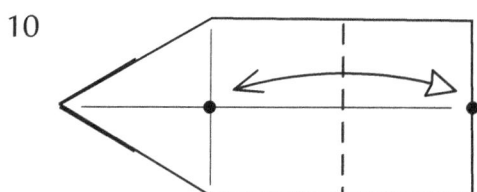

11

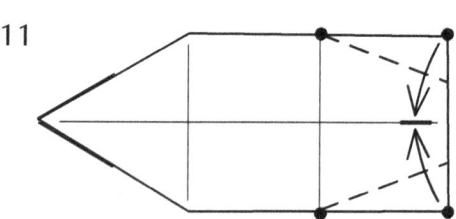

12

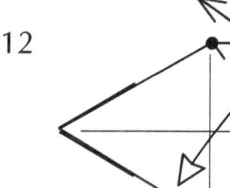

Fold and unfold.

13

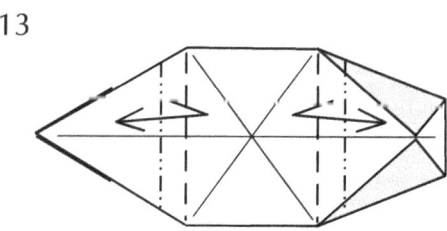

Pleat-fold on both sides.
Valley-fold along the creases.

14

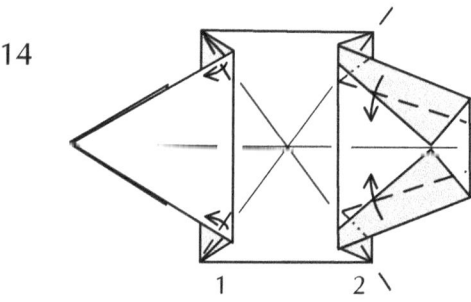

1. Valley-fold.
2. Make squash folds.

15

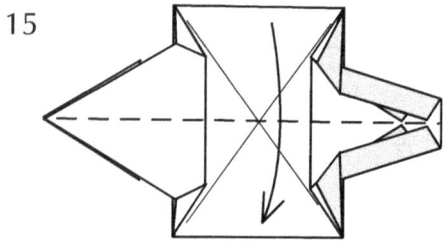

16

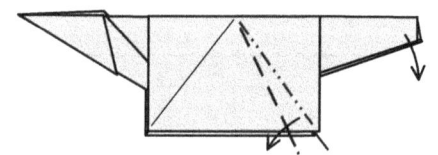

Crimp-fold. Mountain-fold along the crease.

92 *Dollar Origami Treasures*

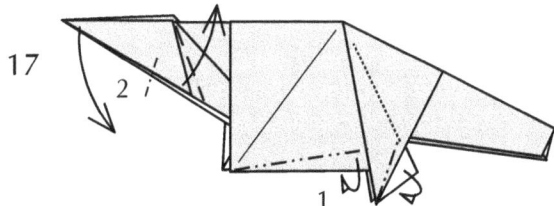

17

1. Squash-fold and repeat behind.
2. Squash-fold the head.

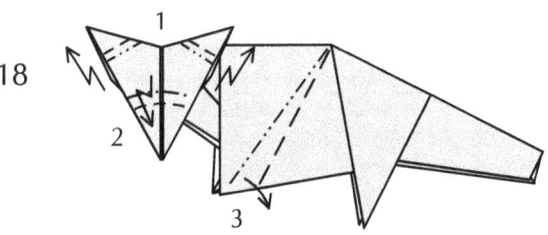

18

1. Crimp-fold the ears.
2. Fold back and forth.
3. Crimp-fold the front legs.
Mountain-fold along the crease.

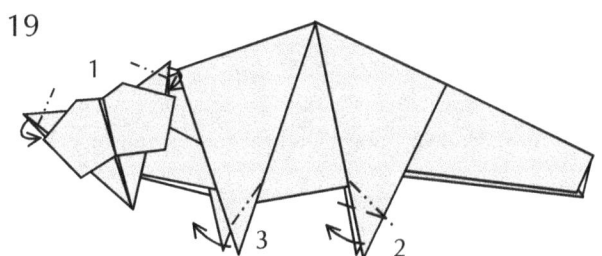

19

1. Reverse-fold the ears.
2. Crimp-fold the hind legs.
3. Reverse-fold the front legs.
Repeat behind.

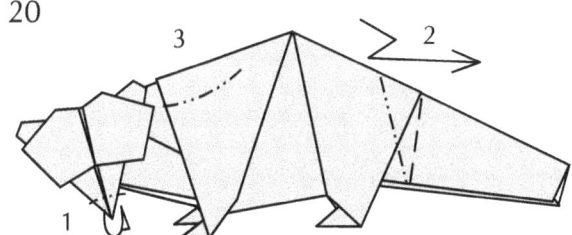

20

1. Fold behind.
2. Crimp-fold.
3. Shape the back.

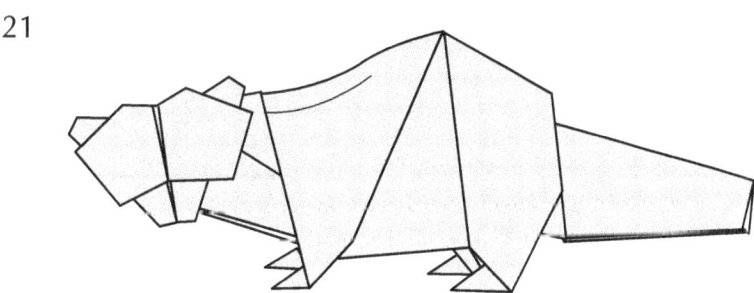

21

Raccoon

Anteater

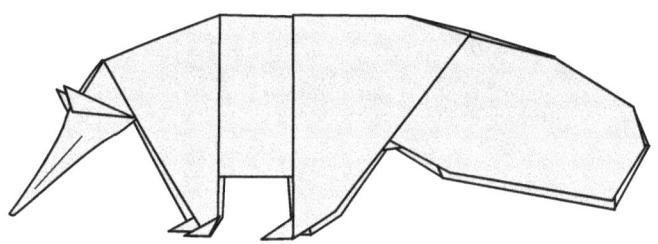

1.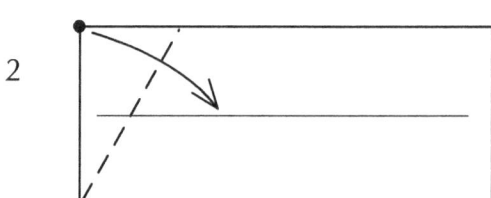
Fold and unfold.

2.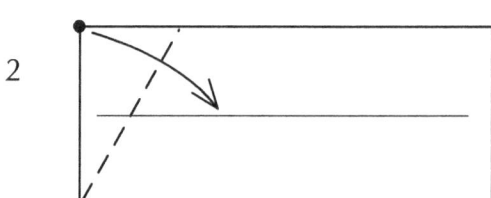
Fold the corner to the line.

3.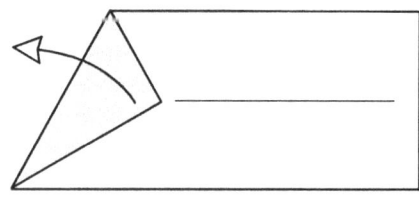
Unfold.

4.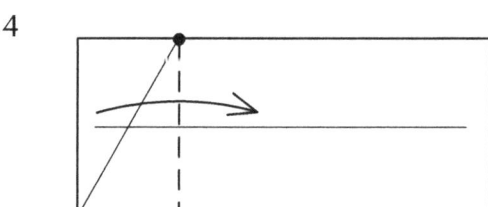

5.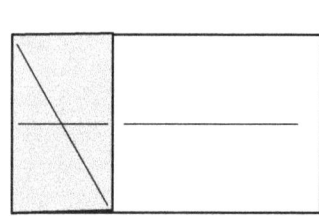

6.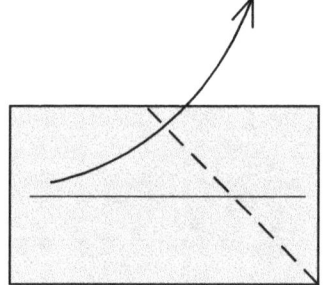

7.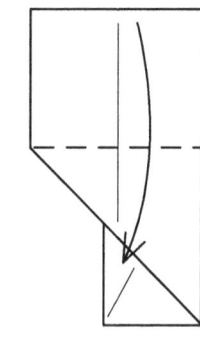

94 *Dollar Origami Treasures*

8

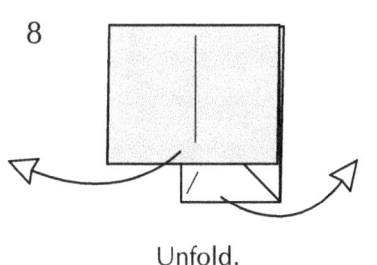

Unfold.

9

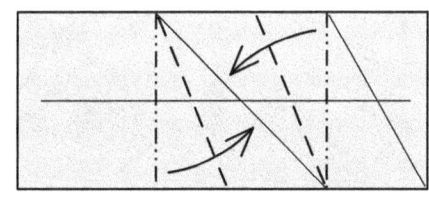

Mountain-fold along the creases. Fold to the diagonal.

10

Unfold.

11 12 13

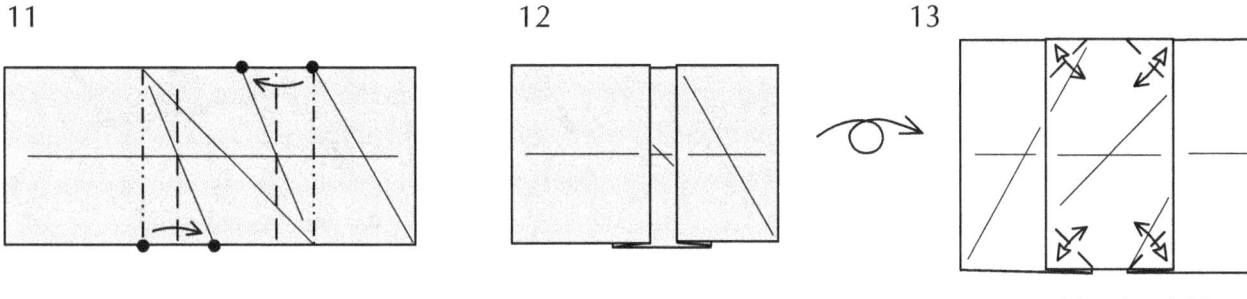

Fold and unfold.

14

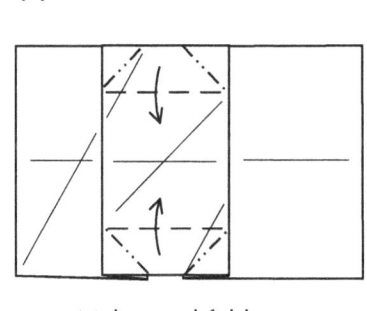

Make petal folds.

15 16

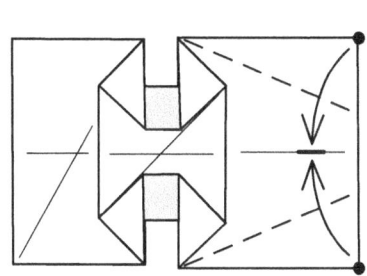

Fold and unfold to bisect the angles.

17

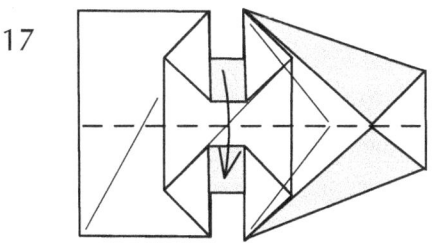

18

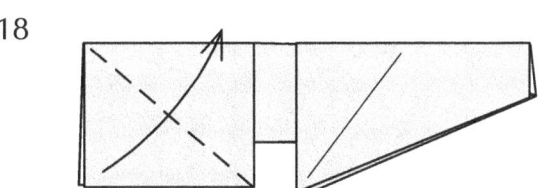

Fold the top layer and repeat behind.

Anteater 95

19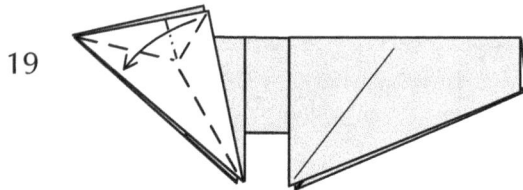

Rabbit-ear. Repeat behind.

20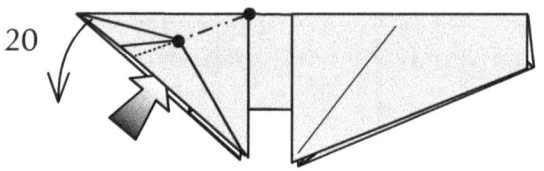

Reverse-fold.

21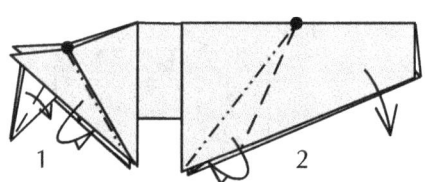

1. Squash-fold and repeat behind.
2. Crimp-fold the tail.

22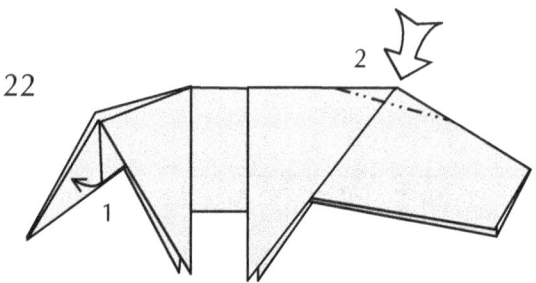

1. Slide the ear and repeat behind.
2. Sink.

23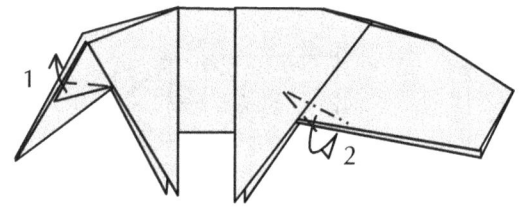

1. Fold the ear.
2. Squash-fold.
Repeat behind.

24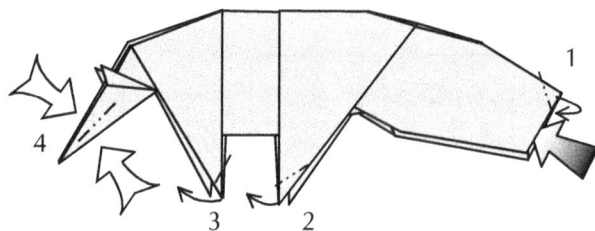

1. Reverse-fold.
2. Reverse-fold.
3. Outside-reverse-fold.
4. Squeeze the head.
Repeat behind.

25

Anteater

Dromedary

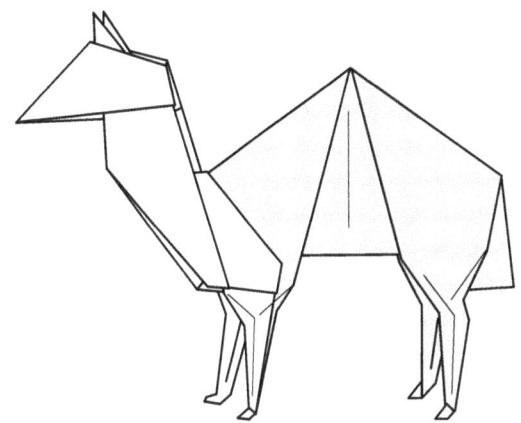

1
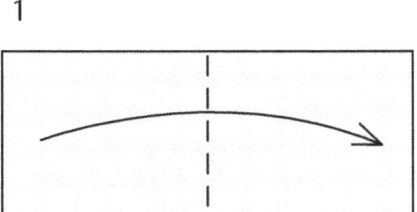

2
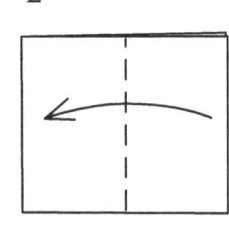

3
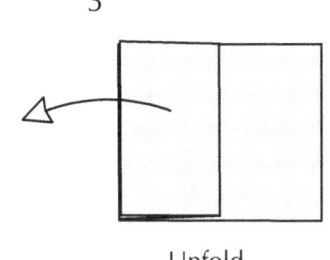
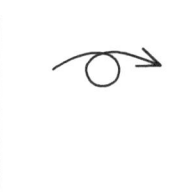

Unfold.

4
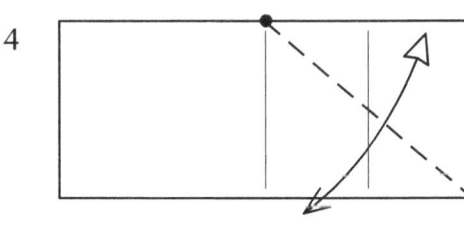

Fold and unfold.

5
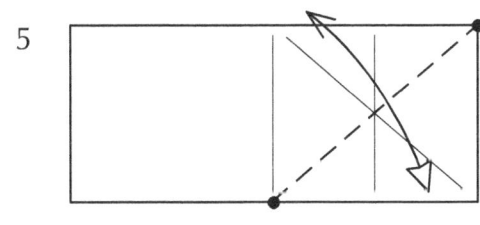

Fold and unfold.

6
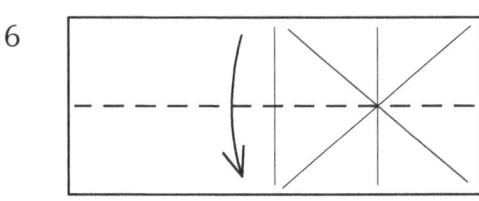

7
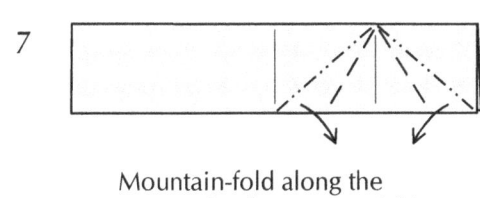

Mountain-fold along the creases for these crimp folds.

Dromedary 97

8

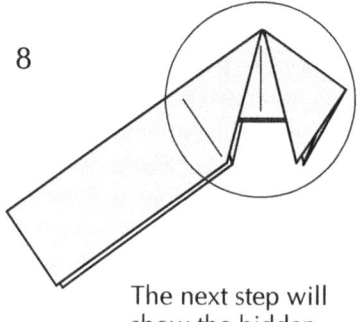

The next step will show the hidden layers in the circle.

9

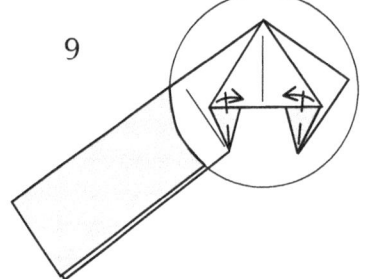

10

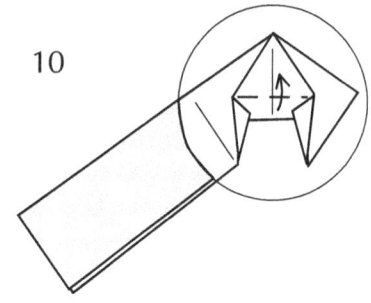

11

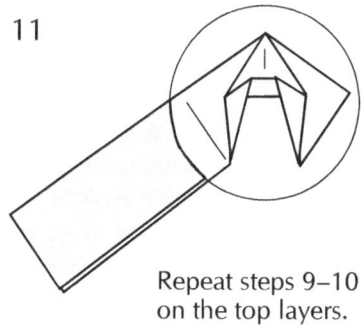

Repeat steps 9–10 on the top layers.

12

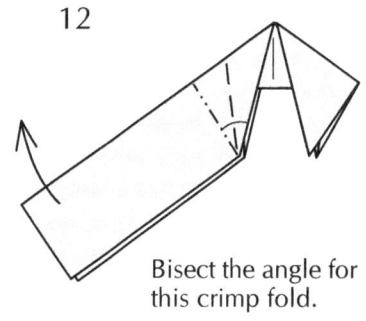

Bisect the angle for this crimp fold.

13

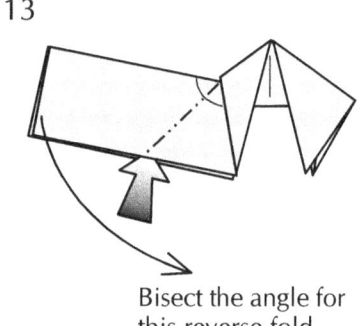

Bisect the angle for this reverse fold.

14

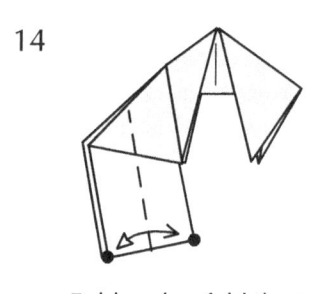

Fold and unfold the top layer. Repeat behind.

15

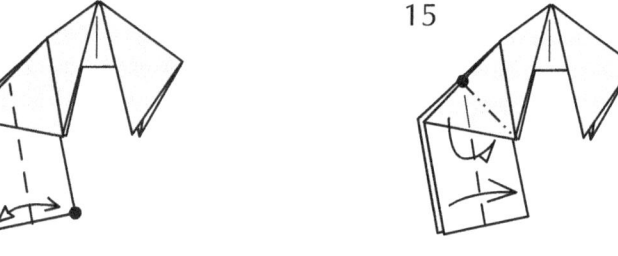

Repeat behind.

16

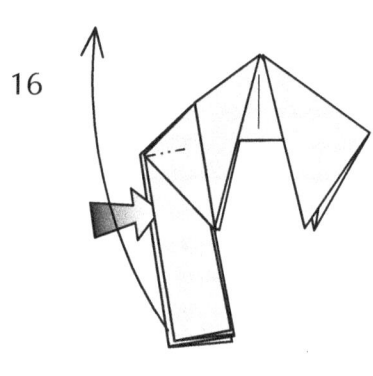

Reverse-fold.

17

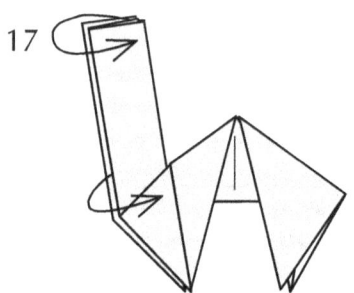

Wrap around. Repeat behind.

18

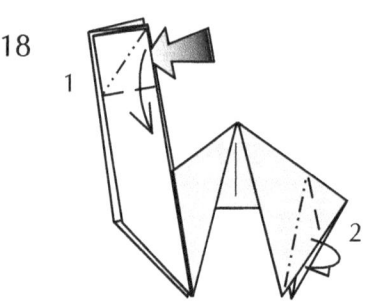

1. Squash-fold and repeat behind.
2. Crimp-fold.

19

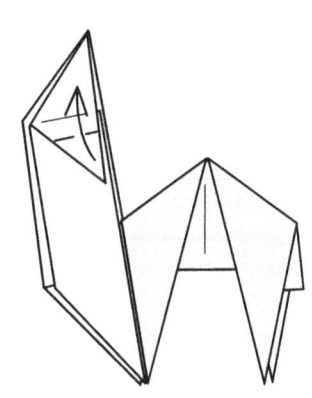

Repeat behind.

20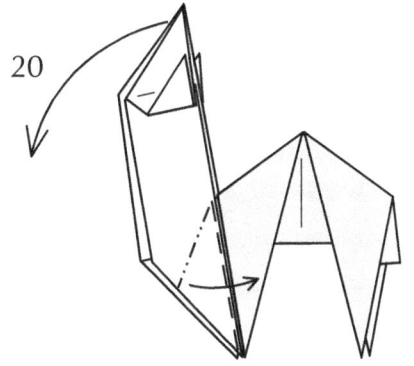

Crimp-fold.

21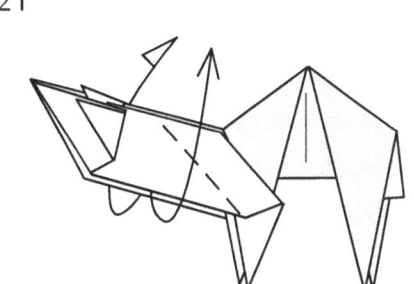

Outside-reverse-fold.

22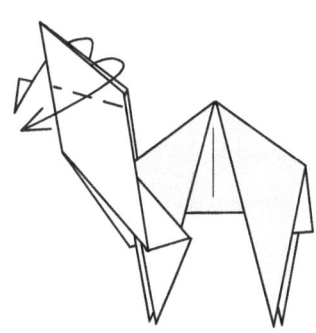

Outside-reverse-fold.

23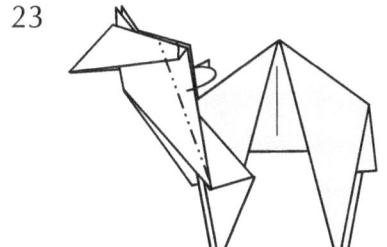

Repeat behind.

24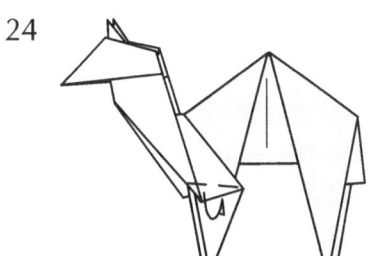

Repeat behind.

25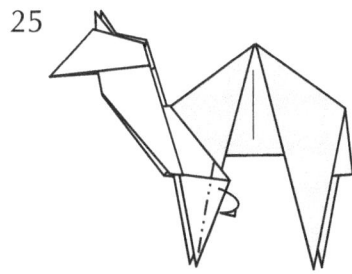

Repeat behind.

26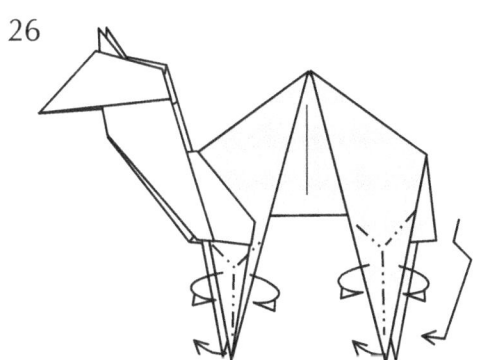

Shape the legs and feet. Repeat behind.

27

Dromedary

Piggy Bank

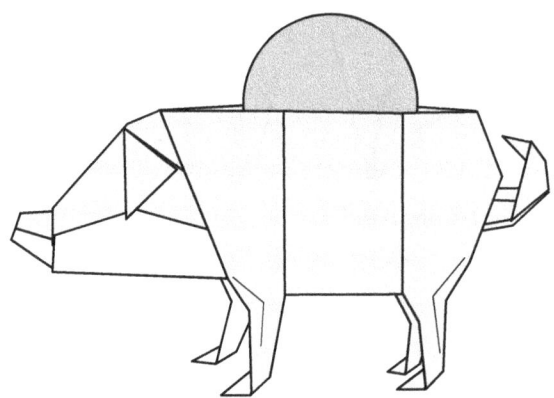

The piggy bank can hold a quarter.

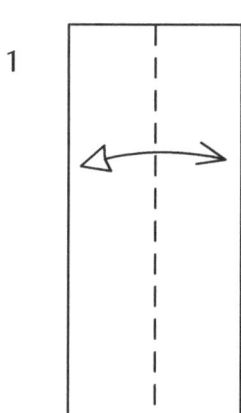

1

Fold and unfold.

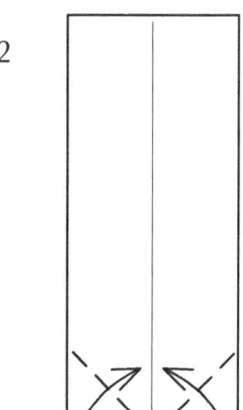

2

Fold to the center.

3

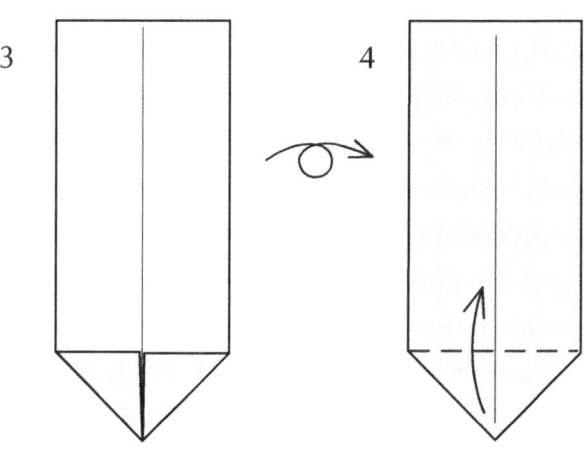

4

Fold up.

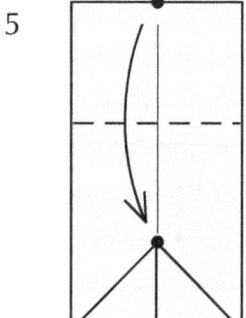

5

The dots will meet.

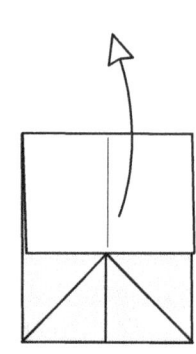

6

Unfold.

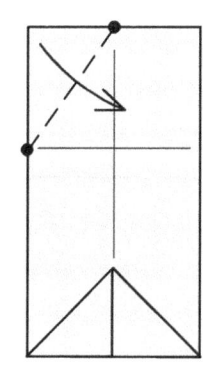

7

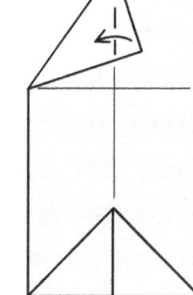

8

Fold along the partially hidden crease.

100   Dollar Origami Treasures

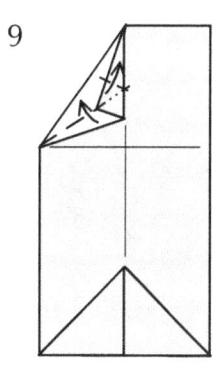

9

Squash-fold.

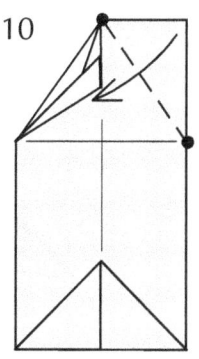

10

Repeat steps 7–9 on the right.

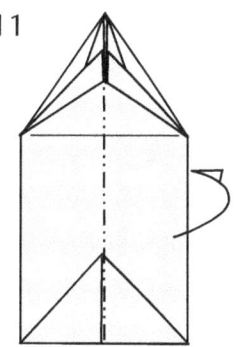

11

Fold in half.

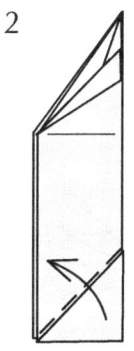

12

Fold all the layers.

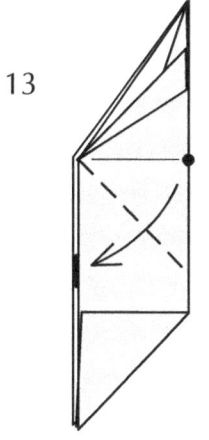

13

Fold all the layers.

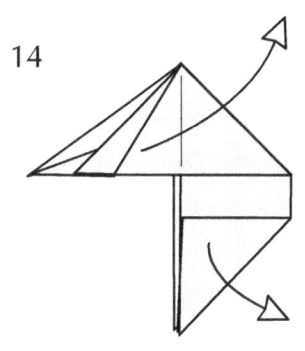

14

Unfold.

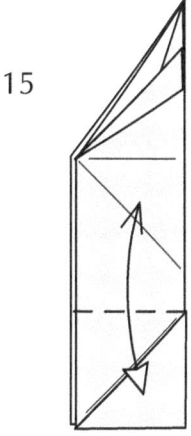

15

Fold and unfold.

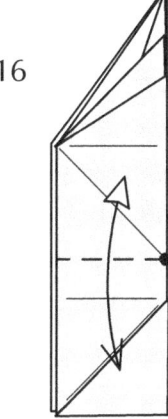

16

Fold and unfold.

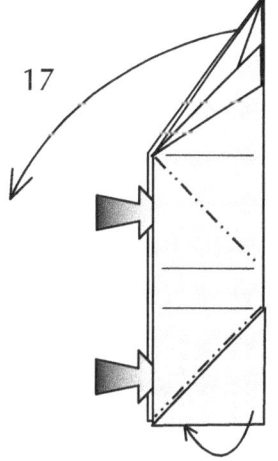

17

Reverse folds. Rotate 90°.

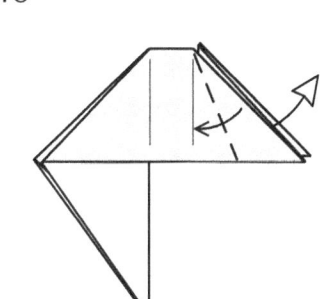

18

Fold to the crease and swing out from inside. Repeat behind at the same time.

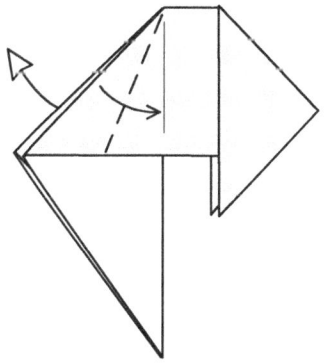

19

Fold to the crease and swing out from inside. Repeat behind at the same time.

Piggy Bank 101

20

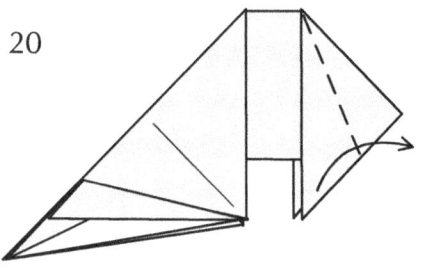

21

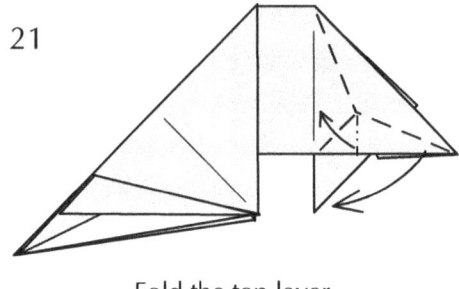

Fold the top layer.

22

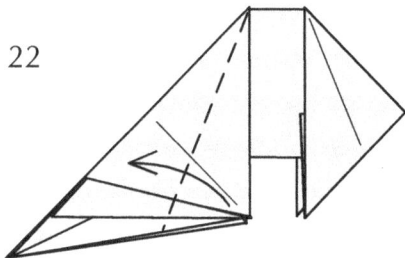

23

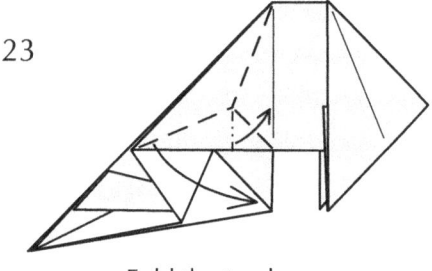

Fold the top layer.

24

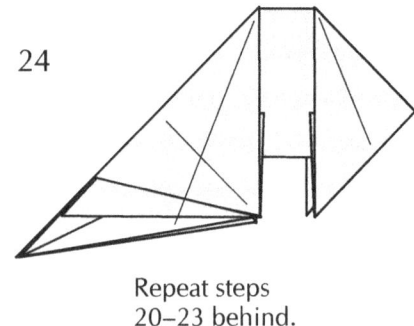

Repeat steps
20–23 behind.

25

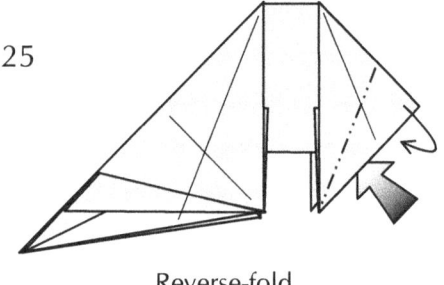

Reverse-fold.

26

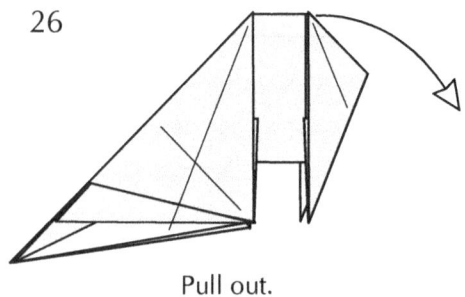

Pull out.

27

Crimp-fold. Valley-fold
along the crease.

102 *Dollar Origami Treasures*

28

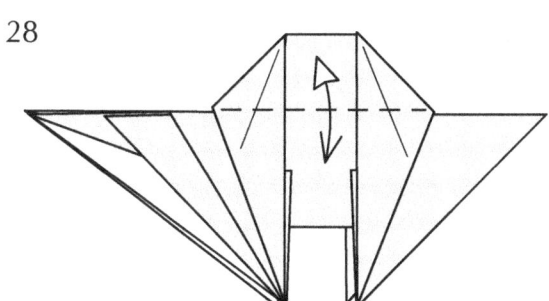

Fold and unfold.

29

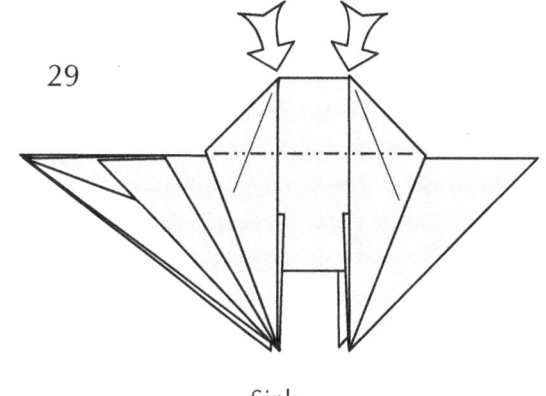

Sink.

30

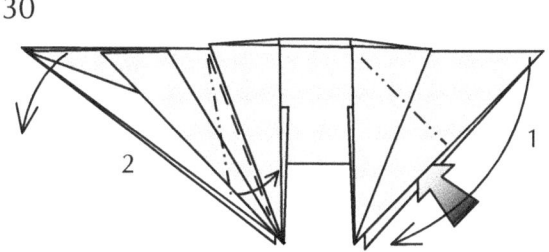

1. Reverse-fold.
2. Crimp-fold.

31

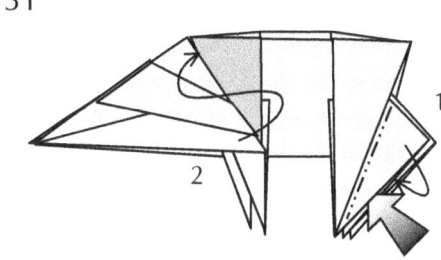

1. Reverse-fold.
2. Tuck under the dark paper.
Repeat behind.

32

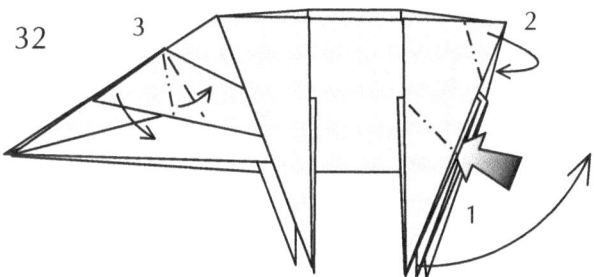

1. Reverse-fold the tail.
2. Reverse-fold.
3. Fold the ear.
Repeat behind.

33

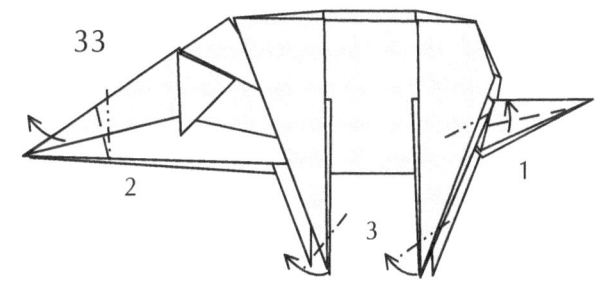

1. Thin the tail.
2. Crimp-fold.
3. Little reverse folds.
Repeat behind.

34

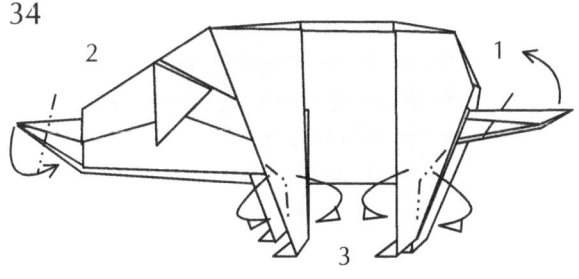

1. Outside-reverse-fold the tail.
2. Reverse-fold.
3. Thin and shape the legs.
Repeat behind.

35

Place a quarter in the piggy bank.

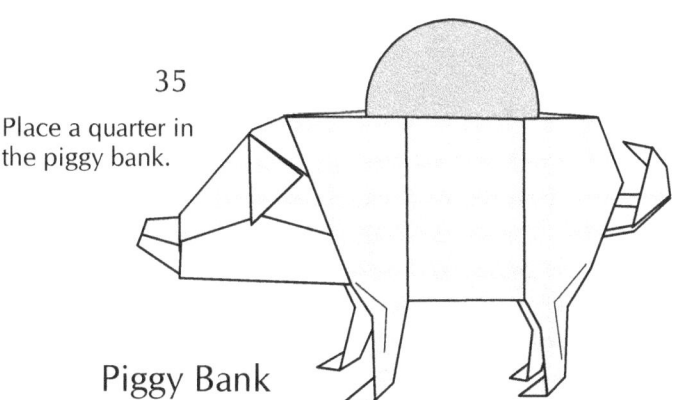

Piggy Bank

Piggy Bank 103

Elephant

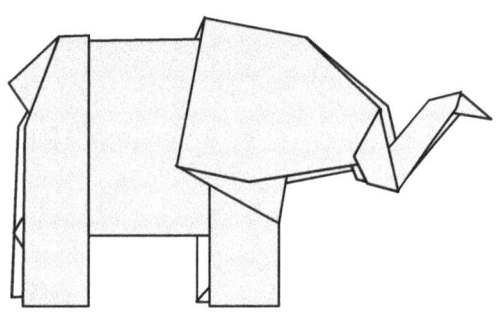

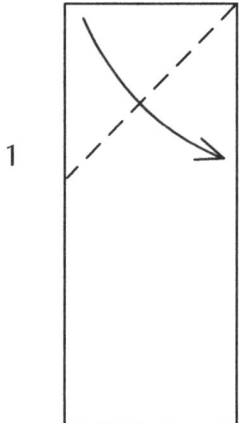
1

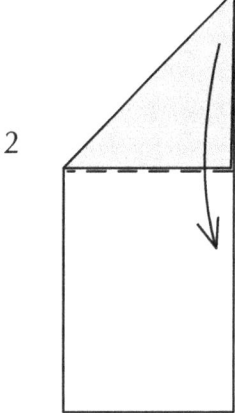
2

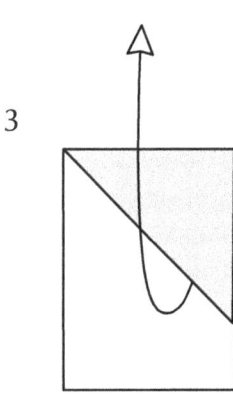
3
Unfold.

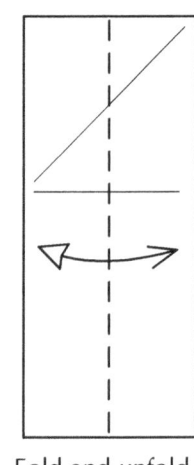
4
Fold and unfold.

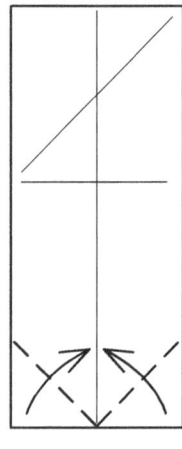
5

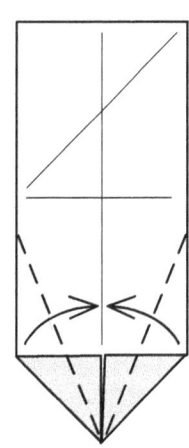
6

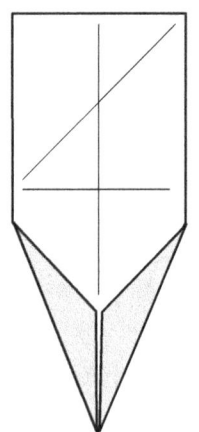
7

104   *Dollar Origami Treasures*

8

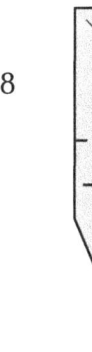

Mountain-fold along the crease.

9

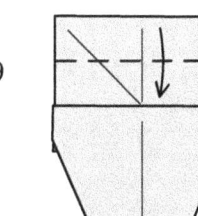

10

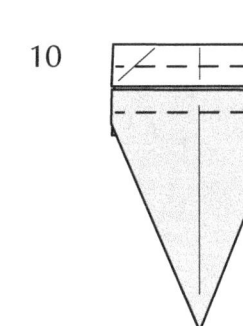

11

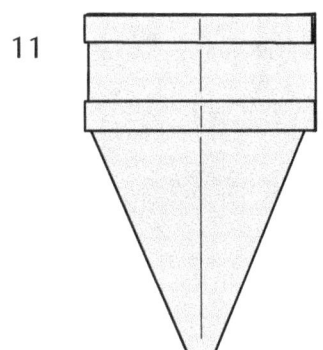

12

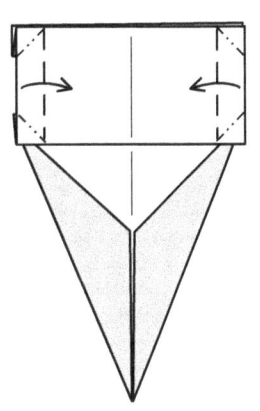

Petal folds.

13

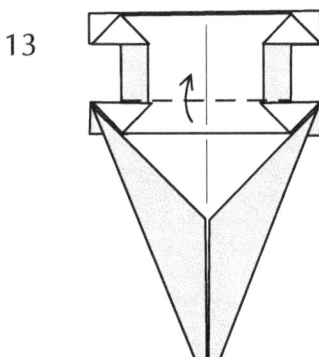

14

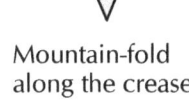

Squash folds.

15

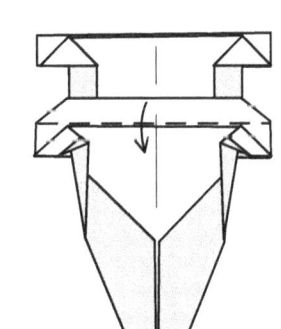

16

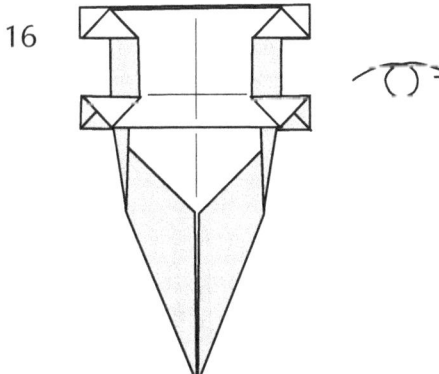

Elephant 105

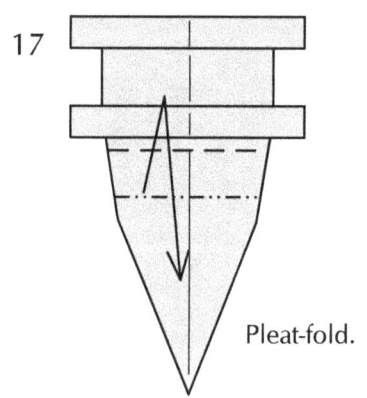

17

Pleat-fold.

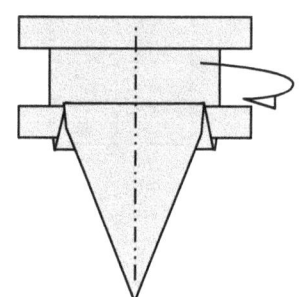

18

Fold in half and rotate.

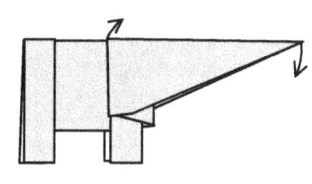

19

Pivot the head.

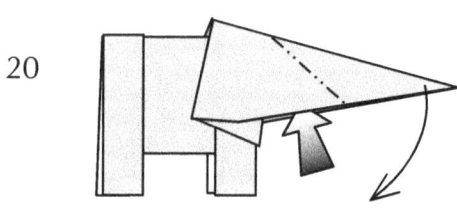

20

Reverse-fold.

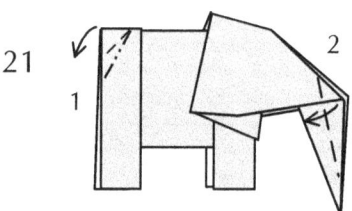

21

1. Crimp-fold.
2. Repeat behind.

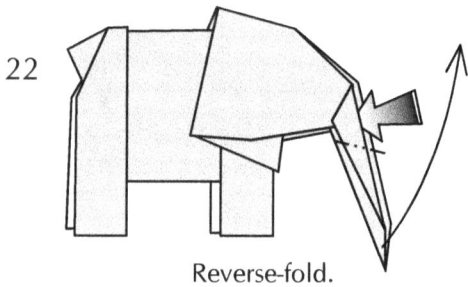

22

Reverse-fold.

23

Reverse-fold.

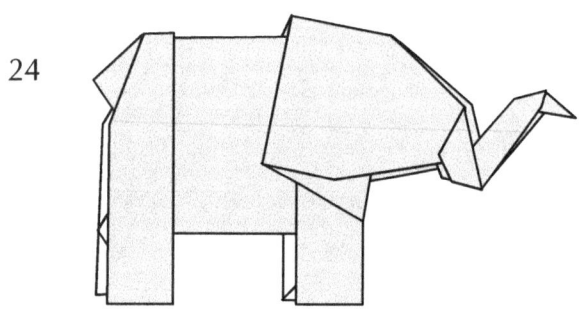

24

Elephant

106 *Dollar Origami Treasures*

Dinosaurs

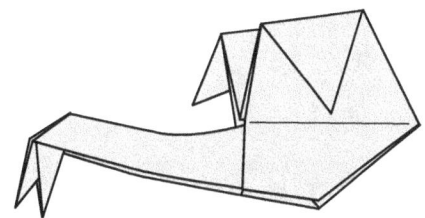
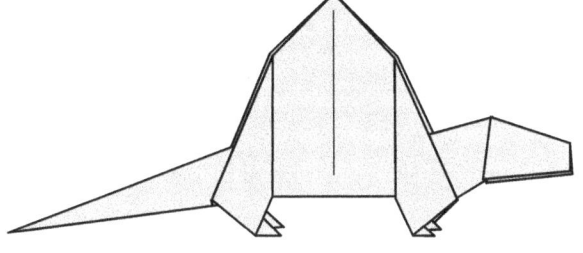
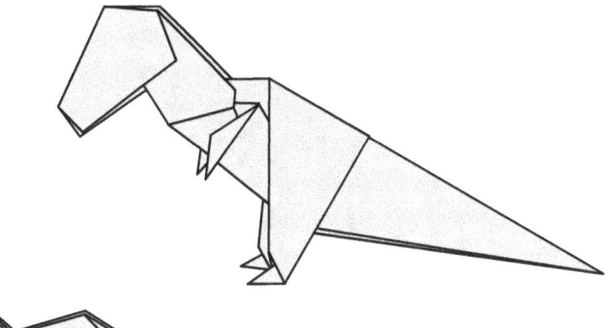

Dollar bill dinosaurs are stunning. The green texture adds realism to the models. Here are seven land and air prehistoric creatures.

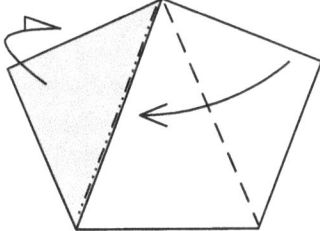

Quetzalcoatlus & Pteranodon

1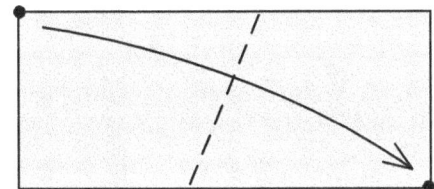

Bring the corners together. Rotate.

2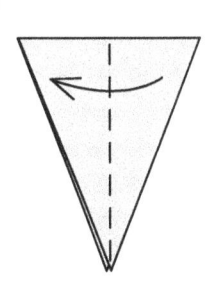

3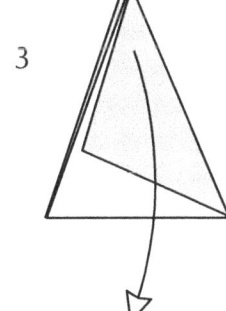

Unfold.

4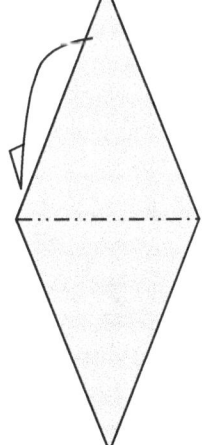

5

Fold in half and rotate.

6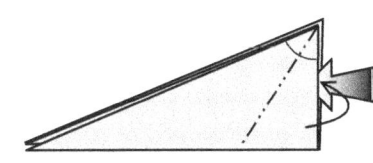

Reverse-fold.

Quetzalcoatlus 107

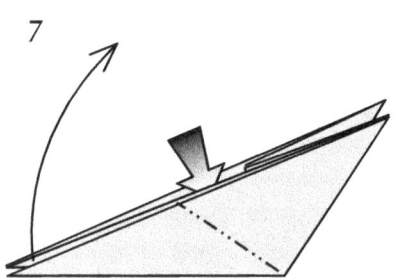

7

Reverse-fold and rotate.

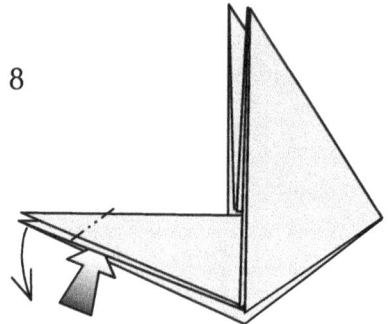

8

Reverse-fold all the layers.

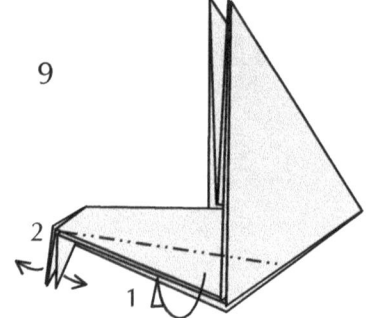

9

1. Fold inside and repeat behind.
2. Spread the beak.

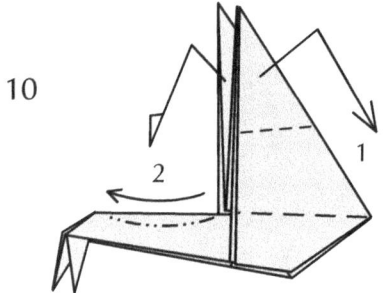

10

1. Spread the wings.
2. Shape the neck.

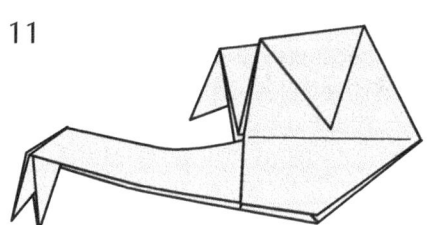

11

Quetzalcoatlus

Pteranodon

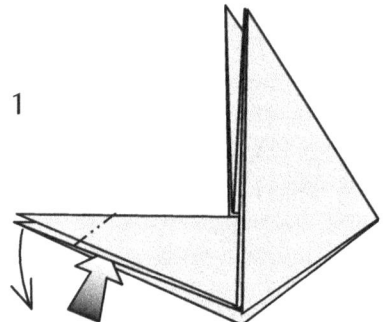

1

Begin with step 8 of the Quetzalcoatlus. Reverse-fold so the beak is slightly larger than that of the Quetzalcoatlus.

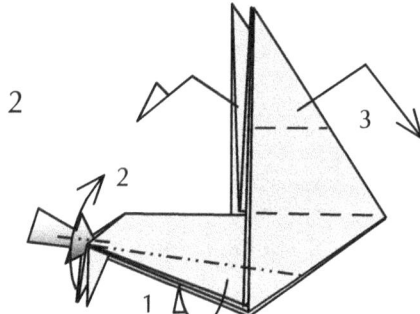

2

1. Fold inside and repeat behind.
2. Reverse-fold.
3. Spread the wings.

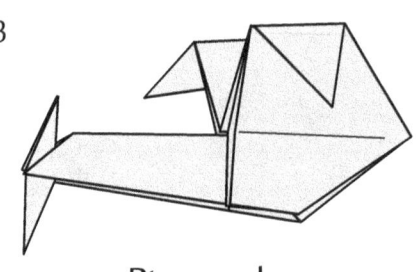

3

Pteranodon

108 *Dollar Origami Treasures*

Pterodactylus

1. Fold and unfold. 
2. 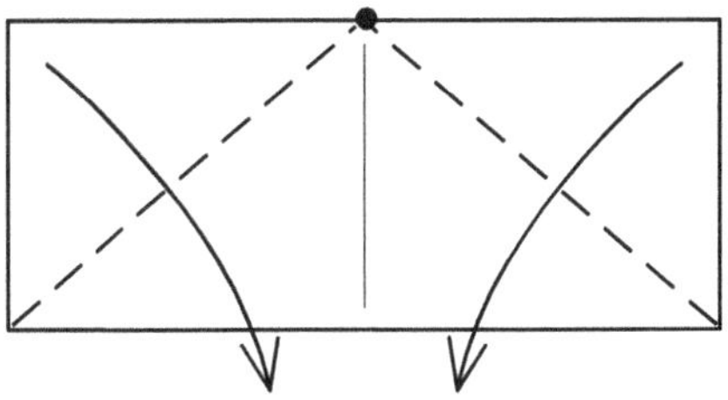
3. 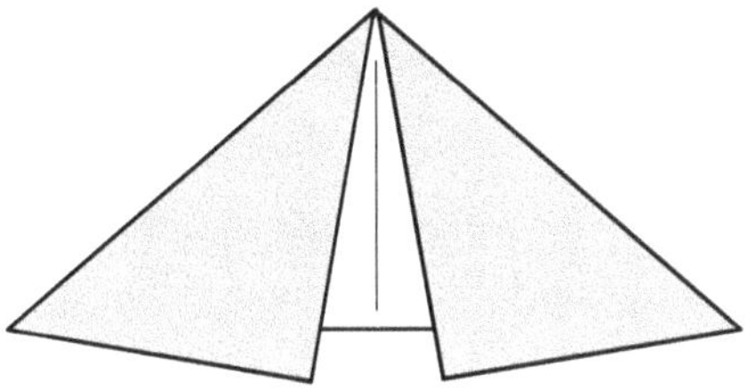 
4. 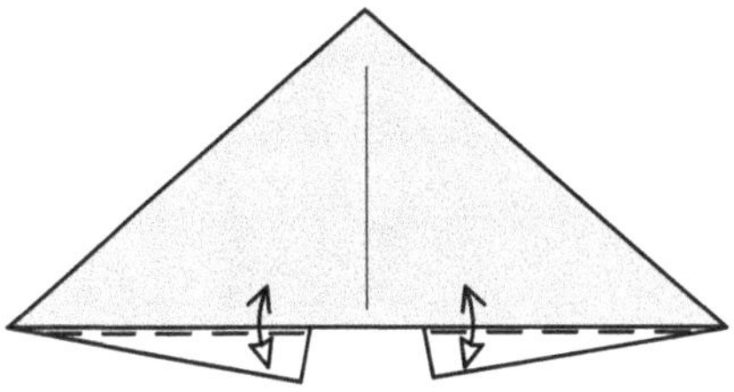 Fold and unfold.
5. Tuck inside.
6. Fold and unfold.
7. Fold in half and rotate.
8. Repeat behind.
9. Squash-fold and repeat behind.
10. 1. Reverse-fold.
    2. Fold inside and repeat behind.
11. Spread the wings.
12.

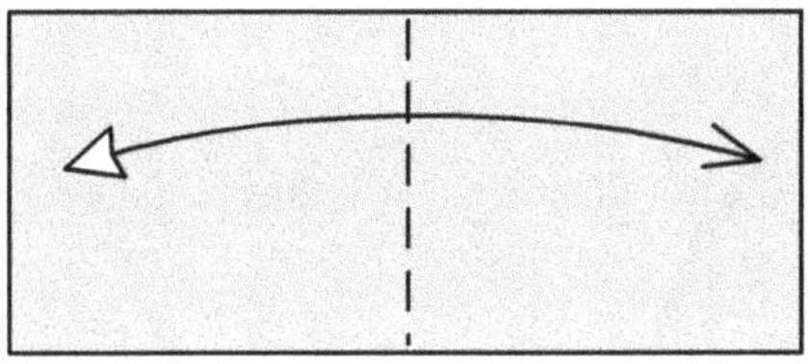

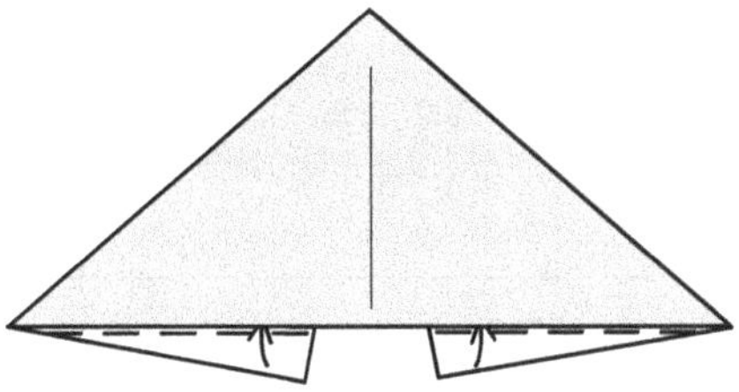

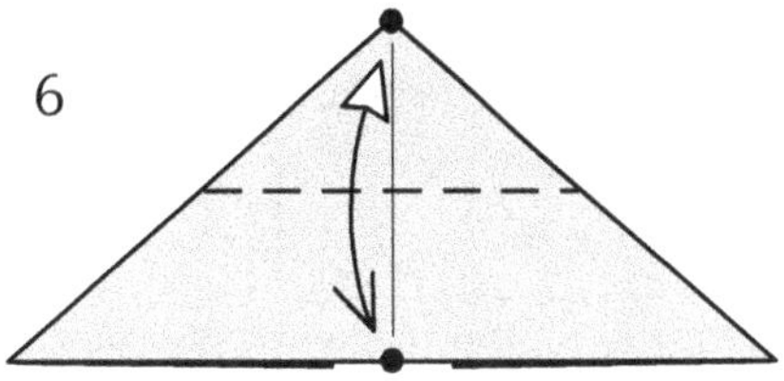

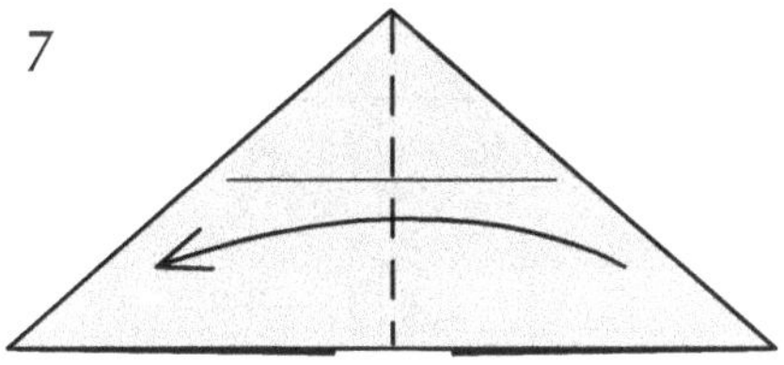

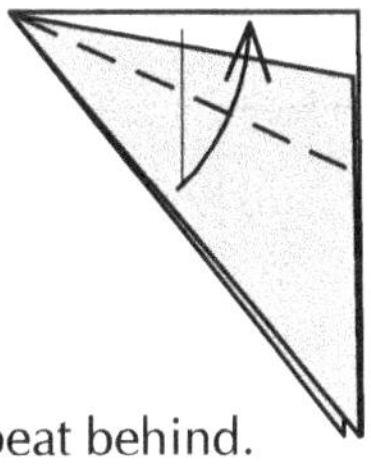

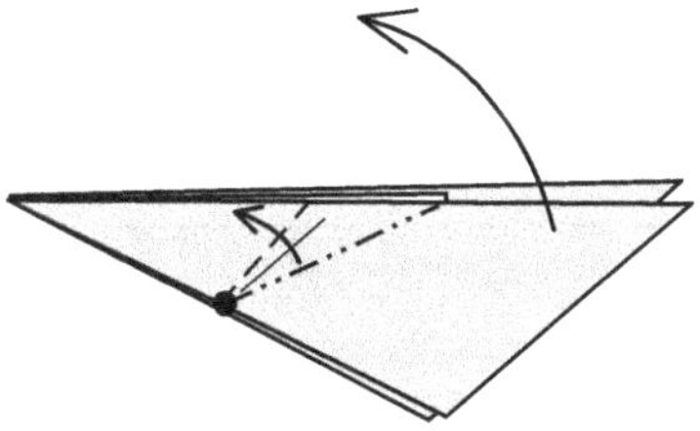

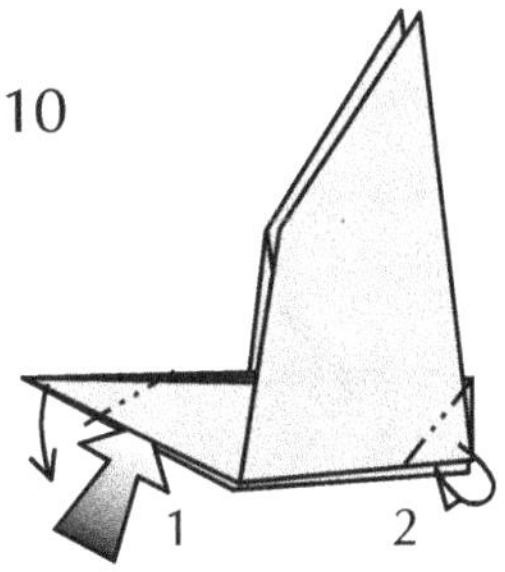

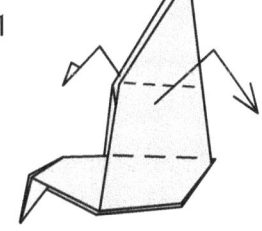

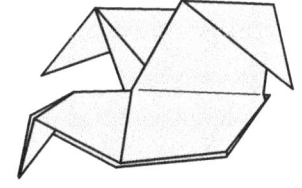

Pterodactylus

Dimetrodon

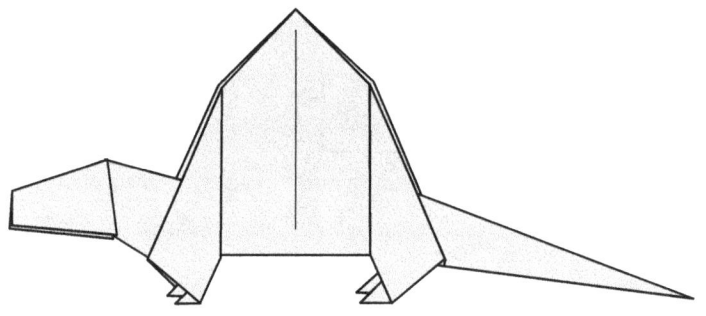

1. 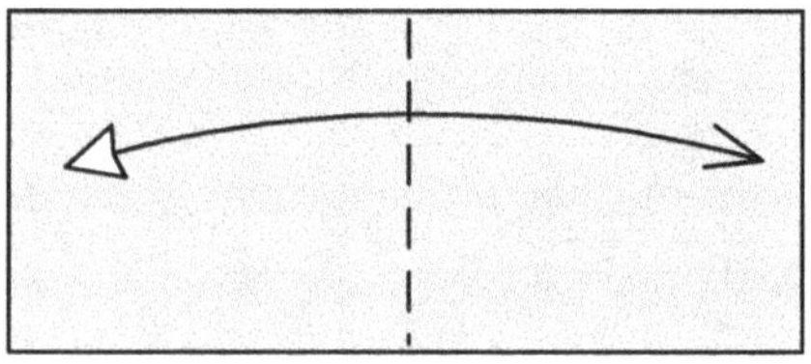 Fold and unfold.
2. 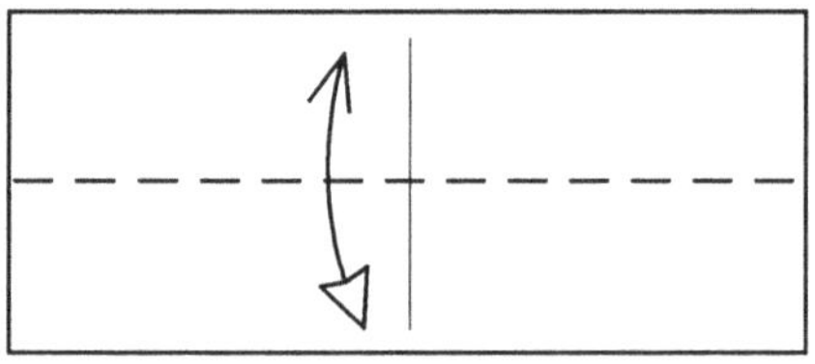 Fold and unfold. 
3.
4. 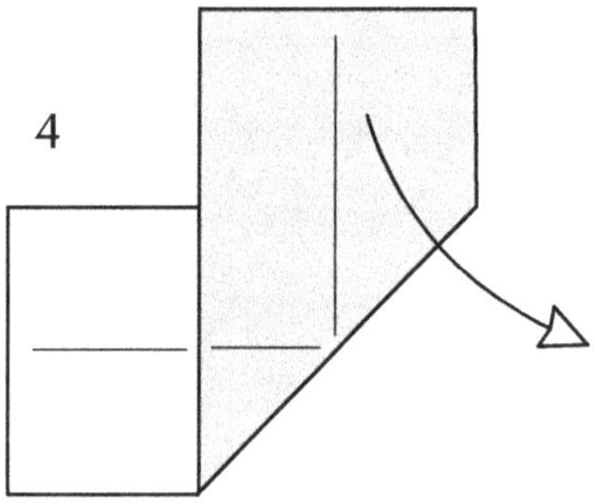 Unfold. 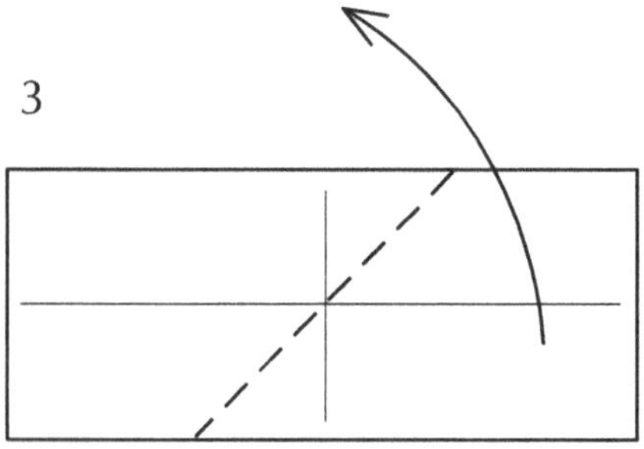
5. Fold and unfold.
6. Fold along the creases.
7. Repeat behind.
8. Repeat behind.

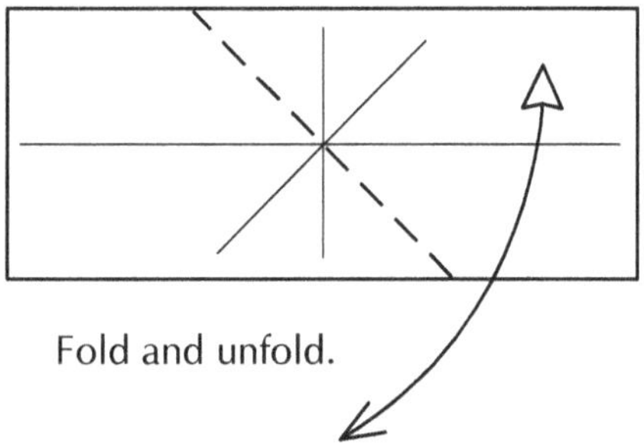

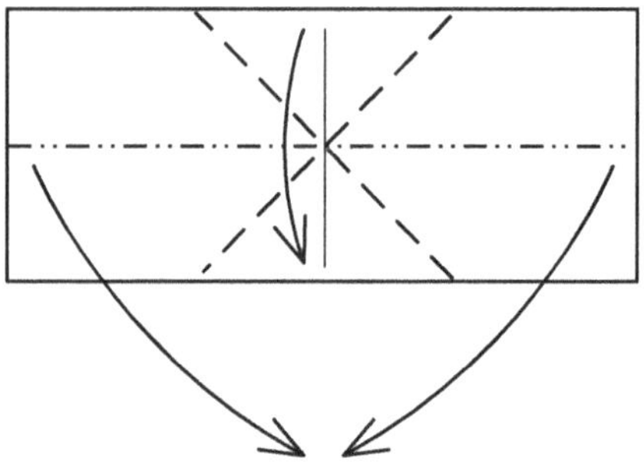

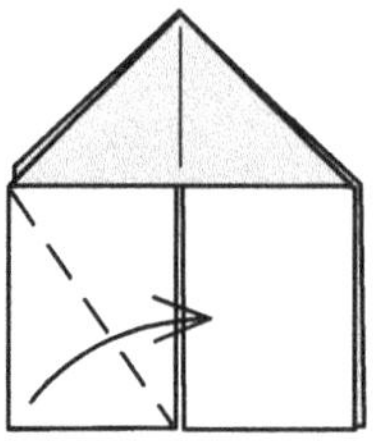

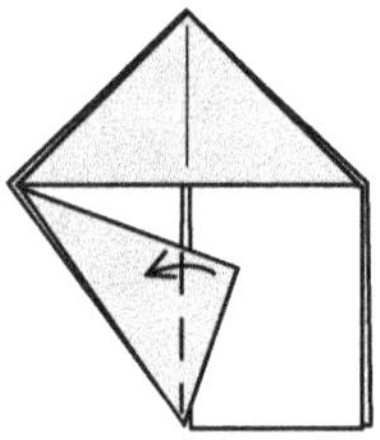

110 *Dollar Origami Treasures*

9

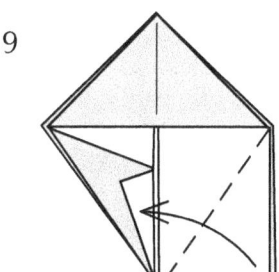

Repeat steps 7–8 on the right.

10

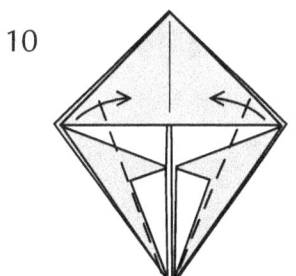

Fold at an angle of one-third. Repeat behind.

11

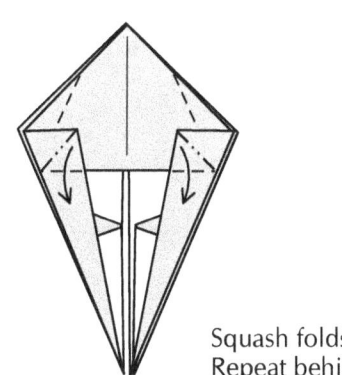

Squash folds. Repeat behind.

12

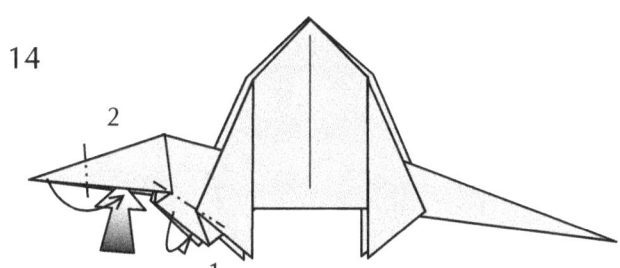

Reverse folds.

13

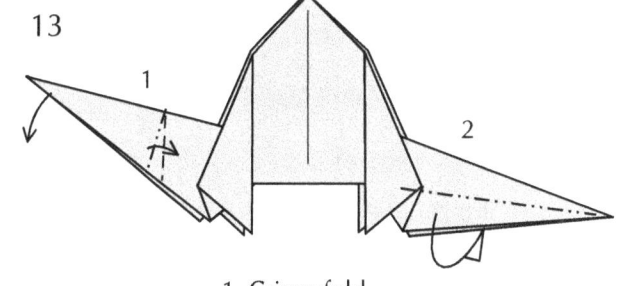

1. Crimp-fold.
2. Fold inside and repeat behind.

14

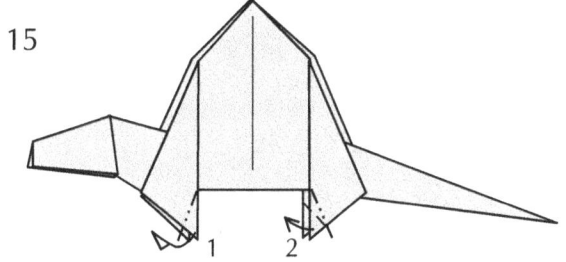

1. Fold inside and repeat behind.
2. Crimp-fold.

15

1. Mountain-fold.
2. Pleat-fold.
Repeat behind.

16

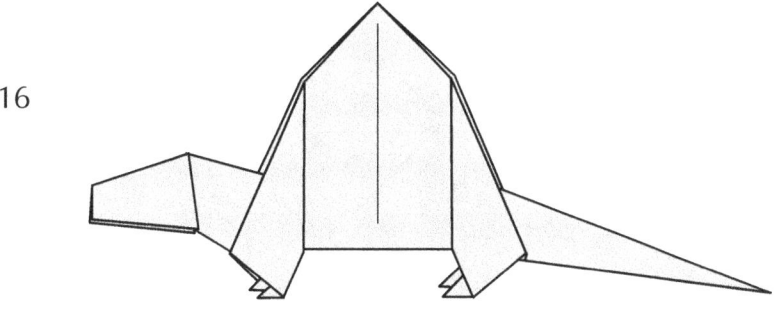

Dimetrodon

Dimetrodon 111

Apatosaurus

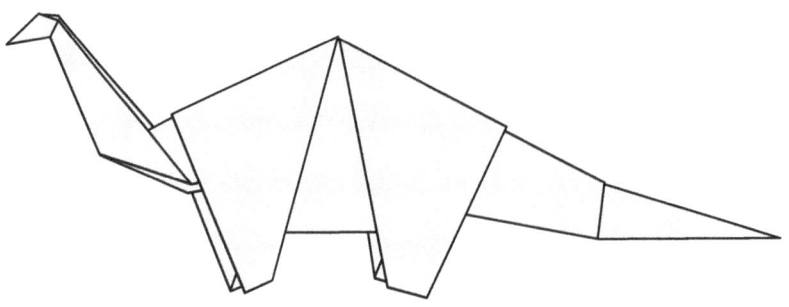

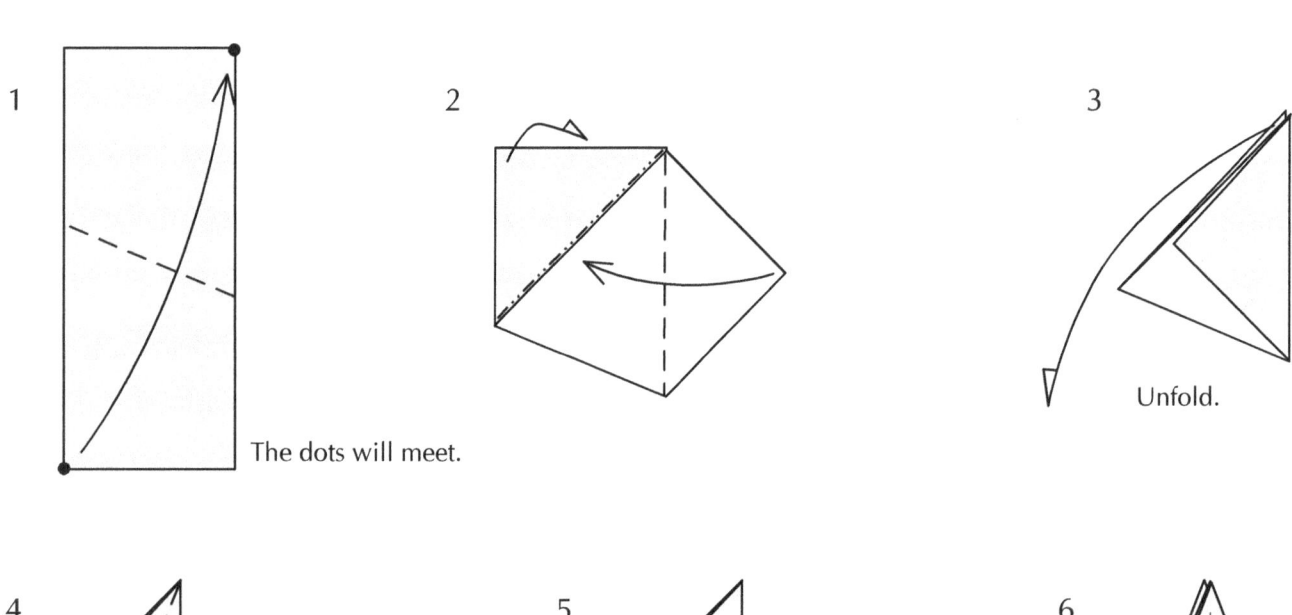

1

The dots will meet.

2

3

Unfold.

4

Fold and unfold.

5

6

112 *Dollar Origami Treasures*

7

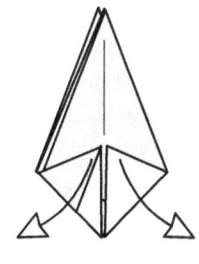

Unfold.

8

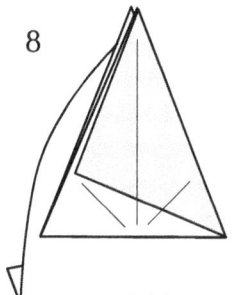

Unfold.

9

10

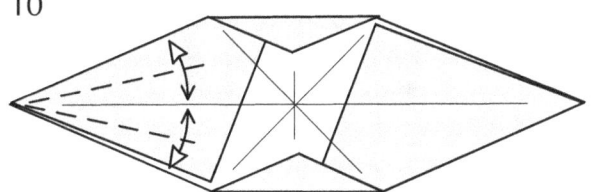

Fold to the center and unfold.

11

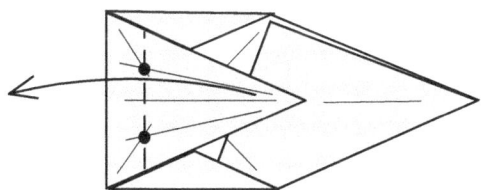

12

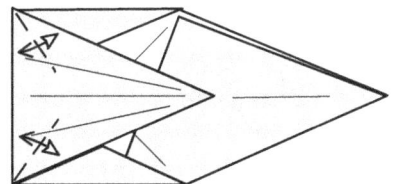

Fold and unfold.

13

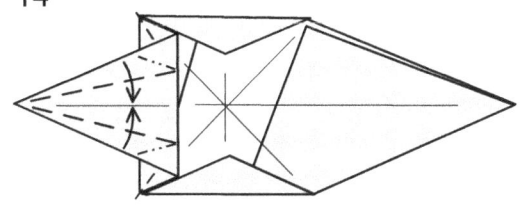

14

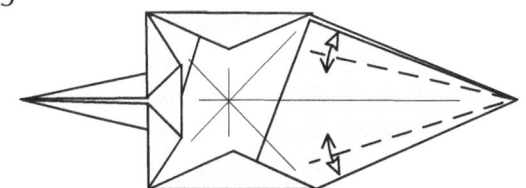

Squash folds.

15

Fold at an angle of one-third and unfold.

Apatosaurus 113

16

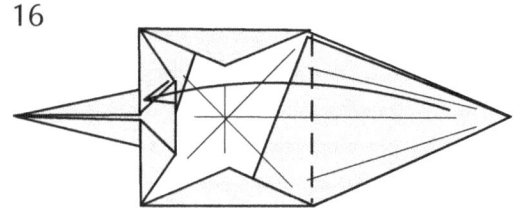

17

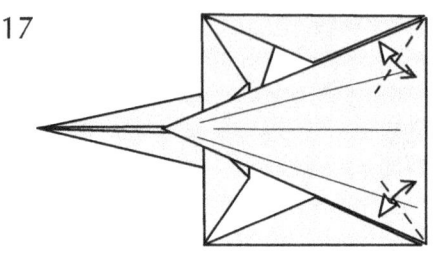

Repeat steps 12–14 on the right.

18

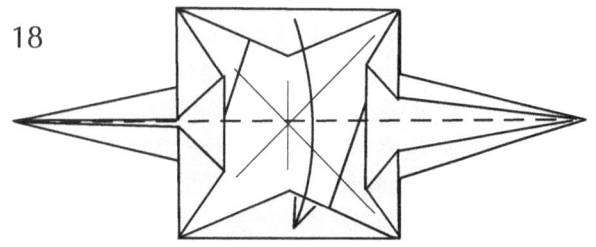

19

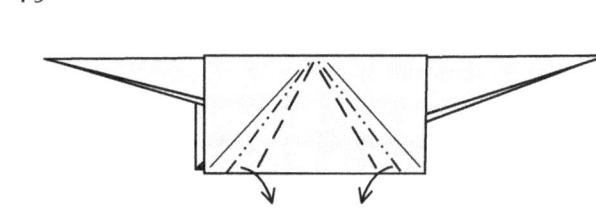

Crimp folds.

20

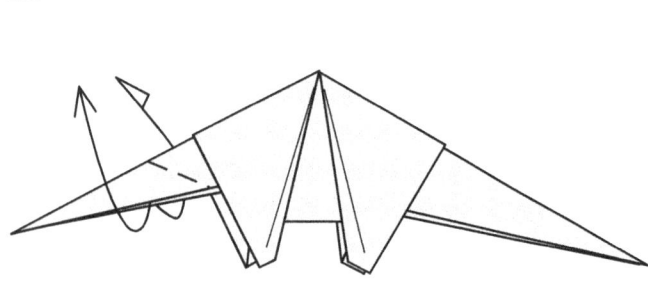

Outside-reverse-fold.

21

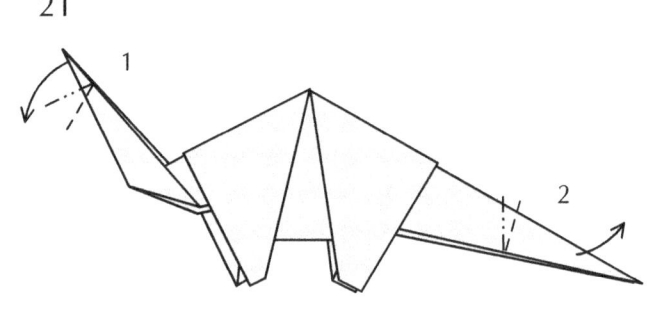

1. Open the head.
2. Crimp-fold.

22

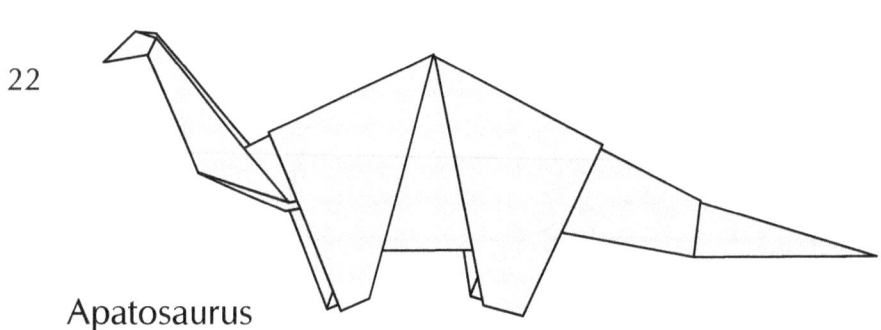

Apatosaurus

114 *Dollar Origami Treasures*

Protoceratops

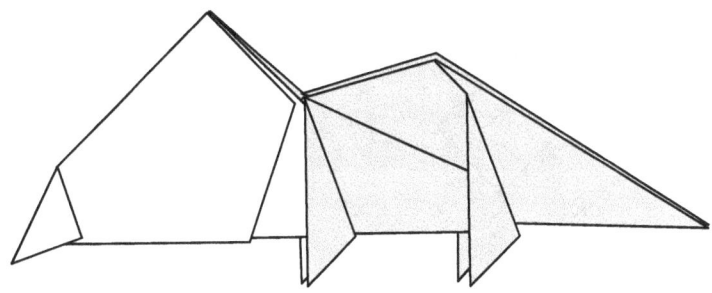

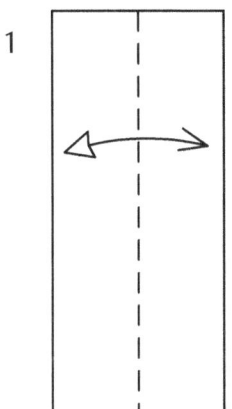

1. Fold and unfold.

2. Fold to the center.

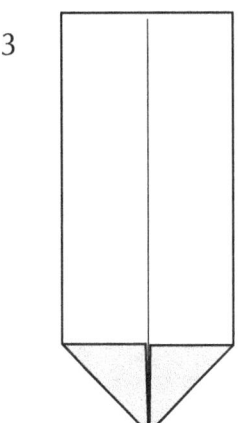

3.

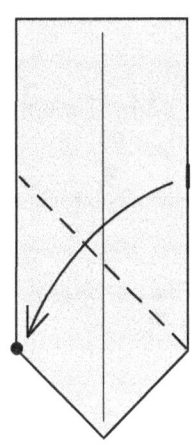

4.

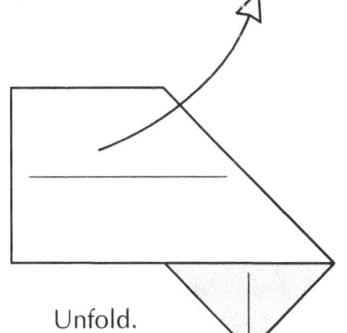

5. Unfold.

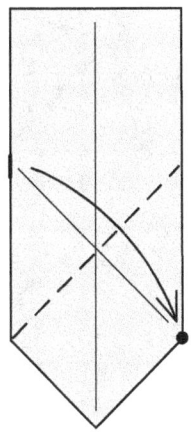

6. Repeat steps 4–5 on the right.

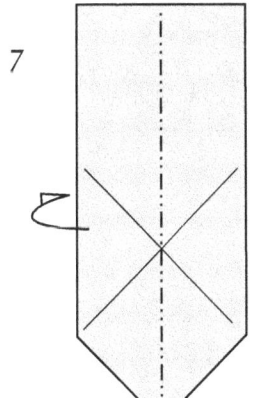

7.

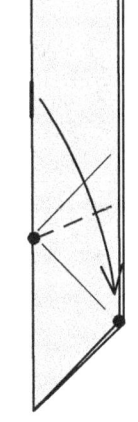

8. Bring the edge to the dot.

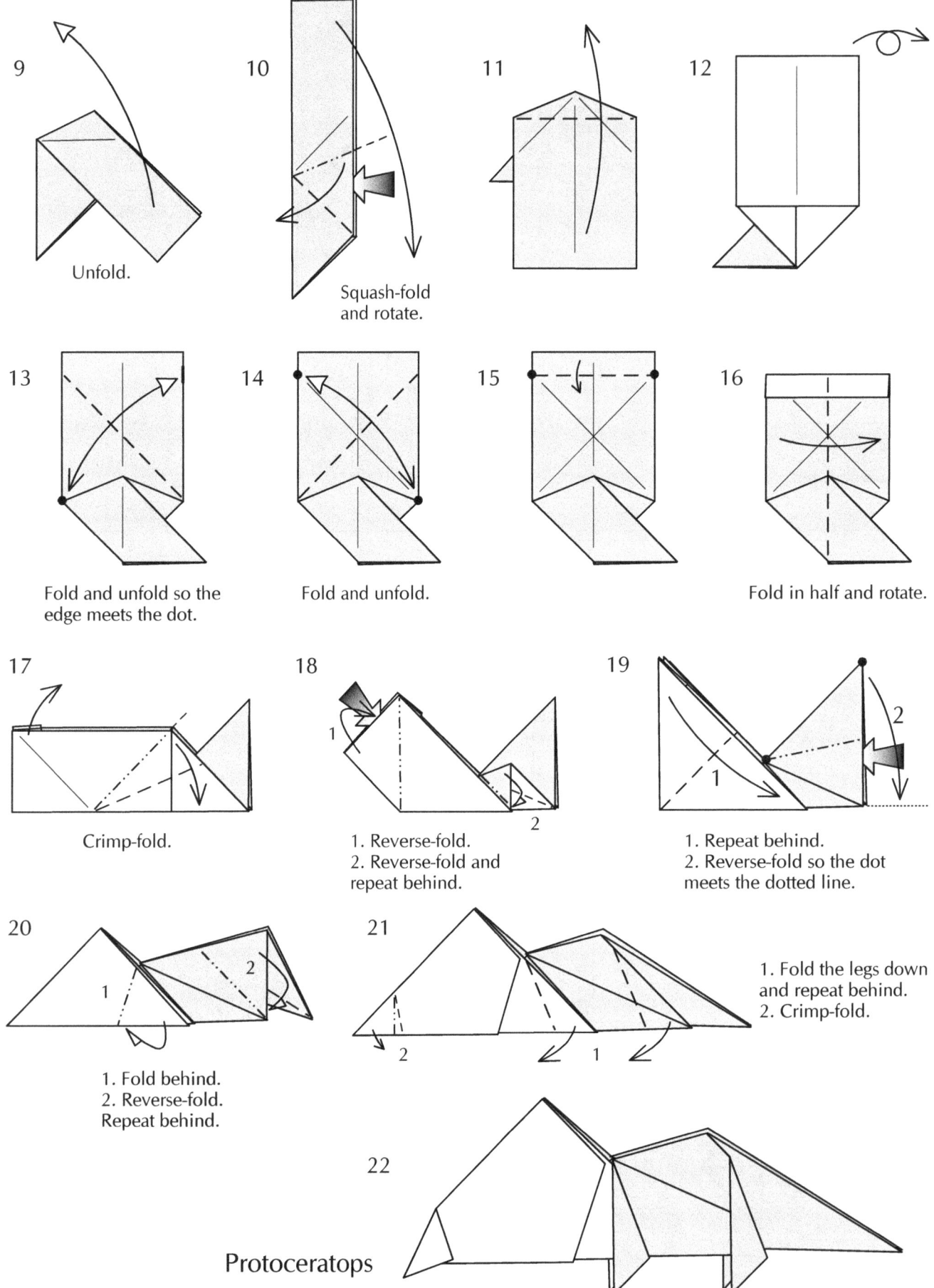

Protoceratops

Tyrannosaurus

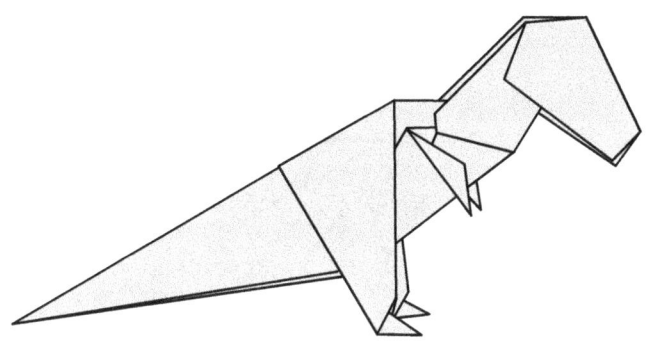

1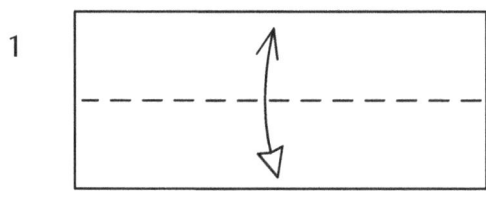

Fold and unfold.

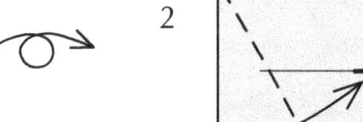

2

Bring the dot to the line.

3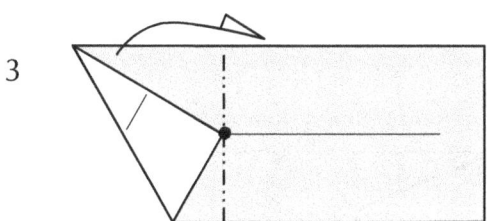

4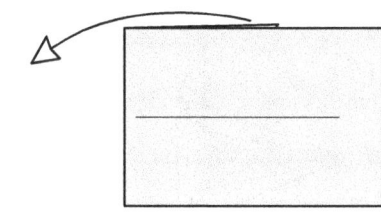

Unfold everything.

5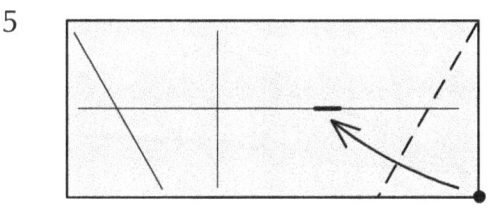

Repeat steps 2–4 on the right.

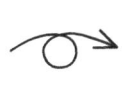

6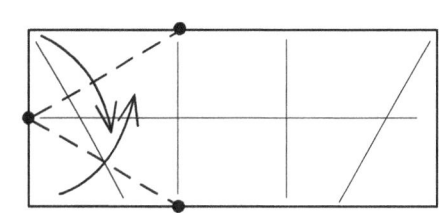

Tyrannosaurus 117

7

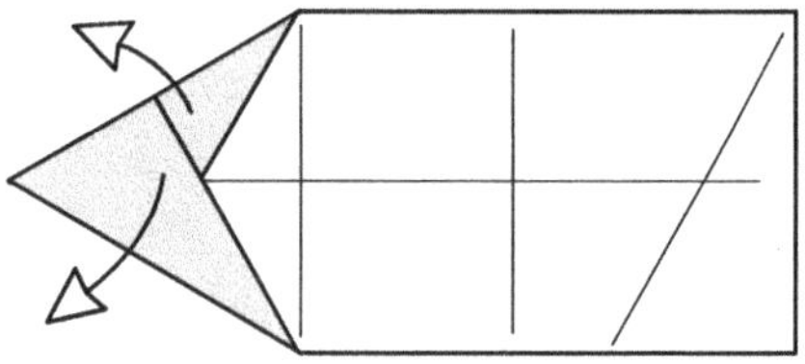

Unfold.

8

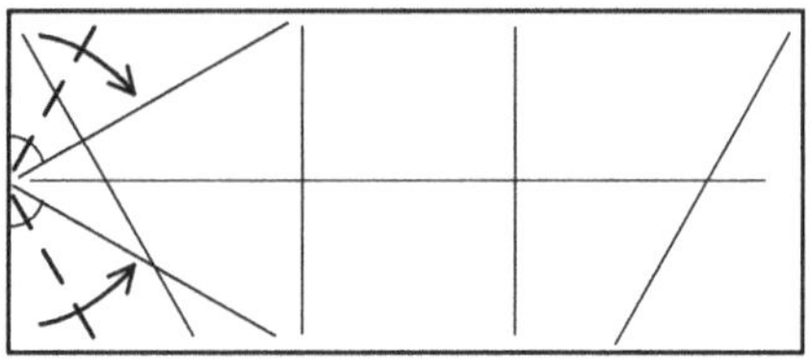

9

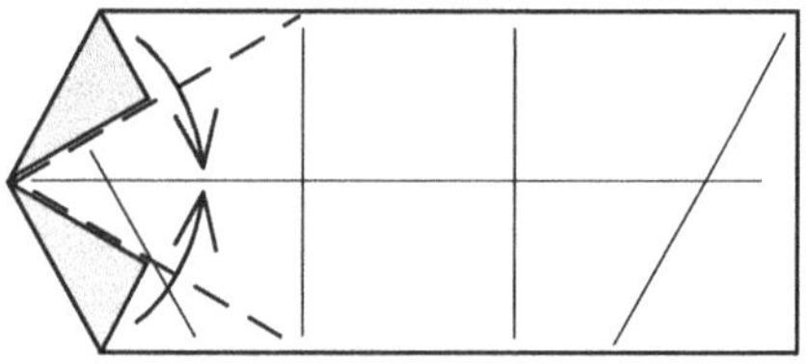

Fold along the creases.

10

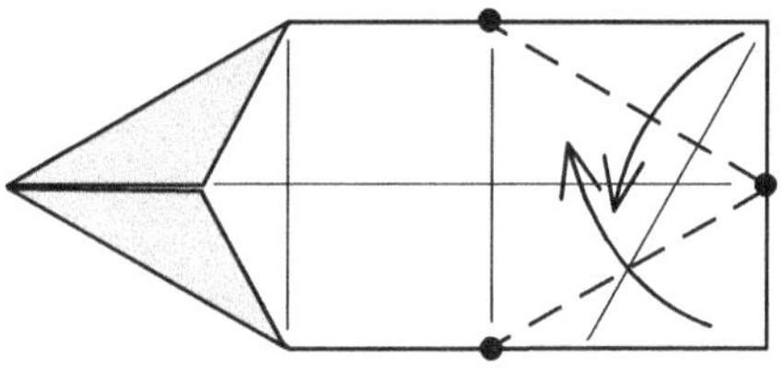

Repeat steps 6–9 on the right.

11

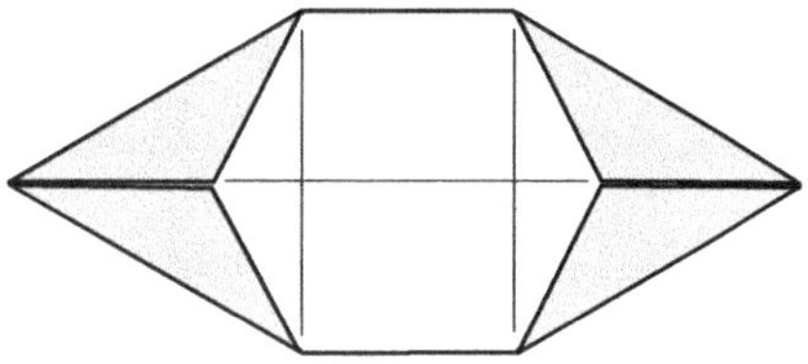

12

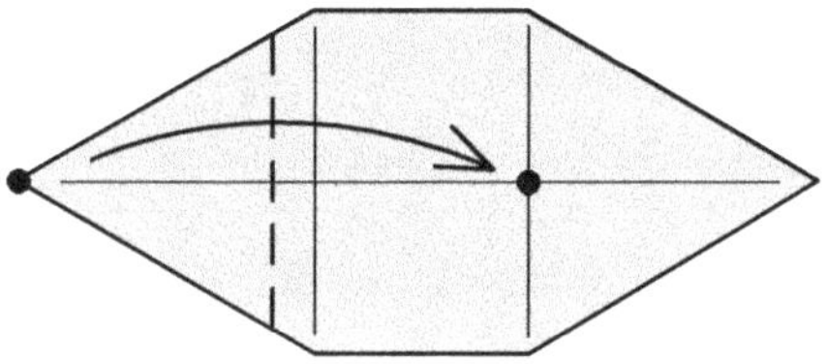

13

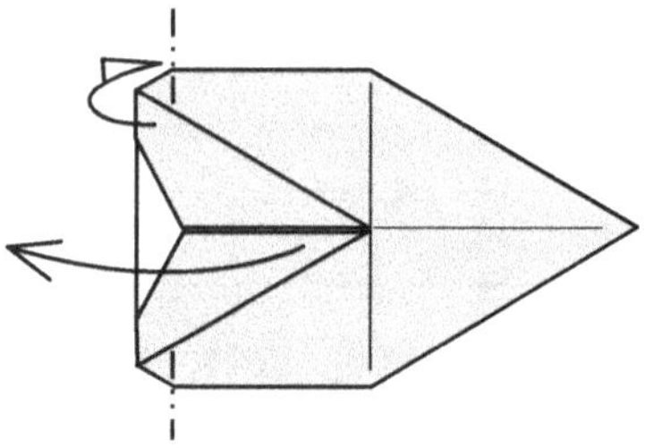

Fold along the creases.

14

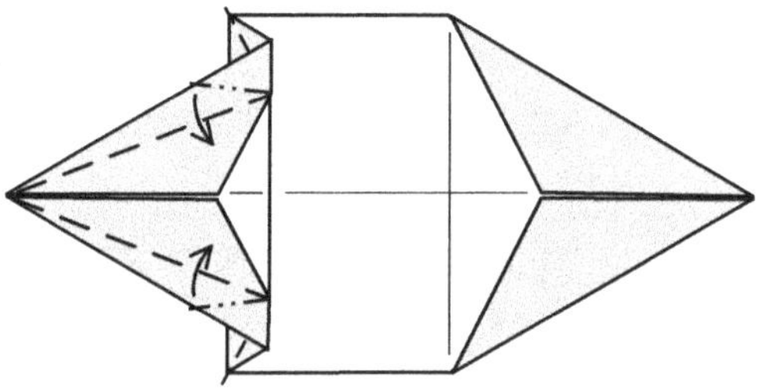

Squash folds.

15

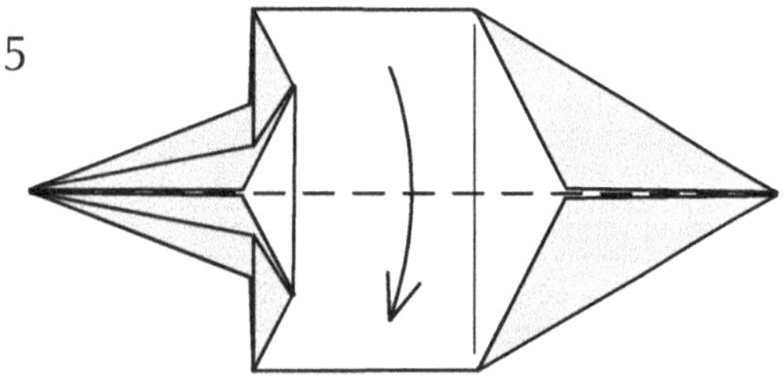

16

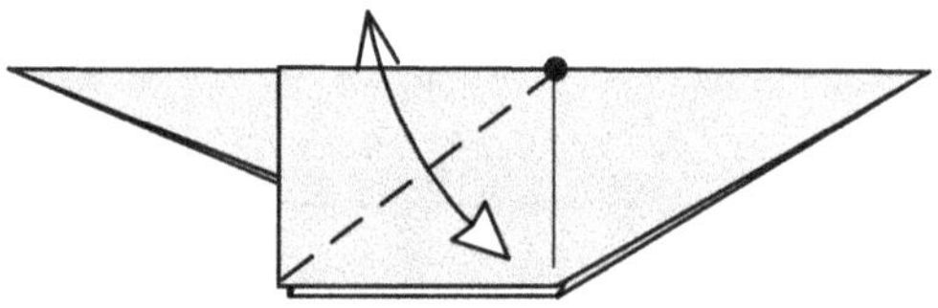

Fold and unfold all the layers.

17

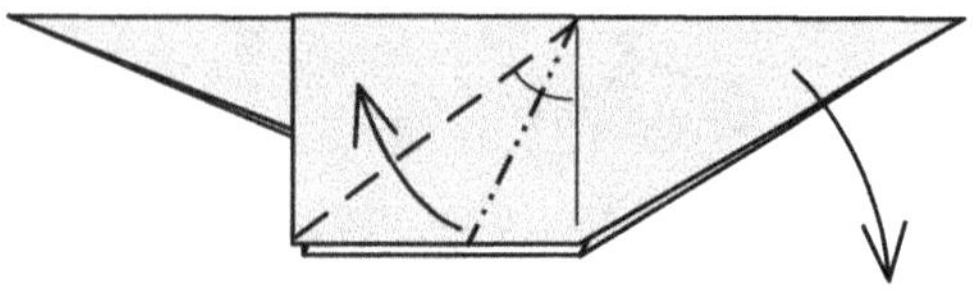

Bisect the angle for this crimp fold. Rotate.

18

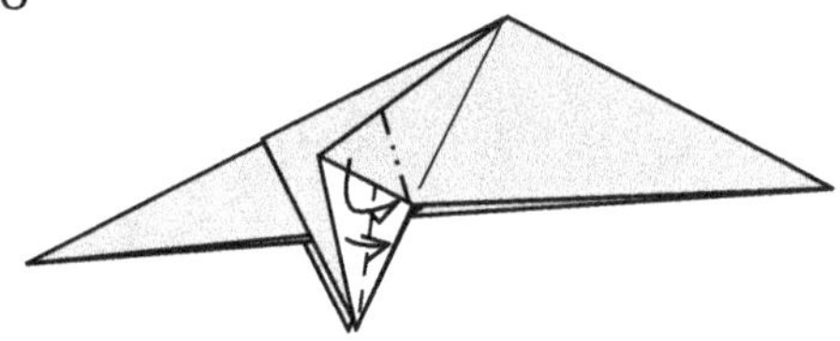

Reverse-fold and repeat behind.

118 *Dollar Origami Treasures*

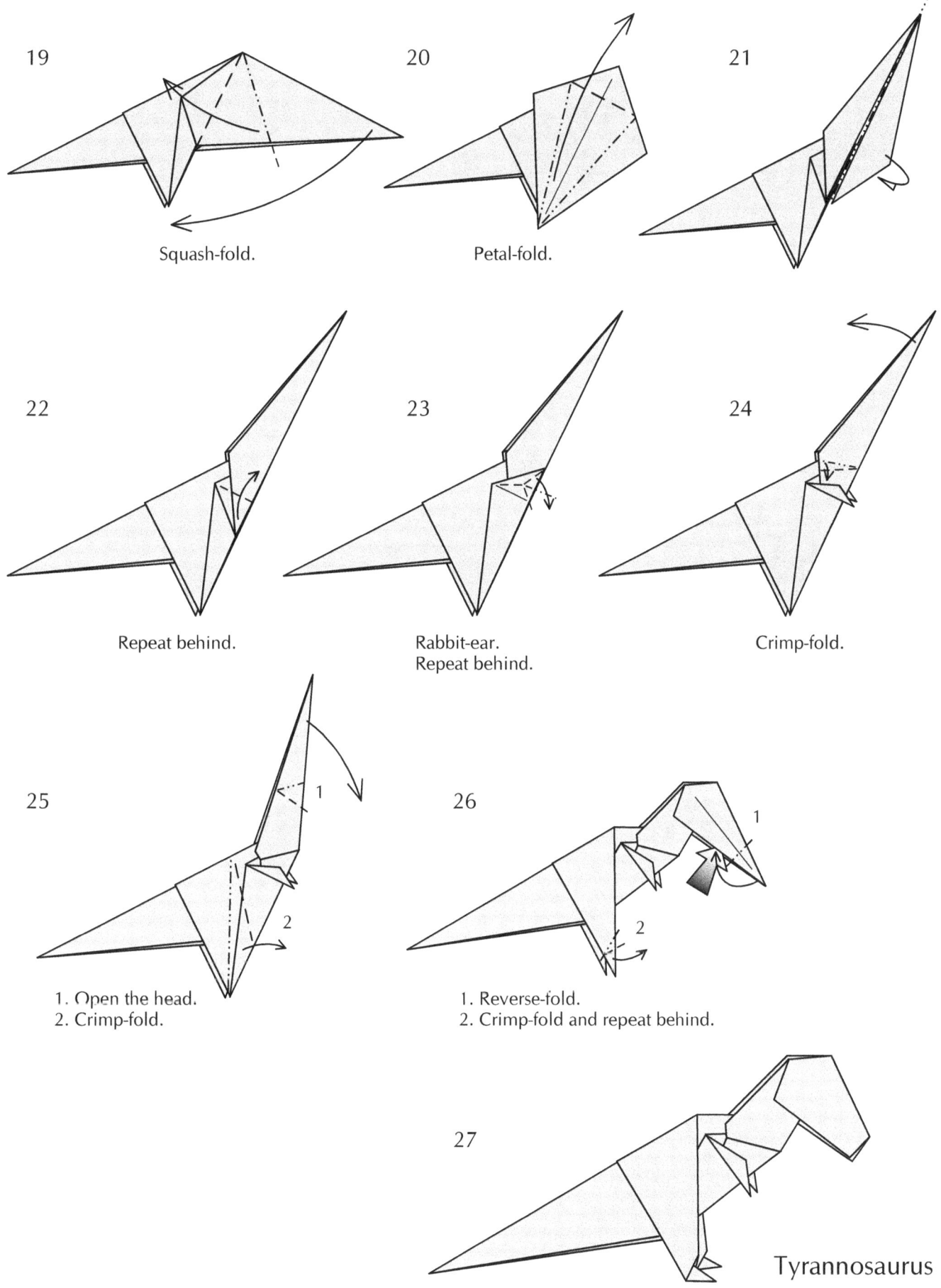

Tyrannosaurus

www.ingramcontent.com/pod-product-compliance
Lightning Source LLC
Chambersburg PA
CBHW081116080526
44587CB00021B/3620